THE BASS
FISHERMAN'S
BIBLE

REVISED EDITION

Erwin A. Bauer

THE BASS FISHERMAN'S BIBLE

REVISED EDITION

DOUBLEDAY & COMPANY, INC., GARDEN CITY, NEW YORK 1980

Library of Congress Cataloging in Publication Data

Bauer, Erwin A.
The bass fisherman's bible.

1. Black bass fishing.   I. Title.
SH681.B34   1980   797.1'7'58

ISBN: 0-385-14993-X

Library of Congress Catalog Card Number 79–7680

CONTENTS

1 THE BLACK-BASS "FAMILY"   9

2 BASIC BASS FISHING   23

3 BASS CASTING TACKLE   33

4 BAIT-CASTING AND SPINNING TECHNIQUES   40

5 GUARANTEED TECHNIQUES AND TIPS FOR TAKING BASS: I   50

6 SURFACE PLUGGING   63

7 FISHING THE ARTIFICIAL WORM   71

8 WEATHER AND WATER   78

9 FLY-RODDING FOR BASS   87

10 GUARANTEED TECHNIQUES AND TIPS FOR TAKING BASS: II   100

11 LIVE BAITS FOR BASS   113

12 BASS BOATS AND OTHER ACCESSORIES   124

13 BASS IN THE PAN   133

14 THE SOUTHEAST   138

15 THE MIDWEST   149

16 THE NORTHEAST   158

17 THE SOUTHWEST   164

18 THE WEST   169

19 BEYOND U.S. BORDERS   173

   APPENDIX   178

THE BASS
FISHERMAN'S
BIBLE

REVISED EDITION

Fishing for black bass is the most popular and among the most exciting forms of sports angling in the world.

Chapter 1

THE BLACK-BASS "FAMILY"

It probably was a warm and beguiling day in June when Dr. James Henshall, a Cincinnati physician, snuffed out the gas light in his office for the last time and hurried to a nearby livery stable for his buggy. That was almost eighty years ago. He carried an umbrella, to conceal a fly rod, and his black valise contained a reel, hooks, and rooster hackles rather than a stethoscope and other tools of his trade. He was starting on a fishing trip from which he never returned.

For several decades Doc Henshall traveled up and down the Ohio Valley, fishing with an enthusiasm that was uncommon in his time. Sport fishing around the turn of the century was confined almost entirely to eastern trout and salmon, but this pioneering doctor had "discovered" another fish—the black bass—which was abundant in local waters.

Henshall not only caught bass wholesale with hook and line, but he also devised new and better tackle to take them. He studied their habits and their physiology with a scientist's eyes and skills. He seined, netted, collected, autopsied, and kept valuable records, meanwhile swatting mosquitoes, losing sleep, and sometimes falling into

Mug shot of a largemouth bass in his natural environment: the deep, dark water near the bottom of a lake.

chilly rivers. He wandered down into Kentucky's blue-grass country and later north through Michigan. During the periods when he returned to Cincinnati, he wrote about his experiences and with his frequently reprinted *Book of the Black Bass* became the father of bass fishing as American fishermen know it today. He was the bass fisherman's Boone and Audubon rolled into one.

It was Henshall who claimed that "inch for inch and pound for pound" the bass was the gamest fish of all. There's much room for argument there because, with times and transportation methods being what they were, Henshall never really knew such fish as the dolphin or the dorado, the tarpon or the bonefish, or even the western steelhead. But still he had a point. All characteristics considered, the black basses easily rank among the great game fishes in the world today, just as they did in Henshall's day.

Of the twenty-five thousand or so species of fish now living on earth, none arouse more interest among American anglers than *Micropterus salmoides,* the largemouth black bass, or *Micropterus dolomieu,* the smallmouth black bass. By sheer weight of numbers, by the extent of their range and availability, the two black basses are easily the most popular game fishes in the United States.

Bass are easy to catch, but not too easy, which is a distinct asset. They are strong and fast and pretty fair jumpers. They are far from the best on the table, but still, here is good, robust fare. But best of all they are the most widely distributed freshwater game species in the Western Hemisphere and, except perhaps for the brown or rainbow trout, in the whole world.

A wandering angler nowadays can stow bass fishing tackle in his car trunk or station wagon and hit the highways optimistically. No matter where he is going, and often no matter when, he can probably put the tackle to good use. Except in Alaska, there is no state in the Union where an angler cannot find bass and no month during the year when, somewhere on the map, they will not be striking.

Bass fishing wasn't always this convenient. For Henshall it was a day's trip to the next county and a week just to West Kentucky. Now turnpikes, toll roads, new automobiles, bass boats on trailers, modern outboard motors, and assorted

Almost every largemouth bass is an exciting jumper when hooked.

Every smallmouth bass is also likely to make at least one thrilling leap when hooked.

flying machines from pontoon-equipped Cubs to giant Boeing jets place any fishing hole within one day's reach of almost any sportsman anywhere.

Early records are so incomplete that no two fishery authorities agree on the exact original ranges of the basses. But all that really matters, generally, is that largemouths were natives of the Southeast, the Midwest, and the fringes of the Great Lakes. Smallmouths shared certain sections of the Midwest and lived in all the Great Lakes except Superior. A lesser-known relative, the spotted bass, existed in certain streams of the Ohio and lower Mississippi drainage areas. Curiously, spotted bass weren't even identified as separate species until the late 1920s. None of the three existed in the western half of the United States, or specifically west of 100 degrees West Longitude, which runs from near Laredo, Texas, to Pierre, South Dakota. But no matter where you find them today, bass aren't really bass at all. Instead they are sunfish, the largest members of a purely North American family that includes crappies, bluegills, warmouths, shellcrackers, punkinseeds, rock bass, Sacramento perch, and more than a dozen other smaller sunfishes. The only true freshwater bass are the white and yellow bass, but common names are not too important, as we will see.

The Largemouth Bass

The largemouth bass, *Micropterus salmoides,* is the most adaptable and widely distributed of the clan. They are still plentiful in nearly all of their original haunts, and they have thrived wherever humans have seen fit to relocate them. Once it seemed that largemouths would never again be as abundant as in pre-Henshall times, when commercial netting for them was possible. For example, in the 1880s the commercial catch in just one place (largemouths and smallmouths together in southwestern Lake Erie) ran to 599,000 pounds a year. Modern outdoorsmen are surprised to learn that largemouths were also netted in such old Ohio canal reservoirs as Buckeye, St. Marys, and Indian lakes, as well as in many southern sloughs. But changing habitats and the gradual introduction of carp (which devoured vegetation and completely changed the ecology of watersheds), which began in 1880, have made such concentrations impossible. Just the same, while cold-water trout and salmon have suffered from the impact of civilization, bass have adapted to it.

Largemouths thrive today in all the water-supply reservoirs of the East and Midwest, which are still abuilding. Fishermen find them behind the high hydroelectric dams of the South

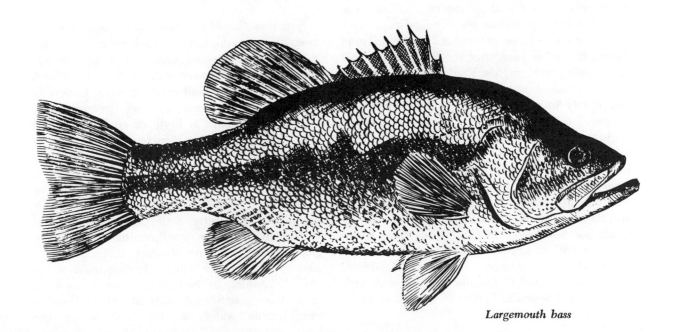

Largemouth bass

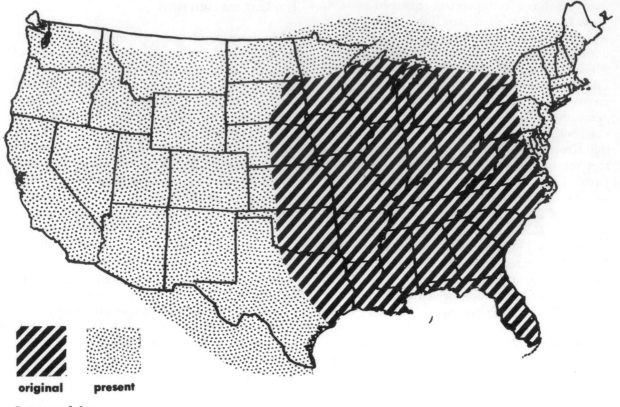

original   present

Largemouth-bass range

and in the giant desert reservoirs of the West. Bigmouths have found almost two million new homes in farm ponds across our landscape—just as they have become naturalized in tepid Texas "water tanks," in *resacas* of the Rio Grande, and in old mill ponds of New England. They've even occupied many a trout pond where they are completely unwelcome and eventually must be poisoned out. They like the slow rivers, clear or slightly roily of the Mississippi watershed as well as the rum-colored "jungle" streams of Florida; and they've found northern flood-control reservoirs as suitable as the swamps, sloughs, oxbows, and bayous of Dixie. They grow firm and strong in pine and birch-rimmed lakes as far north as southern Canada. And they grow stronger still in brackish, tidal waters at many points along the Atlantic Seaboard. Of course, they have invaded California in a big way and were carried over the Pacific to Hawaii as early as 1897.

The Smallmouth Bass

Smallmouths, *Micropterus dolomieu,* have not been quite so adaptable as their more numerous, more tolerant cousins, and that is easy to explain. There are fewer suitable waters without vegetation and without earth bottoms. Generally smallmouths need cool, moving streams where the oxygen content is high, or cool, rockbound lakes where there is a "current," or where the wind gives a wave action something like the tumbling of a stream.

Milton B. Trautman, whose book *Fishes of Ohio* is one of the finest volumes on fish ever compiled, has pretty well pinpointed the requirements of river smallmouths. The largest populations occur in streams that consist of about 40 per cent riffles flowing over clean gravel, boulder, or bedrock bottom; where the pools have a noticeable current; where there is considerable water willow; and where the

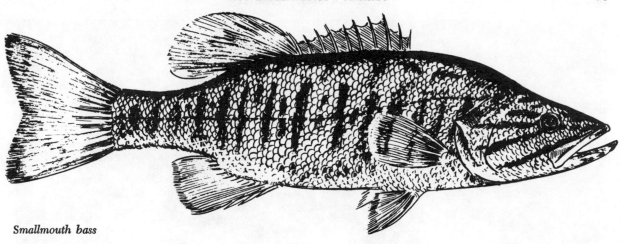

Smallmouth bass

stream drops from four to twenty-five feet per mile. The last can be determined for any stream by consulting a topo map.

Today smallmouths are at home in Maine and New Brunswick as well as the four lower Great Lakes. They are the fish of Kentucky's moonshine country, of those lonely Ozark waterways still unimpounded, and of eastern rivers like the upper Potomac, the Shenandoah, the Susquehanna, and the Delaware. They grow fat, bronze-colored, and wild in many lakes across southern Canada, where, in most cases, they were only released in recent years. Smallmouths also have recently adapted to some of the larger deeper southern reservoirs, such as Dale Hollow, Kentucky.

Smallmouth-bass range

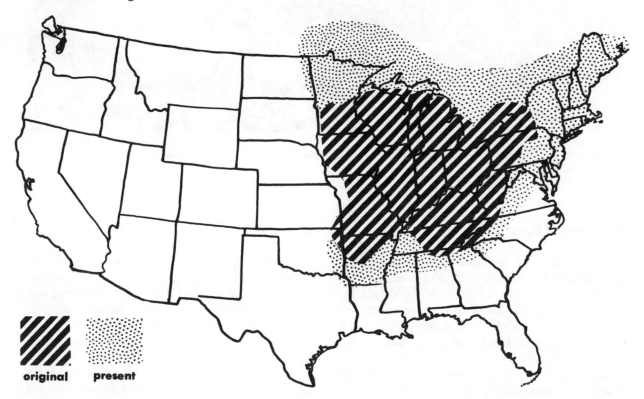

original **present**

Smallmouth bass inhabit rocky, gravelly bottoms in cold, pure lakes and streams. Photo by Karl H. and Stephen Maslowski.

The Spotted Bass

The spotted or Kentucky bass, *Micropterus punctulatus*, has nine rows of scales between the lateral line and the forepart of the dorsal fin. The upper jaw does not extend beyond a vertical line projected through the eye, and most individuals have a large black (or dark) spot on the point of the gill cover. A spotted bass also has a small patch of teeth on the tongue. Neither the smallmouth nor the largemouth has these teeth.

Distribution

Any history of bass distribution would be fascinating, and it would sound almost fictional. Actually it has been so haphazard a process and so unplanned that to compile an accurate history is impossible. Just for example, one early unofficial shipment of smallmouths was carried across the Virginia mountains in the tender of a Chesapeake and Ohio coal train. Many years ago the state of Ohio, as well as neighboring

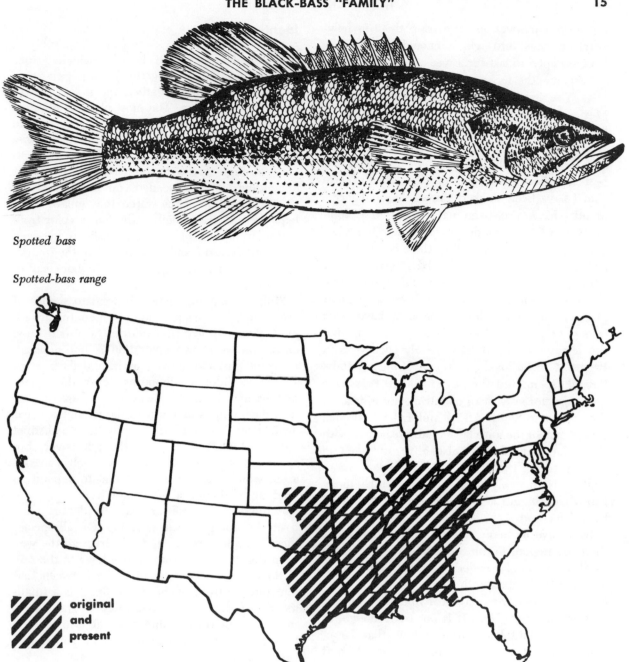

Spotted bass

Spotted-bass range

original
and
present

states (Pennsylvania, Indiana, New York), operated a railway "fish car" that transported bass from Lake Erie to streams statewide. More than once, in the early years of this widespread fish transplanting, a local politician won an election when he just happened to show up at the same moment a load of fish arrived to stock his constituents' lake. Bass were stocked by accident in Nebraska when a train wrecked crossing the

Elkhorn River, and the fish, en route to new homes in California, escaped on the spot.

Bass have been transported by hand, in milk cans by game wardens, on farm tractors, and via canal barge. Eastern states have traded bass eggs to western states for wild turkeys, and there even is a record of shipping bass to Mexico in exchange for quail. In recent years aerated tank trucks have been doing the job, but among the newest innovations is to ship them in polyethylene bags into which enough oxygen has been pumped to last for a week.

Largemouths have even become global travelers. The first shipment of five hundred went to Mexico in 1898; now the fishing is great in many large irrigation reservoirs south of the border. In 1915, Cuba and Puerto Rico were first stocked, and today the fishing in Cuba ranks with the best anywhere (see Chapter 19). New lakes in Brazil have been stocked since 1926, and largemouths have also been naturalized in Colombia, Costa Rica, Ecuador, Guatemala, Honduras, and Panama. However, all of these releases have not been wise because the bass have all but eliminated some valuable native fishes and birds.

Fish swapping has always been a popular practice, and for a long time bass have been traded or given to twenty European countries, the releases being at least mildly successful in Britain, Czechoslovakia, France, Hungary, Italy, Poland, Spain, and the Soviet Union. Bass have gone to a dozen African countries, but appear to thrive best in South Africa and Lake Naivasha, Kenya, where the author has had great luck with them. Largemouths are also alive and well in some waters of the Philippines and Japan, where angling is the only legal means to take them. Elsewhere the introduced bass may be harvested by any method.

Bass have as many names and nicknames as there are regions in the country. The largemouth is also commonly called bigmouth and even widemouth. In the South it is a trout or a green trout. Elsewhere you may hear linesides, jumper, Oswego, or green bass. It is not true, though, as one angler told his mother-in-law, that largemouths are the females of the breed, and smallmouths the males. Almost everywhere, but especially in the South, very heavy largemouths are known as "hawgs."

Smallmouths have fewer names, bronzeback being the most popular since it is an apt description of the fish in many waters. But smallmouths are also known as trout, brownie, or bronze bass, and occasionally as striper or striped bass for vertical bars on his flanks.

Spotted bass are also called Kentuckies, Kentucky bass, Kentucky spotted bass, or (rarely) redeyes.

Identification

Distinguishing which bass is which (since they occasionally live together) is a popular pastime wherever anglers gather, and it isn't always too accurately done. The most obvious physical characteristics are sometimes similar enough to allow a margin for error. For instance, all three species have a wide variation in color, from silvery through green to bronze or solid black, depending, it is conceded, on the color and chemical content of the waters they inhabit. Perhaps there is also a slight variation in color from season to season in individual fish—as between spawning season and fall or when the murky waters of early spring become alcohol-clear in autumn.

Still, largemouths generally tend to shades of green or green-black, while smallmouths are almost always tinged in shades of tarnished brass or bronze. A brown coloration is not unusual. Largemouths may have a horizontal dark stripe along the side; smallmouths never do. Smallmouths may (but not always) have several vertical dark stripes or blotches; largemouths never have them. Spotted bass usually have a distinct dark spot on the edge of the gill cover, but sometimes largemouths also have such a mark—all of which makes it evident that to depend on markings and color alone is unwise.

Actually, the basses are easy to identify positively by doing a little counting. On all species there is a fine, lateral line that curves all the way from the gill cover at about eye level to the tail. If there are eleven rows of scales between that line and the front of the dorsal fin, it is a smallmouth. If there are seven rows, it is a largemouth. If there are nine rows, it is a spotted bass. Following this scale-row count, you simply cannot miss.

Since spotted bass are the hardest to identify, and since they have actually been called (erroneously) a cross between a largemouth and a smallmouth, try an extra check if the scale-row count measures nine. Run your finger over the tongue, and if you feel a small patch of teeth there, it is a spotted for sure. No other bass have the teeth.

There is still another quick method for making an identification, but it is not so positive as the scale-row count. Project a straight line vertically through the eye of the bass. If the jaw of the fish extends beyond the eye, or your line, you have a largemouth. If not, you have a smallmouth or a spotted.

Size of Bass

Largemouths invariably average much heavier than smallmouths. An exception occurs in waters where both species exist and where the water "type" is most suited to smallmouths. Then the smallmouths will grow larger faster. The world's record largemouth remains a 22¼ pounder taken by George W. Perry in Montgomery Pond near Valdosta, Georgia, in 1932. Perry's catch has been debunked as a hoax, and apparently no really clear pictures of it ever existed. Also, Montgomery Pond no longer exists. But when compiling the original edition of *The Bass Fisherman's Bible*, the writer talked to Perry and was convinced that the catch was genuine. Anything is possible in fishing, but this is one world's record that is likely to last a long time.

The largest fish taken every year in Florida, where largemouths average biggest of all, usually run about fifteen or sixteen pounds, and even these are mighty rare. The best chance for a new largemouth record might result from stocking them in a new, fertile water somewhere, perhaps in Latin America, where there is a year-round growing season. Beginning in 1978 when new reservoirs were opened to fishing, bass of fifteen pounds plus began to appear in Cuba, especially Lake Zaza. Lago Yojoa in Honduras has produced some jumbos. But some of the reservoirs of Southern California now seem to have the best chance for a new record with a strain of bass originally imported and introduced from Florida. In 1973 a largemouth weighing twenty pounds, fifteen ounces was taken in Lake Miramar, San Diego County. It is the second largest bass of which there is accurate record.

The smallmouth world record, an eleven-pound, fifteen-ounce trophy taken in Dale Hollow Lake, Kentucky, stands a slightly better chance of being broken. It was caught by D. H. Hayes of Leitchfield, Kentucky, in 1951. Paul Richardson, Jr., of Carthage, Missouri, caught what is probably the record spotted bass in the nearby Spring River on March 9, 1958. The fish weighed seven pounds, two ounces, and it was taken on a live minnow.

Nationwide, largemouths taken by anglers will average between one and two pounds. Smallmouths will average a pound. Generally both species run larger the farther south they're found, the main reason being a longer active feeding and growing season. North of the Ohio River, a six-pound largemouth is bragging size. South of there it takes a larger fish, say an eight- or ten-pounder, to raise a serious bass fisherman's eyebrows.

The bass of each individual lake and stream have different rates of growth and development. Although a largemouth might reach a pound or more after only six months under ideal conditions, the national average largemouth needs two years to reach ten inches and from one half to three quarters of a pound. Smallmouths need three years to reach comparable growth.

Together, bass and bass fishing are important economic factors in our lives whether we fish for them or not. The best estimates available reveal that 85 per cent (or twenty-five million) of all anglers fish in waters that at least contain bass. Figuring that they spend an average of $750 a year for their sport—and that figure is perhaps conservative—bass fishermen pick up an annual check that runs into billions of dollars—more than is spent on baseball, basketball, and football put together. That expenditure includes travel expenses, gas, lodging, boats, motors, special clothing, and meals, as well as tackle, bait, license, guides, and the like.

Black bass are important game fish no matter how you regard them.

Life Histories

Toward the tag end of April, in a belt that would stretch from New York to Nebraska, any careful observer can detect a restlessness among the smallmouth bass in any clear stream in which they live. It might even resemble a migration. But actually it's the beginning of spring spawning—the beginning of life for the species.

As water temperatures climb above fifty-five degrees Fahrenheit, the male bronzebacks spend more time in shallow water, continually searching for a suitable nest site. Then, as if on signal, these same males begin to scoop out nests, or redds, on gravel, coarse sand, or rocky bottoms just as the mercury passes sixty degrees. It is almost as if spawning is triggered by the thermometer. These male-built nests, incidentally, are saucer-shaped depressions from fourteen to thirty inches in diameter, which are "fanned out" by vigorous movements of the tail fin. This "fanning" causes the deformed or reddened tails that anglers often find on bass in early spring.

When the nest is completed the male selects a "ripe" female and drives her to the nest by nudging her with his snout—or by actually biting her on the flank or gill flap. The female usually refuses to remain on the nest the first time; instead she retreats to deeper water. But male bass are persistent, and after several such attempts from a hundred to several thousand eggs are deposited.

Female bass have been found to carry as many as fifteen thousand eggs, but seven thousand is much nearer the average. However, all of these are not deposited at once, nor do all of the deposited eggs mature at the same time. This is a safety mechanism that permits renesting in case predatory fish or spring freshets destroy the first nest. In any case, after egg laying is finished the female either retires or is driven to deeper

A happy angler holds three hefty largemouths at the end of a good day.

water by the male, who takes over caring for the eggs and the young.

Smallmouth eggs hatch within three to five days, and at first the young fish sink into crevices in the rocks. From one to two weeks after the eggs are deposited the fry rise and hover over the nest in a school, under the protection of the male parent, who will attack any other fish— or fisherman's lure—that passes close to them. The fry are nearly black in color at this time. They move about rather slowly until all the nourishment in the egg yolk sac is absorbed and until they are a little more than an inch long. This is usually the most critical period in a bass's life, because by now the male parent has grown hungry enough to eat as many of them as he can catch. The lucky ones escape to feed on tiny water creatures called crustaceans and perhaps to grow to catchable size.

About the same time that things are stirring in smallmouth streams and lakes, there is activity in largemouth waters too. Depending on the latitude, this species will spawn sometime between March (south) and June (north)—although largemouth spawning has actually been observed in Florida and points south during every month of the year. In any case, the restlessness in largemouths begins somewhat later than with smallmouths, and serious spawning occurs somewhere between sixty-three and sixty-eight degrees.

Largemouths' nests are seldom as elaborate as those of smallmouths; sometimes a male will select a site and nothing more. Largemouths prefer to deposit eggs on rootlets of submerged plants or grass, on aquatic vegetation, on either a mud or soft-sand bottom. An average bass nest will be in water three or four feet deep, but the extremes run from a few inches to ten or twelve feet, which is the case in some clear, glacial lakes of Michigan. Eggs hatch within three to six days and are cared for by the male parent—until his appetite gets the better of him. Young largemouths that survive feed on tiny water animals called Cyclops and Daphnia. As they grow older they add larger and larger insects to the menu.

It is obvious that the entire procedure of spawning is a precarious business. Weather is a factor because a sudden cold spell can interrupt everything. Rains and floods can take a toll; conceivably they can wipe out an entire year's "hatch" overnight in one lake or in one region. Turbidity—the presence of silt or earth in suspension—can interfere with spawning, too, because it filters rays of sunlight necessary to hatch eggs by slowly heating the water. In lakes, smallmouths sometimes like to spawn in fairly deep water—perhaps in eight or ten feet. If the sun cannot penetrate that far, the eggs will not hatch.

From the moment the original egg is deposited, a bass's life is one of eating and being eaten. It is an aquatic rat race to survive. Crayfish and an endless host of formidable water insects and amphibians compete to eat the eggs as soon as they are dropped. After they hatch, larger fish are always seeking the fry. Even when a bass reaches several pounds there is no escape, since the sport fishermen then become his problem. But it's only fair to add that anglers are the least serious threat in the entire life cycle.

Just as bass are always hunted in the eat-or-be-eaten underwater world, so are they always hunting. They may eat anything they can swallow, and there have been many known cases of bass tackling creatures they *could not* swallow. All this is fine for fishermen who show up at streamside with many strange lures. For the record, though, the following have been found in largemouth bass stomachs: an adult red-winged blackbird, muskrats, common water snakes, ducklings, a bottle cap, mice, Micronite cigarette filters, a sora rail, flip tops from beer cans, and a shoehorn. But the truth is that once they have passed twelve inches in length, 95 per cent of any bass's food consists of crayfish and smaller fishes with a few of the larger insects thrown in. In some waters the entire diet might consist of crayfish; in others it might consist of gizzard shad. Those are the staples, but they will feed on anything alive and moving, depending mostly on what is readily available.

Because bass often live in very weedy fresh waters that are never as clear as ocean salt waters and therefore not as available to observation by divers, all that is known of bass movements after spawning is what can be determined by netting from the surface, from what fishermen can learn, from stomach analysis, and by circumstantial deduction. That doesn't give a biologist as complete a picture, say, as the one a game biologist has of pheasants and white-tailed deer, which live where anyone can watch them.

The point being made here is that, in large lakes and reservoirs especially, comparatively little is known about the habits, activities, and movements of bass after they desert the shallow water where they spawn. As we will see later, some topnotch fishermen suspect that even largemouths of medium size school up and concentrate in "packs" (at least for certain periods in the year) far more than anyone believes. It has been definitely established by trawling experiments that smallmouths in Lake Erie gather in vast schools and travel aimlessly about. The word "aimlessly" is used here only because no one has been able to find a predictable pattern to these travels.

On the other hand, there is evidence that some largemouths particularly are sedentary—that they establish "territories" that they defend against trespass by all other fishes. This trait has been most evident among bass in captivity.

Summed up, bass are not often "cruising" fish. They commute from shallow to deep water and they even migrate in streams, but this is not a continual or seething movement, such as that which white bass make in fresh water and which tuna, mackerel, and other species make in the salt. At least half of a bass's life will be spent relatively motionless near the bottom—no matter whether the bottom is only inches deep or a hundred feet straight down.

One other point is most evident to any observers of bass. Largemouths especially like "edge"—or, in a sense, cover. Fishermen today refer to this as "structure," and that is a word you will read often throughout the rest of this book. Edge or structure may be a sunken log or a stump, a channel or opening in a weedbed, a point of land or a shoal, an old car body, a barn, a flooded fencerow, a dropoff, an old river channel, or the edge of the lake itself. To repeat, there are exceptions, but the "rule of edge" is a valuable one to remember.

Of the three basses, the least known of all is the spotted. In *Fishes of Ohio*, however, Dr. Trautman does point out that they usually inhabit moderate or large-sized streams having gradients of less than three feet per mile with long, sluggish, rather deep pools. Spotted bass spawn in the shallows when water temperatures reach the low sixties, and they appear to be more tolerant of turbid waters than either smallmouths or largemouths.

Angler Dick Kotis with a nine-pound bass, bragging size anywhere, anytime.

Dr. Trautman reports that about the time water temperatures reach fifty degrees, there is a pronounced upstream migration into smaller streams, but that by early summer most adults as well as the young of the year retreat again to larger streams and to deeper holes. It isn't unusual for the spotted bass to share some water with other bass. Except in a few southern reservoirs, though, the species is not, a dweller of lakes.

Water temperature plays the major, critical role in governing the life of any bass, but this is especially true, we think, of the largemouth; he is a wise angler who takes advantage of this knowledge. A cold-blooded bass's temperature is the same temperature as the water, and until it rises above sixty degrees, the fish are not really active. Cold slows down their metabolism, their digestion, and their nervous systems. When win-

ter comes, smallmouths apparently hibernate, clustering together under logs, debris, or in crevices until the coldest months pass.

Largemouths become very inactive, but do not hibernate. They concentrate in deep water and continue to feed, although not vigorously. They will catch an available minnow, also rendered inactive by cold, and then take days, if not weeks, to digest it. To catch winter bass is a matter of finding the concentrations and fishing slowly on the bottom for them.

A largemouth's life expectancy is also affected by water temperature. The higher the average (year-round) temperature of a lake, the shorter the average life. A northern largemouth from Wisconsin, for example, might reach fourteen to sixteen years, while a Louisiana bass would only average (if never caught) half that age. A largemouth of Ohio or Illinois—in between—could

Bass fishing takes an outdoorsman to some of the most beautiful fresh waters left in America.

reach ten or eleven years if never hooked.

But how do you tell the age of a bass? Fish scales can be "read" in almost the same way as the annual rings on a tree stump. Each ring around a bass scale designates one year. Since scales are never shed, each one remains a history of growth; the wider the space between rings, the faster the growth.

Among the biologists who have studied bass the longest is George W. Bennett of the Illinois Natural History Survey, and one of his most interesting conclusions is that the largemouth is the most "intelligent" of game fishes. They are extremely curious, and this results in a good many getting hooked early in life. But they soon become wary—maybe "educated" is a better word—and often this leads to what anglers call "fished out" ponds. In other words, a largemouth soon learns that lures, especially those it sees most often, can get it into trouble. By comparison, according to Bennett, smallmouths are high-strung, excitable, and not as smart as their larger cousins. But many anglers, this one included, have good reasons to question that.

Another controversial Bennett theory is that closed seasons, creel, and minimum-length limits are unnecessary on any bass waters because it is virtually impossible to fish them out. He points out that some bass will become too wary to strike before all are taken, and the fish and game bureaus (that regulate the fishing) in many states have subscribed to the theory. But again not all anglers agree, and there is evidence that the quality can indeed be diminished by too much angling pressure—or at least by too much removal of large, breeding-size bass. In fact, a counterproposal gaining popularity among bass anglers is to permit unlimited removal—catch—of small bass, but to require that all larger bass be returned to the lake.

One final revealing word about bass biology. In other experiments of the Illinois Natural History Survey, it was discovered that a black bass's vision is similar to that of a human's, but through a strong yellow filter. Therefore bass have the poorest vision at the blue end of the color spectrum. This could explain why the blue and purple lures that anglers so long rejected as unnatural colors do seem attractive to bass today.

Only one thing is certain about bass and bass fishing, though: Both are entirely unpredictable. But still the fisherman who knows the most about them and what makes them tick has a better chance of ending the day with a heavy stringer.

Chapter 2

BASIC BASS FISHING

On every lake or lake region in America, a few bass fishermen catch most of the largemouth bass. According to creel or stringer censuses conducted in many states from Maine to Texas, as few as 10 per cent of the anglers account for 80 per cent to 85 per cent of the fish and an even larger percentage of the heaviest fish. They are the individuals whose pictures most often appear in local newspapers (holding up their catches) and who regularly win tournaments sponsored by local bass clubs. But exactly how can those lopsided success stories be explained?

First, there is no secret, sure-fire formula for catching bass all the time, and no "never fail" lure has yet been invented. And we hope there never will be, because such a miracle would destroy the sport. But it is true that experience and dedication—in other words, putting in plenty of time on the water—will make one sportsman a much better fisherman than another who has only limited time to spend. The veteran has (and has had) plenty of time to develop the techniques that work best on "his" lake, but that might not necessarily be so successful elsewhere.

This is a good place to insert a very valuable tip, one that might spare an angler a lot of fruitless casting: Hire a guide. Especially on most of the larger and more popular bass waters, professional bass guides are always available. For any sportsman who has neither the time nor the inclination to search for bass on his own, a capable guide is the answer. A day or so with a knowledgeable guide may be the best possible bass-fishing clinic.

A guide offers a number of valuable services: He furnishes the boat, motor, perhaps even the tackle if you make special arrangements for this. But mostly he offers expertise on where to go on "his" lake, where each spot may look like every other. He gives advices on lures, on proper cast-

ing and techniques. Usually he is a genial, willing companion. In other words, a guide is a shortcut to faster fishing action, and at the end of the day he will probably dress the fish.

At the time this *Bible* was being compiled (late 1979), bass guides were drawing from $100 to $175 per day for either one or two fishermen, and the best ones were booked far in advance and nearly every day. As in all other endeavors, there are some bad apples in the barrel. Mostly these are guides primarily interested in their own fishing (rather than the client's) and they take a client along only to pay the way. But

A few fishermen catch most of the bass, especially the large ones. One of the most successful anglers anywhere is professional fisherman Roland Martin of Oklahoma.

This bass was hooked by casting around the deadfalls just behind the boat. Always look for bass in such places.

most are reliable and hard-working. Before hiring a guide anywhere, it is wise to check locally on his reputation. The best ones normally are booked well in advance, which means that you will have to plan ahead.

But without a guide, no matter whether the lake is a flooded bottom-land forest in Louisiana or a pond in Pennsylvania, it is impossible to catch bass until you find them. So locating where they live is basic. Fortunately it is possible to predict fairly well where bass are located at any given time or place.

A fisherman without a guide has a number of options. The one too often selected is trial and error, which is really a matter of probing a strange, unseen, underwater world, literally casting in the dark. The goal here is to cover a lot of "territory" at random, presenting baits and lures over widely scattered areas until the proper depth and climate (and therefore bass) are located. Once found, these places—structures—will probably produce for a long time.

And also these same places will prove productive year after year at approximately the same season. Given long experience—practice—in fishing one lake, a bass angler eventually can build up his own inventory of good bass-fishing spots.

Where to Find Bass

Sometimes finding largemouths is easy; more often it takes a little time. In Chapter 1 it was established that bass usually will be on the bottom no matter whether the water is shallow or deep. They seldom stay suspended long in mid-depth. We also believe that they prefer "edge" and a water temperature in the vicinity of seventy degrees. So let's put these three concepts together.

On a typical midwestern lake in May, or a southern reservoir in March or April, an average largemouth bass will probably spend most of its

In spring, when water temperature approaches seventy degrees Fahrenheit, bass will be in shallow water, probably near shore, as this angler well knows.

time on the bottom in shallow waters (because the water there has just reached seventy degrees) and near some kind of edge (which may be around a newly emerging weedbed or along a strip of shoreline). The odds are good it will linger in this same area as long as all conditions are "right"—as long as the water doesn't become too warm, the vegetation too dense, or food fishes too scarce.

Two months later, on this same lake, this same largemouth will have moved, but it will be in the same sort of position—on the bottom, in water of approximately seventy degrees, and near some sort of edge. The only difference is that the edge will be deeper, possibly as deep as fifty feet, but usually wherever the seventy-degree water layer exists. The availability of food or of suitable edge may alter the exact position somewhat, but—an angler must remember this—bass will never be too far away.

Of course, there are exceptions to this seventy-degree-layer theory, and the most obvious occurs in all-shallow lakes where the temperature soars well above seventy in the summer and where no cooler patches of water exist. Largemouths have managed to survive briefly in eighty-five-degree water in Ohio and eighty-nine degrees in Florida. But these are extremes.

Now back to the typical midwestern lake. Although largemouths will spend most of midsummer in deep water, they often will make regular migrations into shallow water to forage heavily. These migrations occur most often at night. Of course, bass are easier to reach with bait or lures when they are in shallow water because they are more accessible, and the odds on catching them are better because they're actually feeding at the time. Still they will strike just as readily while in the depths—if a suitable presentation of a bait is made.

A largemouth bass feeds most frequently, consumes the most food, and grows most rapidly when water temperatures are between seventy and seventy-five. Beginning in midwinter when the water is just above freezing, the basal metabolism of a bass, and of most freshwater fish, increases steadily as the water warms up. This means that a bass requires more and more food to live—until a critical point is reached. Beyond that point, or that temperature, which cannot be pinpointed, the metabolic rate diminishes rapidly until the fish can no longer survive. Among northern "strains" of largemouths that critical point arrives somewhere between seventy-five and eighty. In the South it is slightly higher.

Still another point is worth making, although it is not a hard or fast rule. The larger bass become, the more likely they are to prefer deeper water. On the average they will spawn in deeper water than smaller bass, and, if the seventy-degree layer of water is very thick, they tend toward the deepest part of the layer. It cannot be overemphasized that the deeper the bass, the harder it is for a fisherman to find them.

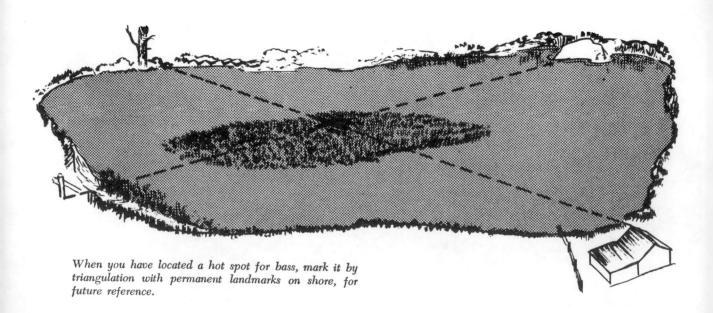

When you have located a hot spot for bass, mark it by triangulation with permanent landmarks on shore, for future reference.

Remember the Hot Spots

Since many of these productive structures may be located far out beneath open water rather than close to shore, a wise fisherman will mark each spot by triangulation—that is, by carefully orienting the spot with landmarks on-shore. It is always a good idea to make more than a mental note and to mark the favored location on a chart or notebook.

Frequently it will be necessary to be absolutely accurate in marking a bass area, because it may be no more than a sharp dropoff, such as a submerged river channel, that curves for any distance from a few yards to several hundred feet along an underwater contour. It is not an easy matter to find such a thin target. But to be able to locate it precisely, quickly, will save much unnecessary exploration later on, as well as valuable fishing time.

As a fisherman gains experience in exploring for bass, he learns that finding abrupt dropoffs or reefs is like finding paydirt. Each one is worth plenty of concentration, even if he doesn't start catching bass immediately. Underwater weed-beds or sunken "islands" are worth investigating, too, because all the bass in a vast area or maybe even in an entire lake might be concentrating there. Many, many limits of trophy fish have been taken without moving from anchor near such spots.

Finding bass in rivers—and most often these will be smallmouths—is similar to finding them in lakes, except that the angler seldom has to deal with such great depths. Once spawning is finished and streams begin to warm, the bronze-backs leave the shallows and retire to deep pools and pockets, at least during midday. Briefly at daybreak, on some evenings, and at night they move out into nearby riffles and runs where hellgrammites, crayfish, and minnows are most plentiful and available.

The consensus among experts is that smallmouths of lakes are a little less inclined to strike in deep water than are largemouths, but nonetheless the species *can* be caught at any time—by someone and by some specific method.

The failure to catch bass has been blamed on the weather more than on any other single factor, and I myself have been inclined to consider certain weather conditions much better or worse than others. Still it is sound scientific theory

A heavy bass is the reward for a fisherman who found action on the fringe of bullrushes.

rather than suspicion that weather has far more effect on fishermen than on fish anywhere. This does not refer to water temperatures, which are important, or to floods and droughts, which could make fishing impossible. But if you can find bass at all, it is possible to catch them whether it is raining and windy or calm with bright sunshine. This becomes more evident all the time as newer, more effective tackle is designed and as biologists learn more about fishes. Still, finding bass is only half of successful bass fishing; it is possible to fish all day in water that is full of them and yet never have a strike.

Obtain a Map of Your Bass Lake

Before exploring any bass lake for the first time, there are three items that can make your exploration much more successful: an accurate topo (topographical) map, a depth finder, and a water-temperature gauge (or thermometer that works well beneath the surface). Consider the important map first.

Topo, or at least detailed physical, maps are available from a number of sources. Many fish and game departments have prepared them for the major lakes within the state, and these are available for a small fee or just the postage. Excellent topo maps for some large reservoirs across the nation can be obtained from the U. S. Geological Survey, Denver, CO 80225, or USGS, 1200 South Eads Street, Arlington, VA 22202. Maps of lakes west of the Mississippi should be ordered from Denver; east of the Mississippi from Arlington. Most topo maps available are in ten-foot or twenty-foot contour intervals. The smaller the interval, the easier the maps are to read and the more detailed for a bass fisherman's special needs. So try to get the smallest interval, or the largest scale, map that happens to be available for your lake.

The U. S. Army Corps of Engineers also supplies free maps of most of America's large reservoirs. These are not topo maps such as the USGS sheets, but each one does clearly reveal what the reservoir looks like beneath the surface. The USED maps can be obtained by writing or calling the nearest Corps of Engineers office, the locations of which are included in the Appendix. Incidentally, the marinas and tackle shops around important lakes may carry the exact maps that are needed.

The main value of a topo or underwater map is that it quickly shows the potentially good bass-fishing areas. It reveals the very deep water that can be skipped over. At the same time, like a highway map, it shows the best, shortest ways to reach potential bass structures.

Let's assume a situation here. You are on mythical *Bible* lake for which you have a good topo map. With your temperature gauge, you have determined that the ideal sixty-eight-to-seventy degrees layer of water is about fifteen feet below the surface. So on your map you locate—trace—those areas of the lake that are fifteen feet deep. Using your depth finder plus the map to locate these areas exactly, you can soon be fishing in areas where the odds are greatly tipped in your favor. You are wisely plotting, rather than depending on luck or trial and error.

Reading a Bass Lake

With and without maps and other helpful devices, a bass fisherman who knows how to "read" a lake can also increase his chances for catching a large stringer of largemouths. And maybe there is no greater reward for a serious bass fisherman than challenging a completely unfamiliar lake—and winning.

Start out by asking questions around docks, marinas, from guides and successful fishermen. Don't bother to ask exactly where they caught fish, because they will not tell or probably will lie. But you can certainly ask (and get an honest answer) in what kind of situation or structure and perhaps how deep the fish were found. Largemouths will be found in similar situations elsewhere. That's a good start.

Your next step is to get out on the lake and start looking around, which may be bewildering at first. Especially larger lakes tend to be vast expanses of shimmering surface, with countless bays and many miles of shoreline, a lot of it looking like all the rest. Just the same, you can start fishing by *not* fishing those sections of lake that obviously are too deep to be worthwhile. In many bodies of water, this quickly eliminates a lot. You can usually tell, but of course not always, that a very steep or clifflike shoreline drops off sharply into deep water.

On the other hand, you can read some structure by what you can see on the surface. Tips of trees or brush mean sunken bass cover below. Parallel lines of treetops in the water may mean an old country road or lane below; cast a lure along both sides of it. By checking on the nearest shore, you may see where the abandoned right-of-way actually entered the water, and even without any visible roadside trees, you can follow it and fish both sides.

Underneath the giant reservoirs all across America, remember that roads lead to old homesteads, cemeteries, barns, fencerows, woodlots, bridges, and countless other human structures that after flooding became bass structures. Often you can find your way around them from above.

When starting out "cold"—new to a lake—it is always good advice to head initially for points of land and start working out in different directions from there. As you work outward, watch especially for sudden dropoffs and weedbeds, particularly if the weedbeds are sunken beyond sight,

Where do you look for bass in an unfamiliar lake? The point of that peninsula in the center is a good place to start.

Largemouth bass fishing often calls for casting in flooded forests such as this one.

and spend a little extra time prospecting these places. As you cast, you will notice more and more visible signs, which you at first did not notice, of likely places to find bass. In other words, you are suddenly reading the lake.

Places where tributary streams enter a reservoir are also worthwhile starting places. If the tributary is a meandering (as opposed to a straight) stream, chances are that now the flooded part is also meandering beneath you. Because curving, crooked creeks offer much more cover—structure, again—than straight ones, you have read another likely place to find large bass, if not a whole concentration of them. Present a variety of lures right here, giving the spot thorough coverage.

This will seem fundamental to experienced bass fishermen, but there are two main methods to present a lure or bait—by casting or by fly-rodding. Trolling, drifting, and a vintage method called skittering are possible too. But with just a few local exceptions, casting and fly-rodding are the most important methods of bass fishing. The latter is effective only in shallow water—usually in water less than six feet deep and seldom in water over ten feet deep. Casting (and this category includes bait casting, spin-bait casting, and spinning, all of them essentially the same except for the operation of the reel) is adaptable to both deep and shallow water.

Casting is delivering a lure and then retrieving it either in a lifelike manner or in some other manner designed to cause fish to strike it. A better bass fisherman, then, is a man who casts his lure more often into productive water—into water of about seventy degrees, along the bottom and near some kind of structure. But the best bass fisherman of all will also retrieve slowly, and he will experiment with lures of various designs, actions, and finishes until he finds the one that does the job. Much more on this later.

But remember that there are no absolute rules for bass fishing. Although seven or eight times in ten the slow retrieve will be best, there will be days when a fast one is more effective.

The importance of retrieving a lure close to the bottom, or rather right along the bottom, simply cannot be overemphasized. Even the best anglers will have their lures snag to cause delays and inconvenience, but the trouble is worth it. A retrieve that occasionally touches bottom along the way will often catch two or three times as many bass as the same lure retrieved at the same speed just a few inches higher.

In fly-rodding (or surface or top-water fishing), a floating lure is cast (by any tackle) and retrieved in a lifelike manner or in a manner calculated to tease bass into striking it. This is a most exciting as well as a deadly method, but it has limitations because it's confined to use over shallow water. Since bass, except those in shallow swamp and marsh ponds, are only present in the shallows in springtime and for very brief morning, night, and evening periods later on, top-water fishing is practical for only a fraction of each fishing season.

The more quickly a bass fisherman learns the tricks of the sport—and then practices them unconsciously—the better the odds will build up in his favor. For example, there is the matter of noise. The more quietly an angler behaves, the better his chances. It has been written often that banging a tackle box against the bottom of the boat or knocking the ashes from a pipe against a gunwale are to be avoided because they frighten the bass. Well, that is true. I'm convinced that if it doesn't frighten them completely out of the vicinity, it will surely make them uneasy—on guard.

It has also been claimed that the sound or disturbance of an outboard motor will not frighten fish, and in fairly deep water this may be true. But an outboard motor running through shallow water will scatter any bass nearby as quickly as an exploding hand grenade. I've seen it happen. Creaky or loose oarlocks will spook them just as well.

It is possible to multiply the chances of scoring just by making certain types of deliveries. For instance, cast so that the retrieve passes close to and parallel to a sunken log rather than across the log. This simple maneuver puts the lure within reach of lurking bass for a longer period of time—and for a longer distance. Similarly, a cast parallel to the edge of a weedbed or along a dropoff will be better than a cast at right angles.

Except in the case of surface fishing, there is no better advice than always to keep "feeling" for the bottom. It doesn't make any difference which lure is being used, because some will be snagged completely and lost anyway. But this technique not only reaches more bass, it also gives a fisherman a picture of the lake's bottom, of the underwater topography. By constantly feeling the bottom he will find edge or structure features that cannot easily be found in any other way.

It is more than just a homespun saying in the Deep South that the laziest fishermen catch the most and the biggest bass. There *is* some basis for this philosophy. To fish slowly and deliberately is to improve the odds as surely as feeling for the bottom. Put the two together and it's a deadly combination hard to match by any means. But always keep a line in the water.

A good, all-around bass fisherman is flexible and persistent. He maintains his tackle in good shape, and he religiously sharpens his hooks. He tries new methods and new lures, new retrieves and new places; he explores and experiments constantly. And he has the time of his life when he's fishing.

Chapter 3

BASS CASTING TACKLE

Serious bass fishermen are as discriminating with their tackle, perhaps more so, than any other breed of anglers today. Rods and reels are selected with care, each outfit to serve a special purpose. And a busy bass angler usually carries more than one outfit whenever he ventures out on the water. He will have at least one plug or bait-casting outfit, but probably two; at least one spinning rig; possibly even a fly-casting outfit or a trolling unit, all set up and ready to use. Because fly casting differs radically from other types of casting and lure presentation, we will consider it separately in another chapter.

Plug- or Bait-casting Tackle

Different anglers have different preferences, of course, but Bill Dance, one of America's most consistently successful bass catchers, prefers just two different actions (degrees of stiffness) in bass rods; but both are of the same length—5½ feet. For top-water plugs and spinners he prefers a rod with about 30 per cent tip action—or with what is normally called a medium action. For the rest of his casting, Dance selects a much stiffer rod with not more than 10 per cent play in the tip. This stiff rod is used to cast jigs, artificial worms, spoons, and deep-diving or "crank baits,"

which are hard-driving and are retrieved rapidly.

The stiff casting rod has enough backbone for setting the hook securely and getting a bass out of dense vegetation (or other cover) before it can get hopelessly snagged. In brush the stiff rod is a necessity. But the tip still is sensitive enough, when worming, to feel a fish taking the worm.

Bait-casting rods today come in Fiberglas or graphite, with very few bamboo models still on the scene. Glass is the least expensive and maybe the most durable. Recently bait-casting rods of graphite have all but cornered the market with fishermen who mostly use plastic worms. The graphite material is light enough in weight to be very sensitive to a bass sucking a bait as it is dragged over the bottom. Also new magnesium rods, sensitive but supertough, have been introduced. These rods are manufactured with three different styles of handles: straight, offset, and double-offset. The reel is positioned lower on the offset handles and therefore may be best for an angler with a small hand or for most women casters. A man with a large hand can comfortably "palm" a straight handle. But the selection depends entirely on which kind of handle feels best to the individual.

Short rods (slightly shorter than 5½ feet, for

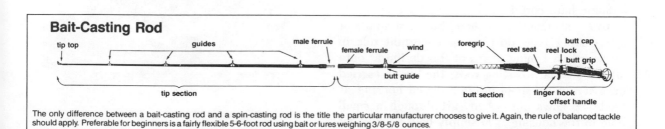

Bait-Casting Rod

tip top · guides · male ferrule · female ferrule · wind · foregrip · reel seat · reel lock · butt cap · butt grip · butt guide · tip section · butt section · finger hook · offset handle

The only difference between a bait-casting rod and a spin-casting rod is the title the particular manufacturer chooses to give it. Again, the rule of balanced tackle should apply. Preferable for beginners is a fairly flexible 5-6-foot rod using bait or lures weighing 3/8-5/8 ounces.

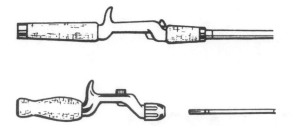

Straight handle (top) and offset handle (bottom).

example) are easy to use in tight quarters, as when tossing lures toward undercut banks or under trees. Longer rods average better for distance casting, for open water, and for use with smaller lures, say ⅜ ounce or less. But on any good rod the ferrules should fit tightly and not twist with use. And to prevent abrasion and wear on lines, the guides should be of a smooth and hard material.

Every plug caster should look for top quality in all his reels—more so even than in his rods. Any reel should have a good antibacklash device, a level wind, and a smooth, reliable drag, plus a capacity for 100 to 150 yards of 10- or 12-pound-test line. Light weight is important in a reel because it reduces casting fatigue. Bass anglers who spend the most time on the water opt for a free spool reel with ball bearings. Check to be certain that the reel spool flanges fit snugly into the frame of the reel. Otherwise your line will be nicked or cut and eventually lose you a good bass.

To prolong reel life, as well as to improve your own casting skill, keep every reel clean and lubricated according to the manufacturer's instructions. Most casters prefer large or oversize handles on their reels and often replace the small ones that come from the factory. It is good advice to carry spare parts, especially for the level wind mechanism, in your tackle box. The bottom line is to buy the best casting reel you can afford and then care for it like the precision, high-performance instrument it is.

Some hard-core bass fishermen have apoplexy at the mere mention of them, but closed-face or spin-casting reels do play an important role in modern bass fishing. Reels of this design fit onto all the standard casting rods; the line is carried on a stationary spool inside a closed housing. It feeds—or flows out—when cast through a small hole in the housing. You simply hold your finger on a button until you cast forward (with the

Typical bait or plug-casting reels.

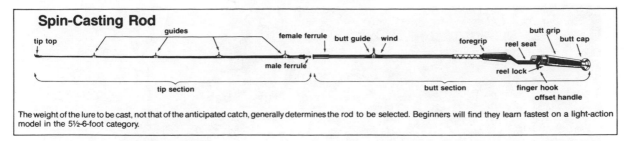

Spin-Casting Rod

The weight of the lure to be cast, not that of the anticipated catch, generally determines the rod to be selected. Beginners will find they learn fastest on a light-action model in the 5½-6-foot category.

Typical closed or spin-casting reel.

rod) and then lift your finger. The lure shoots out toward its target. To retrieve, as with usual bait-casting reels, you change hands and turn the reel handle with your casting hand. The closed-face reels are designed to be foolproof, flawless in casting, and to eliminate backlashes. Most work very well, too, although there is a loss in casting accuracy, which is why the experts disdain them. Nonetheless, closed-face

reels have made it possible for many people, who would not otherwise have become addicted, to enjoy bass fishing.

Spinning Tackle

Although plug-casting tackle is the standard—the old traditional reliable—for largemouth bass fishermen, many also carry along a medium spinning outfit designed for (approximately) 8-pound-test line and to deliver smaller or midsize lures (¼ to ⅜ ounce) and/or live bait. Spinning rods are made of the same material as casting rods, and the quality of these should be checked in the same manner. A spinning rod for bass should tend to be on the stiff side rather than limber. It is excellent advice to try out as many as possible in the 6-foot length before actually buying one.

There are just enough times when a year-round bass-fishing addict will need an ultralight spinning outfit to justify its acquisition. That is especially true if the bass are smallmouths and the water is free of vegetation and of great clarity, as smallmouth lakes are likely to be. The ultralight rod will be about five feet and designed to toss midget lures at fairly long distances with line testing about four pounds.

Of all the numerous items of fishing tackle,

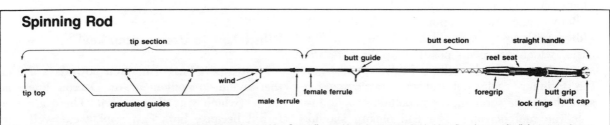

Spinning Rod

Spinning rods are characterized by straight handles and graduated ring guides. Generally speaking, they can be divided into five classes, ultralight to extra-heavy; each class determined by the optimum lure weight range of each rod. (See "Balanced Fishing Tackle.") For class and general tournament purposes, use a light-action, 5½-6½-foot rod capable of casting 1/4-3/8-ounce lures.

Largemouth-bass fisherman fights jumping bass on spinning reel.

none come in such bewildering variety as spinning reels. Fortunately a lot of them are good and differ only in cosmetics, minor adjustments, or the amount of advertising and promotion heaped on them. The main advantage of spinning reels over bait-casting reels is the higher rate of retrieve of the former, as well as the chance it offers to use smaller, lighter lures.

Before acquiring a spinning reel, attach it (filled with line) to a rod and make short flip casts, which are even possible inside a tackle store. Be sure the line flows freely, easily from the stationary reel spool. But when retrieving, be sure that same spool moves smoothly, snugly, inside the reel housing. The bail pickup should work—should flip over—easily, without forcing the reel handle. And, most important, the reel should have a velvet-smooth drag. Set the drag at various settings, and at each one, manually pull line off the end of the reel. If the pressure is not smooth and even, reject the reel and look for another. When you are playing lively game fish on light line, a smooth drag always is essential.

Which Line to Use on Your Reel

Most expert bass fishermen nowadays use either nylon monofilament or Dacron lines, no matter which way they cast it. These are preferred because both cast well, wear well, and apparently have low visibility to fish; the lighter (smaller diameter) the line, the lower the visi-

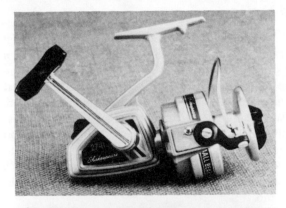

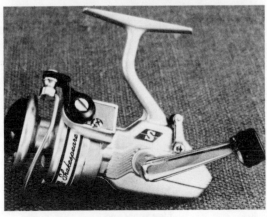

bility. However, a good line must also retain its strength when knotted, resist impact and abrasion, be of low "stretchability," and be very limp both in cold and in warm water. Pick up a coil of line and if it feels either stiff or brittle, it is old or of low quality, and therefore not fit to use. Some fishing lines on the market today contain a fluorescence that is not visible (some tests show) under water, but that is easier to see above water, to the angler's advantage. For example, high above-water visibility helps a large-mouth fisherman to detect the slightest twitch when he is worming.

It should be mentioned here that braided lines are still used by bass fishermen who find the extra limpness to be more "comfortable" or helpful in preventing line snarls. Braided lines also may be a boon to beginners who, later on, with additional practice, can switch over to the monofilaments.

As a rule of thumb, reels should be filled with the lightest monofilaments or Dacron that is practical for the angling situations you are likely to encounter. In other words, you must consider water clarity, weight of your lures, light conditions, season, the size of bass you are most likely to hook, and, most important of all: Is the water open, as full of weeds as a salad bowl, or choked with brush? Obviously, then, your line might range from a frail four-pound-test to a twenty-five-pound-test, in the extreme case of giant bass lurking in heavy brush or vegetation. There are actually some lakes in the Deep South where the latter strength is practically dictated.

Dacron lines are certainly worth considering, no matter what the test strength, for one very

Spool under filled

Spool over filled

Spool correctly filled

Typical spinning reels.

important reason: Dacron has far less stretch than monofilament. This is important when setting the hook because there is less time lag (only a split second, but critical nevertheless) between the raising of the rod tip and the actual bite of the hook.

For most average bass fishing, nationwide, a bass fisherman's reel can be filled with 10-to-15-pound-test line and serve well. The spool of a bait casting reel should be filled to within about ⅜ inch of the flange. A spinning reel works best if filled to within about ¼ inch below the outside diameter of the spool's rim.

Lines and Reels

Any line ever made loses strength from friction, age, and continued use. So it is a good idea to replace a line at least once a year, and maybe more often if the angler fishes frequently.

Line can twist right from the start if a reel spool is filled incorrectly. With spinning and closed-face tackle, the best way to fill a reel is to have a friend hold the packaging spools. The

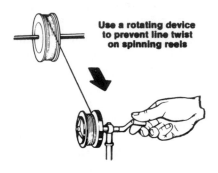

Use a rotating device to prevent line twist on spinning reels

spools must face the reel, and line must spiral off the packaging spools in the same direction the bail is winding line onto the reel spool. Check this by holding up your arms and sighting from behind the reel as you turn the handle. Many reels have bails that turn counterclockwise. Of course, the line pickup pins and winding cup take the place of the bail on spin-casting reels.

Too loose a drag setting can cause line-twist problems on a spinning reel. If the pull from a fish exceeds the drag setting, and you continue to reel, the bail will rotate around the spool, but the line will not actually be wound back on. Each complete turn of the bail puts one twist into the line. Keep turning and you will soon have a badly twisted line. Never turn that handle unless line is actually being retrieved. To pull in a heavy fish or snag, use a pumping technique.

Bass casting reels with revolving spools should be filled by the direct-transfer method to prevent twisting. This method consists of having a friend stick a pencil through the hole in the packaging spool to serve as an axle. As he holds both ends of the pencil, wind line directly onto your reel spool. You can be certain the spool is neatly and compactly wound by squeezing the line between your thumb and forefinger. Incidentally, a slip knot with an overhand knot tied in the free end can be used to fasten your line to the spool.

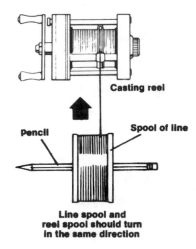

Casting reel

Pencil   Spool of line

Line spool and reel spool should turn in the same direction

There is a temptation to pay too little attention to the fishing line we buy, and too often an angler might settle for the cheapest available. But that is false economy.

The line that any bass fisherman uses is just as important as his rod and reel; the success of a whole expensive trip could depend on it.

Traditional bait-casting tackle accounted for this heavy largemouth bass.

Chapter 4

BAIT-CASTING AND SPINNING TECHNIQUES

As strange as it may seem, distance is not all-important in casting for bass. There may be a few instances when a long toss is necessary, but day in and day out, the short, accurate casts catch most of the largemouth bass. There are a good many guides and professionals today who rarely throw a lure more than thirty or thirty-five feet. Casts of fifty to sixty feet are considered very long. So keep this important fact in mind as we consider correct casting techniques.

The Four Steps to Casting

Accurate casting should be the goal. In many situations it isn't possible to deliver a bait or a lure without snagging it, unless it is accurately placed. And with today's new rods and reels it is an easy matter for anyone to acquire accuracy after a minimum of basic training, plus plenty of practice on the water. Casting is as easy as aim, back cast, forward cast, stop.

The following four steps, correctly performed, tell the whole story of casting. First aim your rod almost as you would a rifle and concentrate on the target. Using your elbow as a pivot, bring the rod back smoothly and halt it when almost vertical. Then snap it forward with a firm downstroke, applying extra wrist power as you do so.

When the rod reaches a point halfway between the vertical and the horizontal position, ease off with your thumb or forefinger to permit the line to pay out. Exactly how this is done will depend on the type of reel—bait casting, close-face or spin-bait casting, or spinning. When the lure approaches the target, feather or thumb it to a stop. It would be hard to describe the technique in a simpler manner. But it wasn't always that easy.

Bait Casting

Bait casting is an all-American technique. It was born when fishing watchmakers in Frankfort, Kentucky, developed a precision-multiplying reel—a reel that would permit smooth and effortless casting of a bait and whose spool, during both casting and retrieve, would make several turns for each turn of the reel handle. Bait casting received its biggest boost when the famous old Dowagiac, Rush Tango, and Pfleuger Tandem Spinner lures were developed and widely distributed. The next great development after that was the level-wind mechanism, which automatically spooled line evenly on the retrieve. Other developments came in the form of continual and ongoing improvements in bait-casting line, resulting in today's monofilament and Dacron lines.

Bait casting is largely a matter of co-ordination between wrist and thumb. The rod is held so that the reel handles are up and slightly pointed toward the caster at the beginning and end of each cast. The grip on the rod handle should be firm but not tight. The thumb should be placed so that it can control the revolutions of the reel spool.

The caster should lower the rod in front of himself to approximately the ten-o'clock position, pointing the tip at the target. When the target is lined up, the caster should bring the rod upright with a snap of the wrist—plus a very little bit of arm movement. The upward motion

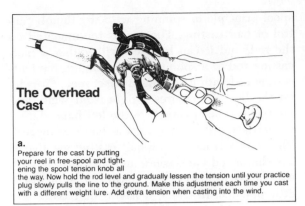

The Overhead Cast

a.
Prepare for the cast by putting your reel in free-spool and tightening the spool tension knob all the way. Now hold the rod level and gradually lessen the tension until your practice plug slowly pulls the line to the ground. Make this adjustment each time you cast with a different weight lure. Add extra tension when casting into the wind.

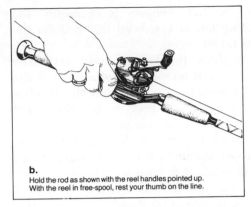

b.
Hold the rod as shown with the reel handles pointed up. With the reel in free-spool, rest your thumb on the line.

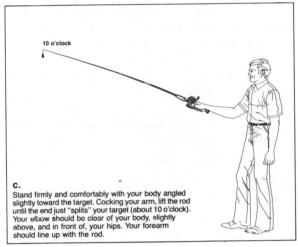

10 o'clock

c.
Stand firmly and comfortably with your body angled slightly toward the target. Cocking your arm, lift the rod until the end just "splits" your target (about 10 o'clock). Your elbow should be clear of your body, slightly above, and in front of, your hips. Your forearm should line up with the rod.

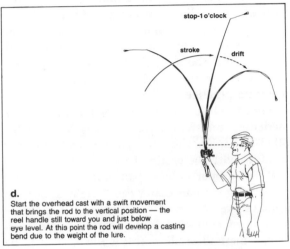

stop-1 o'clock

stroke   drift

d.
Start the overhead cast with a swift movement that brings the rod to the vertical position — the reel handle still toward you and just below eye level. At this point the rod will develop a casting bend due to the weight of the lure.

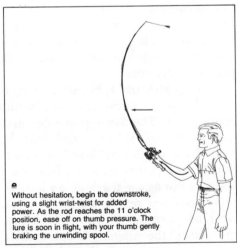

e.
Without hesitation, begin the downstroke, using a slight wrist-twist for added power. As the rod reaches the 11 o'clock position, ease off on thumb pressure. The lure is soon in flight, with your thumb gently braking the unwinding spool.

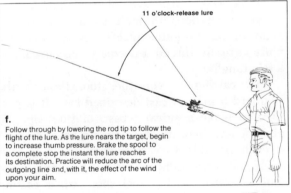

11 o'clock-release lure

f.
Follow through by lowering the rod tip to follow the flight of the lure. As the lure nears the target, begin to increase thumb pressure. Brake the spool to a complete stop the instant the lure reaches its destination. Practice will reduce the arc of the outgoing line and, with it, the effect of the wind upon your aim.

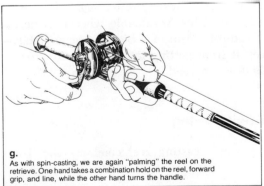

g.
As with spin-casting, we are again "palming" the reel on the retrieve. One hand takes a combination hold on the reel, forward grip, and line, while the other hand turns the handle.

should be fast, and it must be stopped at no farther back than the one-o'clock position. It is better still to stop it at twelve o'clock.

Without a second's hesitation the rod must be snapped forward again to about the ten-o'clock position and the pressure on the reel released so that line can run out. The forward thrust of the rod must be fast enough to put a fairly deep bend in the rod, because it is mostly the straightening out of this bend that delivers the lure to its target.

The thumb is the key to every cast. The thumb should rest on some stationary part of the reel as well as on the spool, because this steadies the thumb—just as a heel on the floorboard steadies a foot on a car accelerator.

When thumb pressure on the spool is removed at the proper instant, the lure will travel to its target. But while it is traveling the caster must maintain contact with the whirling reel spool with the tip or side of his thumb. Too little pressure allows the line to overrun and backlash into a "bird's nest." Too much pressure shortens and stops the cast. This controlling of pressure with the thumb is the most difficult part of bait casting. However the knack comes quickly to any one with practice.

After the lure is cast to a target, the reel is immediately transferred from casting hand to the other hand. The lure is then retrieved (the reel wound) with the casting hand.

When properly done, bait casting is beautiful to see. A good bait caster can literally knock out a gnat's eye at forty feet. Because of its delicate method of control it is the most accurate bass-fishing method of all, and it is *the* method to be used in tight places—in flooded jungles, in heavy vegetation, through stump "fields," in many of the forgotten places where every cast must virtually thread a needle or become hopelessly tangled.

Bait casting is versatile, too. Besides the standard overhand cast described here, it is possible to make a sidearm cast, or sideswipe, to place a lure beneath overhanging vegetation. It is even possible to cast underhand or to cast backhand into difficult spots. And the same thumb control of the reel spool when casting also gives the most positive control over a fighting fish. This is valuable when it is necessary to stop the run of a big fish—immediately—to keep it from getting into a sunken treetop or tangle of smartweed.

Spin-bait Casting

A spin-bait casting reel combines the fixed-spool principle of spinning with the thumb control of bait casting. The reel is top-mounted on the rod, and it can be used with either a bait-casting rod or a spinning rod, although the bait-casting rod with its standard offset reel seat is by far the best. It features a right-hand wind, and the reel can be "palmed" in the left hand during the retrieve just like the regular bait-casting reel. The chief virtues of spin-bait casting are that it has eliminated backlashes, and that anyone with normal co-ordination can master it with just a little practice. In effect, it has made bass fishing easily possible for everyone.

Line peels off the end of the spool of a spin-bait casting reel, and an internal pickup device controls its release and engagement. As in other types of casting, the size of lure that can be used depends on rod action and diameter of the line. Most spin-bait casting reels of bass size operate best with monofilament lines of about eight-pound test. A good, balanced spin-bait casting outfit will deliver lures from ¼ to ½ ounce.

One commonly heard objection to spin-bait casting reels is that the protective housing is such a great source of friction to the outgoing line that it reduces casting distance as compared to bait-casting reels handling lures of equal weight. Maybe that is true at extreme distances, but for all practical purposes, the range of these reels is adequate for any but the most unusual bass fishing. These reels constitute a great advancement in fishing tackle and become more popular every year.

Casting with the spin-bait casting reel is almost the same as casting with a standard bait-casting reel. The same principles apply to all casts—overhand, sidearm, and underhand. The main difference is that there is a push button for thumb control. On some models you press the lever to disengage the line, and on others you press and then release the lever to accomplish the same purpose. With some reels it is possible to "feather" the outgoing line, thereby slowing it down. Re-engaging the line is accomplished either by turning the reel handles or by touching the lever a second time. But the actual motion of casting is always the same.

Nearly all spin-bait casting reels now have antireverse mechanisms and smooth-running, jerk-free brakes.

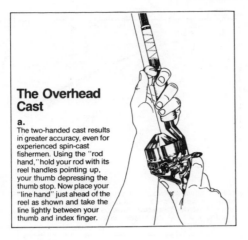

The Overhead Cast

a.
The two-handed cast results in greater accuracy, even for experienced spin-cast fishermen. Using the "rod hand," hold your rod with its reel handles pointing up, your thumb depressing the thumb stop. Now place your "line hand" just ahead of the reel as shown and take the line lightly between your thumb and index finger.

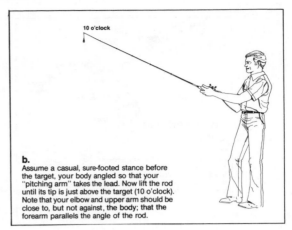

b.
Assume a casual, sure-footed stance before the target, your body angled so that your "pitching arm" takes the lead. Now lift the rod until its tip is just above the target (10 o'clock). Note that your elbow and upper arm should be close to, but not against, the body; that the forearm parallels the angle of the rod.

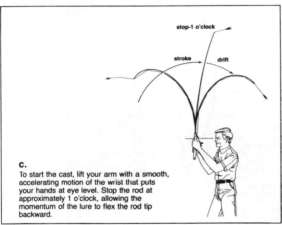

c.
To start the cast, lift your arm with a smooth, accelerating motion of the wrist that puts your hands at eye level. Stop the rod at approximately 1 o'clock, allowing the momentum of the lure to flex the rod tip backward.

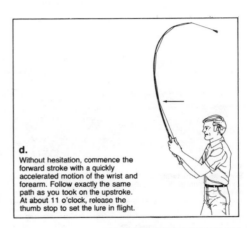

d.
Without hesitation, commence the forward stroke with a quickly accelerated motion of the wrist and forearm. Follow exactly the same path as you took on the upstroke. At about 11 o'clock, release the thumb stop to set the lure in flight.

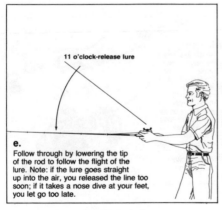

e.
Follow through by lowering the tip of the rod to follow the flight of the lure. Note: if the lure goes straight up into the air, you released the line too soon; if it takes a nose dive at your feet, you let go too late.

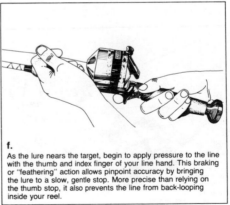

f.
As the lure nears the target, begin to apply pressure to the line with the thumb and index finger of your line hand. This braking or "feathering" action allows pinpoint accuracy by bringing the lure to a slow, gentle stop. More precise than relying on the thumb stop, it also prevents the line from back-looping inside your reel.

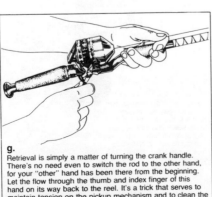

g.
Retrieval is simply a matter of turning the crank handle. There's no need even to switch the rod to the other hand, for your "other" hand has been there from the beginning. Let the flow through the thumb and index finger of this hand on its way back to the reel. It's a trick that serves to maintain tension on the pickup mechanism and to clean the line for another trouble-free cast.

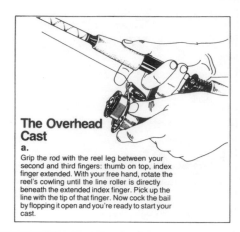

The Overhead Cast

a.
Grip the rod with the reel leg between your second and third fingers: thumb on top, index finger extended. With your free hand, rotate the reel's cowling until the line roller is directly beneath the extended index finger. Pick up the line with the tip of that finger. Now cock the bail by flopping it open and you're ready to start your cast.

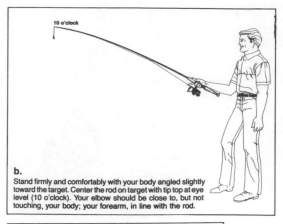

10 o'clock

b.
Stand firmly and comfortably with your body angled slightly toward the target. Center the rod on target with tip top at eye level (10 o'clock). Your elbow should be close to, but not touching, your body; your forearm, in line with the rod.

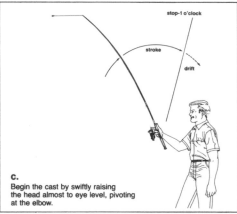

stop-1 o'clock

stroke

drift

c.
Begin the cast by swiftly raising the head almost to eye level, pivoting at the elbow.

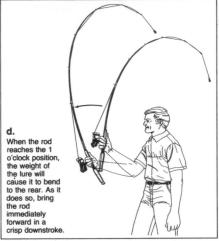

d.
When the rod reaches the 1 o'clock position, the weight of the lure will cause it to bend to the rear. As it does so, bring the rod immediately forward in a crisp downstroke.

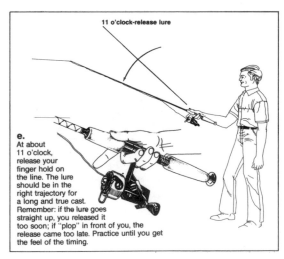

11 o'clock-release lure

e.
At about 11 o'clock, release your finger hold on the line. The lure should be in the right trajectory for a long and true cast. Remember: if the lure goes straight up, you released it too soon; if "plop" in front of you, the release came too late. Practice until you get the feel of the timing.

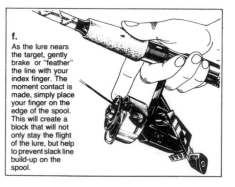

f.
As the lure nears the target, gently brake or "feather" the line with your index finger. The moment contact is made, simply place your finger on the edge of the spool. This will create a block that will not only stay the flight of the lure, but help to prevent slack line build-up on the spool.

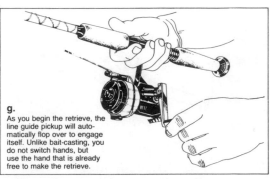

g.
As you begin the retrieve, the line guide pickup will automatically flop over to engage itself. Unlike bait-casting, you do not switch hands, but use the hand that is already free to make the retrieve.

Spinning

A generation or so ago only a handful of anglers believed that European spinning with its fixed-spool, open-faced reels of radically different designs would ever be popular in America. But ten years after World War II ended, spinning was firmly entrenched in this country. Nearly every angler owned a spinning outfit, and its ease of operation had made it possible for many more citizens to take up a fascinating sport. Spinning was simple, trouble-free, and easy to learn. It eliminated the backlash, and that was to fishing history what inventing the wheel was to world history.

But today, spinning with the standard open-faced reels is only secondary in importance to most largemouth bass fishermen. However, many smallmouth anglers fishing in the Great Lakes region use the open-face reels almost exclusively. Spinning owes its important place in bass fishing to its ability to deliver the very small lures—of ¼ ounce and even smaller—that are so necessary to take bass at certain times and in certain places. It is not as accurate a method as bait casting, but it is accurate enough for most open-water situations or in waters where fishing pressure is extra-heavy and where bass are so sophisticated that very light line must be used.

Spinning is an easy, uncomplicated technique with many applications in bass fishing.

The actual act of spinning is much the same as bait and spin-bait casting. You aim, back cast, forward cast, and stop. The back cast should stop at the vertical or one-o'clock position, and the forward cast should follow without even a split second's pause to about ten o'clock. Only the use of thumb and fingers is different in spinning. And retrieving (for a right-handed caster) is done with the left hand. You do not switch hands after each cast.

Just before aiming, the caster picks up the line with his right forefinger and holds it away from the bail. Meanwhile, with the left hand the "bail" is turned or flipped over to the open position. Then midway of the forward cast the line is allowed to slip off the forefinger and to peel off the fixed spool of the reel. It can be feathered by the forefinger as it peels off, and it can be stopped on target by placing the forefinger on the spool or by a quick forward turn of the reel handle, which also closes the bail.

Some delicate timing is involved in releasing line at the proper instant, but usually this comes quickly with practice—backyard practice if no water is readily available. Otherwise, spinning is as easy—and as pleasant—as that.

Practice Casting at Home

Any fisherman can become a fairly good caster, no matter what kind of tackle he uses, before ever venturing out on the water. He can practice in his own backyard, in a school playground or a nearby public park. Assume that you live in typical Suburbia, U.S.A; you then have a perfect practice area.

First set up your casting tackle with a practice casting weight instead of a regular hooked lure knotted to the end of your line. Next, at different casting distances around your lawn, place a number of inner tubes, bicycle tires, hoola hoops, frisbees, or anything else that will make suitable casting targets. Standing in one place, keep casting at those targets until you hit them almost every time, which shouldn't be too difficult if your tackle is balanced and your casting technique is correct.

Once you have achieved accuracy standing up, take a kitchen chair or box or anything else that most closely resembles a boat seat out into

Plug casting allows anglers to toss lures accurately along tangled shorelines such as this.

the yard. Now start casting toward the same targets while sitting down. Continue until you have reached the same almost automatic accuracy as when standing erect.

The next step is to try to simulate actual bass-fishing conditions as much as possible. Change the position of your targets. Place them beside, beneath, or even behind trees, hedges, and clumps of shrubbery so that hitting them is much more difficult. But keep in mind that these are exactly the kinds of situations you will find on many bass lakes. For example you may have to deliver a lure between two trees standing in water or beneath an undercut bank. Throw underarm and sidearm as well as overhand. Learn to cast well with both left and right hands. This will come in handy later on, when you are actually fishing, to relieve the fatigue of casting for hours with just one hand alone. (NOTE: Changing back and forth from bait casting to spinning tackle also helps relieve monotony and fatigue.) Another tip is to take advantage of any local park ponds or reservoirs for practice casting. In many towns there are casting clubs with their own practice ponds available. During the off-season, find a suitable indoor swimming pool.

It is true that some neighbors may at first regard your backyard practice as slightly bonkers. But pity them because they probably have not yet discovered bass fishing.

Casting Problems

Most fishermen too quickly blame casting problems on tackle, and sometimes a reel or an improper line will indeed be the culprit. If you are having trouble with either distance or accuracy, check with the handiest expert to see if your technique is correct. If it is, a simple cleaning or servicing job on the reel might solve the problem. But often the most common cause of casting problems, especially with spinning or spin-casting, is an insufficient quantity of line on the reel spool. In the previous chapter, we indicated exactly how and how much line should go onto a reel. Recheck this.

Rather than completely filling a reel spool with line, which is not inexpensive, many bass fishermen first install a cork arbor on the spool, thereby reducing the line capacity to about half. Only very, very rarely, if ever, does a bass fisher-

man really need more than seventy-five yards of line on any reel.

Tackle improperly balanced is probably the second most common cause of casting problems. When reel spools are filled to the proper level, and the angler still cannot cast far enough, the odds are good his tackle is not properly balanced. This usually means the line is too heavy for the lures, or the rod is too stiff and the caster is not using enough weight to bring out the rod's action.

Casting distance and accuracy are achieved by matching a light line to lightweight lures, and vice versa. Most quality rods have a decal located on the butt section that indicates the line test and lure weights recommended for the rod. If you stay within these guidelines, and match light lines to light lures and heavier lines to heavier lures, you are on the right track. The manufacturer's line and lure recommendations should always be considered.

Line dig-in is another frequent cause of casting problems with spin-casting reels. This is the result of tightly winding line over underlying loose coils. When casting, the tightly wound coils become caught, causing a decrease in distance. The chances of line dig-in are reduced by palming your reel and squeezing the line between thumb and forefinger as you retrieve. This will eliminate loose coils and still assure a neat, compactly wound spool.

A properly wound reel spool will increase casting efficiency with other types of tackle, as well. This can be accomplished by always maintaining some form of tension on your line when retrieving. But do not overdo this, since excessive tension applied to a monofilament line can crush or crack reel spools.

Backlash or spool overrun is a common problem with bait casting tackle. It happens when the angler uses a stiff, springy monofilament line and does not match it with a heavy enough casting weight. But it can also be caused by an improperly adjusted reel. To adjust the mechanical brake or spool-tension control, rig your rod, reel, and the lure you intend to use. Hold your rod parallel to the ground and depress the free-spool button or lever. The brake or tension control applies tension to the end of the spool axle. This should be adjusted so that the lure drops slowly to the ground and the spool stops turning as soon as the lure hits. The reel should be

checked and readjusted if necessary every time a fisherman changes his line or lure weight. Of course, bait casting does take timing and skill, which come with practice and experience.

Problems with Reels

Often maintenance is the simple solution to reel problems. Periodically, any reel should be disassembled, inspected, cleaned, and the internal mechanism relubricated. Disassemble only those parts that must be removed to facilitate maintenance, in order to save wear and tear on screw threads. Metallic parts can be cleaned with some mild solvent applied with an old toothbrush. Use the brush with a household detergent, or just an old rag, to clean the nonmetallic parts. Be sure to work in a clean, uncluttered area to avoid loss of small parts.

Spinning accounts for good bass whether you are wading or fishing from a boat.

Prior to reassembling a spinning or spin-casting reel, coat each part with a protective layer of light oil. A reel that is kept clean and lubricated sparingly with a light oil will operate far more freely in cold weather. A light silicone-base grease is good. It is also wise to apply a layer of grease around the housing edge before reinstalling the cover plate. This will form a protective gasket and help seal the inside of the reel.

The gears of bait-casting reels should be lubricated with a light oil. The bearings, bushings, spool axle, line-carriage screw, and other moving parts are best lubricated with a lightweight oil. Never overoil your reel, as this is messy, wasteful, and the excess oil only picks up abrasive dirt, sand, and other grit. Too much oil can also accumulate dust and lint, which will clog parts and prevent them from working freely. Just follow the manufacturer's lubricating instructions for the best possible performance.

A serious bass fisherman should keep reels away from all sharp edges to prevent damage to the finish and parts such as the bail, which could cause line abrasion. Never lay down reels in dirt or sand because the abrasive qualities of these substances grind on moving parts. Except on the water, some kind of protective case is recommended to store and keep reels free of dirt. Zippered and draw-string leather or vinyl pouches are made for this purpose by some companies.

Chapter 5

GUARANTEED TECHNIQUES AND TIPS FOR TAKING BASS: I

Bass fishermen today can choose from a bewildering number of fishing aids: "expert" systems, printed tables, stages-of-the-moon calendars, even complicated computer projections on when, where, and how to go fishing. Thus it may seem that a wholesome, exciting outdoor sport is being transformed into a predictable ho-hum event. But the truth is that an angler might just as well depend on astrology, flipping coins or the arthritis in his joints. At the very best, it is debatable whether any system yet devised for catching bass is ever more than 50 per cent accurate.

However, there are a few elements on which a fisherman can depend—most of the time in most places. Spring usually is the best time of year to fish for bass, since this is when bass move into shallower water (where they are most accessible) to spawn as the water gradually warms to the ideal temperature for the species. Day in and day out, we know that dawn and dusk tend to be better than midday. Somehow the approach of a storm front (but rarely its aftermath) is a top time to be fishing. But what is true one place may be all wrong elsewhere. Local weather conditions can throw a wrench into any system, to any calculation, or, more to the point, to any fishing trip.

So the happy solution is to go fishing whenever you can and try to beat the handicaps with whatever methods work for you. Before you go, read carefully the following techniques and tips. All are tried and true—at least somewhere and some of the time. Among them you just may find

the key to catching the best stringer of bass of your fishing life.

More different bass lures have been manufactured, and more are on the market today, than have ever been counted or catalogued. The total number must be high into five figures and does not even include the homemade, or limited-edition, lures that are few in number but still account for a lot of bass. Lures could be categorized as top-water, shallow-running (when retrieved), medium-running, and deep-running or deep-divers. Artificial baits can also be classed as fast or slow retrieve. Some are weedless (meaning "snagless"); others are not. Another way to view them would be as naturals (which imitate some actual living creature) or unnaturals, such as the spinners, which do not resemble anything that ever lived. All this is too confusing. In this chapter we will categorize the different types of lures by the techniques that call for them, in order to simplify the advice, especially for sportsmen who are not yet experienced or who do not always understand the strange jargon of the veteran bass fishermen.

Jigging

Jigs are the oldest artifical lures in the world, having been used by ancient people everywhere from the Arctic to the tropics. Until the past few decades, their use by American sport fishermen had been confined to salt water. A jig is nothing more than a weighted head (or forepart), usu-

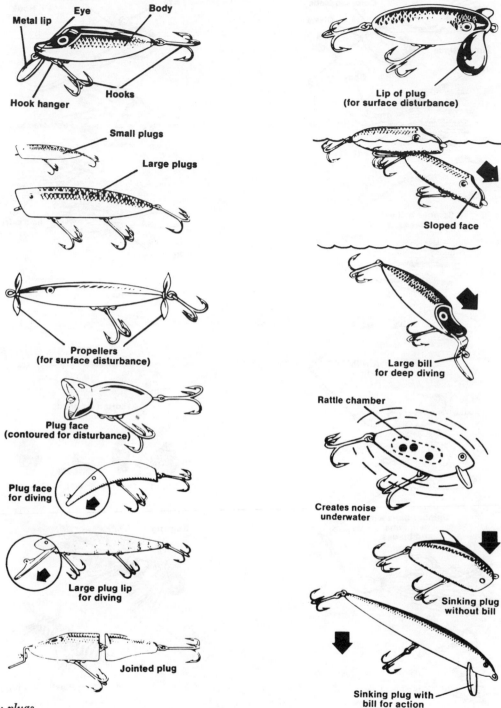

Eye
Metal lip
Body
Hook hanger
Hooks

Lip of plug
(for surface disturbance)

Small plugs

Large plugs

Sloped face

Propellers
(for surface disturbance)

Large bill
for deep diving

Plug face
(contoured for disturbance)

Rattle chamber

Plug face
for diving

Creates noise
underwater

Large plug lip
for diving

Sinking plug
without bill

Jointed plug

Sinking plug with
bill for action

Bass lures: plugs

ally of molded lead, with a tail composed of hair, hackles, yarn, nylon, pork, or plastic. Perhaps bucktail is the most popular tail material nationwide. Depending on how it is fished, a jig can imitate the antics of a crayfish or a bottom-dwelling small fish such as a sculpin. Jigs are versatile enough to be used with live (or natu-

ral) baits, with trailer hooks, or with soft plastic worm lures. Compact and easy to cast, a jig is strictly a bottom or deep-running lure.

Basically, jigging means casting the jig, allowing it to sink to the bottom and then retrieving it slowly in short, sharp jerks along the bottom. There are many variations, especially in the re-

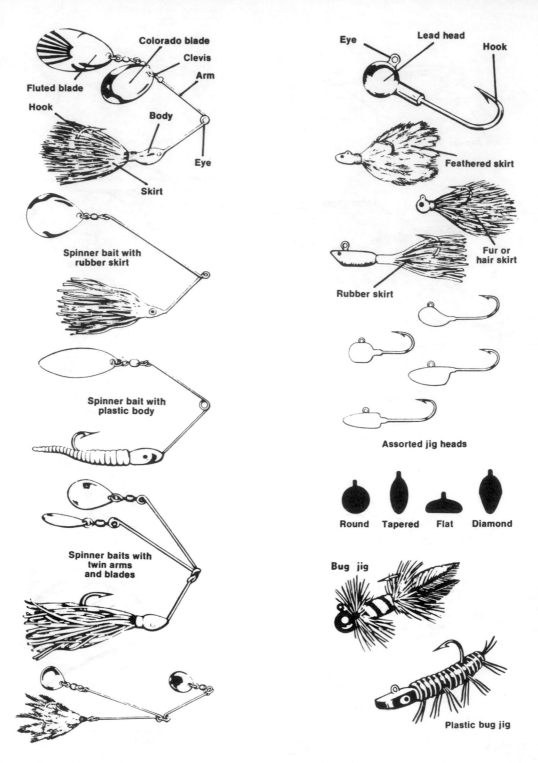

Bass lures: spinner baits and jigs

trieve. But obviously jigging is easier to describe than to execute because the bottoms in very few bass lakes are smooth. When jigging, a bass fisherman also must avoid fouling on underwater obstacles and snags.

Jigging is probably the most consistent technique yet discovered for lake-dwelling smallmouth bass, for two reasons. Smallmouths, even more so than largemouths, tend to be on the bottom of any lake, no matter what the depth.

Smallmouth bass taken on a jig in Tennessee.

Steep, rocky shorelines such as this are good spots for jigging.

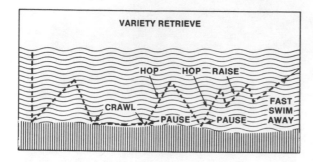

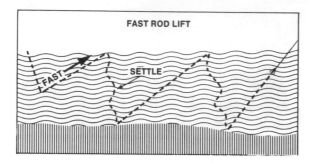

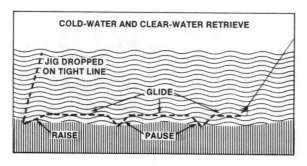

Fishing a jig.

Smallmouths also prefer more open water with gravel or rocky beds, rather than the snag-infested or very weedy waters where large-mouths live and where jigging is a lot tougher. In the bays and over the reefs in Lake Erie and the other Great Lakes, jigs, live bait, or a combination of the two may account for 90 per cent of the smallmouth bass taken. The trick always is to locate the bass first and then to jig the bottom for them.

Unlike many artificial baits, leadhead jigs display little action of their own. A jig's appeal to fish is determined by its appearance and by a particular method of "working" it. You can bounce or hop a jig, or swim it straight, but try all of these variations, fast and slow, until you find the correct combination.

When casting for largemouth or smallmouth bass, variations of a simple "lift and drop" retrieve often work best. While retrieving your jig, repeatedly pull your rod tip forward and let it drop back down. This pumping motion of the rod allows the jig to hop along the bottom. Sometimes you will catch more fish by exaggerating this jigging action with sharp, sweeping strokes of the rod; on other, rarer, occasions you will score with short twitches or even with a straight retrieve.

Use monofilament line as light as any jigging conditions permit. A useful guideline: The smaller the jig, the lighter the line. Also the more open the water, the lighter the line can be. Knot your jig directly to the line. Avoid leaders, snaps, swivels, and extra sinkers. If more weight is needed to cast against wind or to compensate

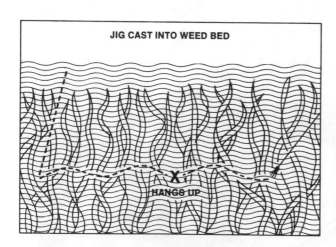

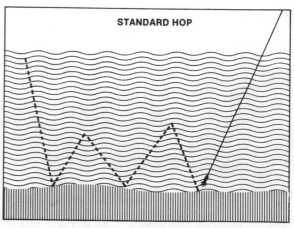

for boat speed (if you happen to be trolling or drifting), go to a heavier jig.

When tipping (baiting) jigs with small minnows, crayfish, or pieces of worm, strike back right away, especially when fish are hitting hard. But with large minnows and whole nightcrawlers (live or plastic), point your rod tip toward the fish for a moment before setting the hook. This brief hesitation allows the fish time to work the bait and more importantly, the hook into its mouth. Smallmouths may even scoop tipped jigs right off the bottom! When tipping with minnows, pork strips, plastic worms, or other bait, you'll get more of these "bottom bites" with a jig that literally stands on its head and elevates the hook, making your bait readily visible and easy to grab.

Slow trolling or just drifting with a breeze allows you to maintain your preferred jigging action without the usual casting and retrieving. How much line to let out will depend on depth level of the fish, the weight of your jig, and the speed of your boat. In unfamiliar lakes, trolling and drifting methods can be ideal for locating fish, or at least fish structures. In time and with experience, it becomes possible to almost "feel" your way over the bottom, somehow avoiding most of the snags.

Very often bass strike jigs on the drop. An alert angler can detect these hard-to-notice strikes by closely watching his line for unusual behavior—such as the slightest telltale twitch or knock on the line. Sometimes the line moves off to one side or just stops while the jig is settling. That is a good signal to set the hook immediately. Many lures, especially the spoons and plugs, have built-in action. But regardless of how you do it with jigs, *you* provide the action and that adds much to the fascination—and also to the success—of jigging.

One jigging variation well worth mentioning here is the use of two smaller jigs in tandem at the same time. The technique is mostly designed for crappies, but in bass waters it catches just as many bass, particularly smallmouths. If you normally cast a ⅜-ounce jig, tie instead a ¼-ounce jig to the end of your line. Then with a short (say, 6-inch to 8-inch) dropper line and a blood knot, tie a second ¼-ounce jig about 2 feet above the terminal jig. As you retrieve the tandem rig, the two jigs will have slightly different actions, one of which may prove more seductive to a hungry bass.

Spoon Jigging

Recently in many waters of the deeper bass reservoirs of the South, the Southwest, and Southern California, a variation of jigging—spoon jigging—has greatly expanded the bass fisherman's season. It is a technique that works well from late autumn through early spring, when bass retreat to find warmer water farther down. And now a few fishermen are pioneering with jig spoons during midsummer dog days when bass also go deep, but this time to locate cooler water.

The more or less standard lure for this is a wobbling spoon of the old, familiar, shoehorn-shaped Daredevil type, weighing ½ ounce to ¾ ounce, with silver or brass finish; the more fluttery its action, the better the spoon for jigging vertically. The technique is as simple as any can be. A fisherman locates his fish or his fish structure from a boat and then drops the spoon straight down to them. No casting skills are required here. The spoon is then jiggled, jigged, fluttered, and manipulated upward in as tantalizing a manner as possible to provoke a strike, perhaps many.

Obviously finding fish first is the secret to success here. If a fisherman does not have an electronic depth and/or fish finder, he must instead have an accurate knowledge of fish structures in the lake and the ability to pinpoint them exactly from geographical features on the shore. Coldwater bass are not very active and (with a few notable exceptions) not very widespread, so spoon jigging will not pay off unless it's done right where bass are living.

Two kinds of bass are targets for spoon jigging. Most important are the largemouths clustered around such likely structures as dropoffs,

HOW TO TIE THE TANDEM JIG RIG

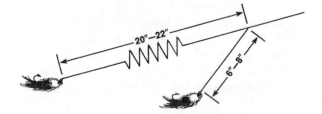

20″–22″

6″–8″

SPOON JIGGING TECHNIQUE

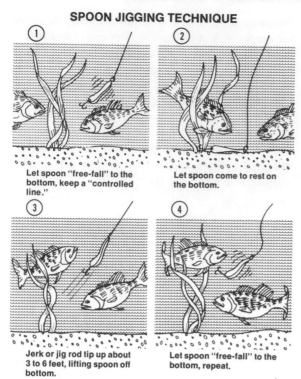

1. Let spoon "free-fall" to the bottom, keep a "controlled line."

2. Let spoon come to rest on the bottom.

3. Jerk or jig rod tip up about 3 to 6 feet, lifting spoon off bottom.

4. Let spoon "free-fall" to the bottom, repeat.

Spoon jigging early in the morning accounted for this bass about to be boated.

ledges, channel or creek bends, and particularly isolated trees or clumps of trees completely surrounded by deep water. A bass fisherman may occasionally find fish in the crowns of such trees, but according to the best spoon jiggers, they will most often be around the base of it. It is feast-or-famine fishing: Find one and you almost certainly have found a whole school.

The other possible target of spoon jigging is a school of suspended or cruising bass at some middepth. As often as not (if the species is well established in that particular lake) these will be spotted rather than largemouth bass and they will be following behind or underneath (perhaps feeding on) a school of shad. While a depth locator is very important for finding deep bass structure, it is an absolute necessity for spotting cruising schools—and for following these fish in their erratic wandering. With a good locator, blips indicating bass will be clearly visible as long as they are beneath the boat.

Spoon jigging is most effective when fish are deeper than twenty-five or thirty-five feet and perhaps as far down as seventy feet or so. At such distances it can be hard to detect the strike of a large bass, but with a little practice, a fisherman soon reacts promptly enough to hook his fish. But almost as important as proper tackle

is what the spoon jigger wears. Jigging may be best when the weather is worst, and that means several layers of the warmest possible clothes. Even the most addicted bass fisherman will have trouble concentrating if he is cold and uncomfortable. But the rewards are worth some suffering. Those largemouths caught around deep winter structures usually weigh, on the average, a lot more than bass taken in balmier weather.

How to Fish Spinner Baits

One kind of bass lure that has long been popular, and that is either incredibly effective one day or a failure the next, is the spinner bait, which is also called the safety-pin lure. That is appropriate because it superficially resembles a large V-wire safety pin with hair or feathers. Spinner baits have lead bodies with either hackle, bucktail, or a plastic skirt tail covering a single hook on the lower wire. One or more spinners are affixed to spin freely from the upper wire. Sometimes the spinners are called blades, and good spinner-bait anglers are known as blademen.

Spinner baits are most effective in shallow-to-medium-depth water—say, down to eight or ten feet. A good many professional bassers use them especially when fishing shorelines where salt brush or tamarisk grows lush (as it does in the Southwest), in flooded timber, and where shoreline trees have been toppled over into the water.

Let's assume the boat is drifting slowly parallel to a shoreline where there is a mixture of deadfalls, sunken logs, new willow growth, and some vegetation—in other words, a typical bass area. As we go along, the best bet is to toss spinner baits right into the thickest portions of this cover, but varying the retrieve all the time. Say we've reached a fallen hickory with its crown far out in the water. The first cast could be toward the base of the trunk and then skittered back out to the boat close to the surface. Succeeding casts can then be retrieved deeper and slower so that the spinner works and flashes right down through the "heart" of the dead tree. If a bass resides there—anywhere within the tree cover—he is likely to see the flash and maybe make a pass at the lure.

Brushy, sloping points of land are good places to toss spinner baits, too. So are the edges of willow, bullrushes, or dead brush islands, as well as the more shallow bays of very deep lakes. Casting accuracy is far more important in spinner-bait fishing than in some other techniques because of snagging up in the brushy places fished. So one secret is to cast into the tiny openings in the brush. But every good spinner-bait caster eventually learns to "feel" his way over obstacles, to raise and lower his rod tip at the proper times. He also learns to flip the lure free of twigs, rather than to try to tear them loose. But exactly how to do these things cannot be adequately described and instead must come from actual experience.

There are times when a blademan will find that largemouth bass strike the lure even while it is sinking, following the cast. That happens most often when there is a sharp dropoff along the shore—and if it happens once, the angler is wise to watch for other sudden strikes this same way.

Spinner baiting is good for fishing cattails and bullrushes. But here, as in brush, the success may depend entirely on the speed of the retrieve. So as in almost all kinds of bass fishing, experiment with retrieve speeds. First try reeling just fast enough to revolve the spinners. Then a little faster. Finally crank the reel as fast as you can.

One technique that many skilled blademen use, especially along shorelines, is to buzz the lure (reel fast, just barely breaking the surface) for the first few feet to attract the attention of any bass nearby. Then allow the bait to sink a few feet before continuing the retrieve rather slowly. On some golden days it works like pure magic.

Another good piece of advice is to cast several times, maybe as many as ten or twelve, into any spot that looks like a genuine bass hideout, or where you may have hooked largemouths on previous occasions. Remember that any good

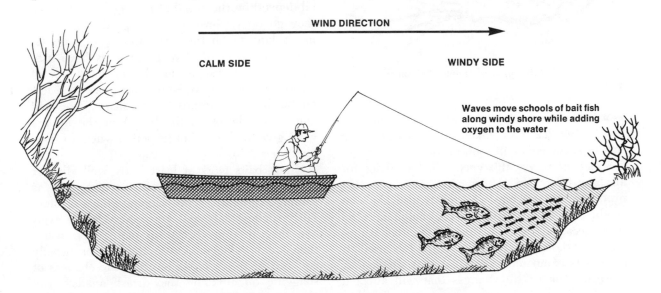

WIND DIRECTION

CALM SIDE   WINDY SIDE

Waves move schools of bait fish along windy shore while adding oxygen to the water

Largemouth bass hooked on a spinner bait.

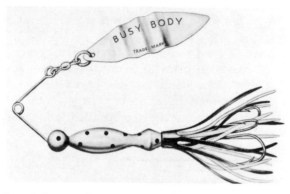

One of the countless types of spinner bait on the market today.

spot is likely to remain a good spot, even after a bass or two has been taken out. Odds are good that replacements will soon move in.

So let me repeat this very valuable advice for all bass fishermen everywhere: Any spot that produces bass on one occasion is also likely to produce bass, largemouths, or smallmouths on other occasions when water and weather conditions are the same. It is one of the few predictable facts of an unpredictable sport. Of course, there can be subtle changes that will affect a

bass's habits or routine—changes so subtle that a fisherman cannot detect them—such as pollution, lack of oxygen, or other deterioration in water quality.

Spinner baits are manufactured and sold in an astonishing variety of sizes, spinner-blade shapes, weights, and tail colors. The most serious blademen carry a large selection, which they constantly change when fishing to find the deadliest combination. The parts—blades and tails—often are interchangeable. Despite the variety available, many fishermen prefer to make their own spinner baits and so just buy a selection of needed parts, which they put together to suit their own whims. The cost per home-made lure averages about one third that of a manufactured bait, and several dozen can be assembled in a spare evening's time at home. But manufactured or home-made, carefully field-test each one before serious use. Be certain that the lure rides vertically in the water, spinners on top, and does not tilt or quarter to the side at any speed of retrieve. Also, the spinner should turn freely at even a very slow retrieve.

How to Use Crank Baits

Somewhere every year, especially on larger impoundments, so-called crank baits make bass-fishing headlines. But the term "crank bait" covers a fairly wide variety of artificial lures. Some float when at rest on the water, a few sink slowly, and the rest sink rapidly after a cast. But all depend on the speed of reeling for how deep they go on retrieve. Reeling speed also determines how much the lure vibrates or wobbles during a retrieve. All of these lures have fish-shaped bodies, usually of plastic, but a few of wood. They also have large plastic or metal lips on the head, or forepart. The shape, size, and angle (in relation to the body) of the lip are what give the lure all of its action when a fisherman reels it in.

Crank baits work at least fairly well all year long and in many kinds of structure such as sloping shorelines, gently sloping points of land, fairly shallow flats, and grassbeds. On the average they produce better in more open water than spinner baits because the one or usually two sets of treble hooks increase the chances of snagging on anything they brush against. But

A 12½-pound bass caught by Larry Helin on crank bait in Florida's Oklawaha River. Photo by Karl H. Maslowski.

steady bottom-bumping retrieve back to the boat. Incidentally, it is perfectly possible to fish from deep toward shallow water, as well as vice versa, by starting with a fast retrieve to gain depth and then gradually slowing down. Spawning bass that see a lure thus approaching the spawning bed (as might be the case anywhere in springtime) very often charge the lure.

Another tactic that pays off when casting over fairly level bottoms is to bottom-bump the lure

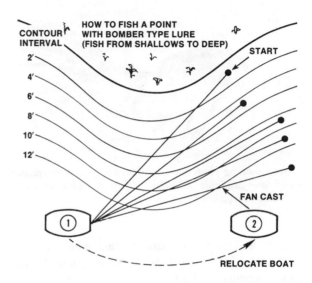

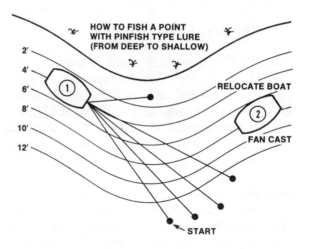

the percentage of hookups from strikes is high.

Again let's assume here a typical bass-fishing situation. A point of land slopes steadily out into the water for a long distance, creating a large area of shallow-to-medium-depth water. A good possibility here is a crank bait that floats at rest. So from either a drifting or an anchored boat, a very likely tactic is to broadcast (or fan-cast) the area thoroughly by casting toward shallowest water first and slowly dragging—bottom bumping gently—the crank bait into deeper and deeper water. The action or vibrations from most of these lures is such that a fisherman (even an inexperienced one) can soon feel his lure touching its way along the sloping lakebed. Slowing or increasing the rate of retrieve regulates the depth, and this is a satisfying as well as a productive way to find bass.

There are a few tricks to crank baiting, too. When casting toward shore, manipulate the lure exactly as a surface lure (see later) by jiggling it gently on top. Only after that delay, begin the

on retrieve, but with pauses in the reeling at brief intervals to allow the crank bait to rise slowly before bottom-bumping again. In the Southeast, bass seem to strike crank baits most readily where crayfish form a good to substantial part of their diet. In the Southwest crank baits also

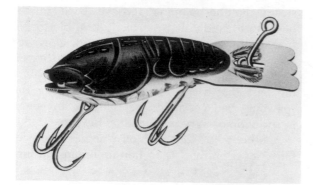

Deep running plugs such as these are great bass catchers and are available in many different styles on tackle shelves everywhere.

work well in those same waters where anglers are most successful with spring lizards—live salamanders—as bait.

Tailspinner Fishing

The tailspinner is a small, heavy-weighted (usually of lead), minnow-shaped lure with a fluttering metal tail and one set of treble hooks. Used in the right way and in the right places it can be a sensational fish-catcher. The lure was designed originally for making long casts in clear water and also for fishing fairly deep areas where a fast lure is necessary. Many good fishermen who specialize in tailspinning use a fairly long and fairly stiff spinning rod with a high-speed spinning reel instead of the standard plug-casting outfits they use to cast other types of lures. Ten-to-15-pound-test monofilament is recommended. The lighter the line, the deeper a lure of the same weight will run underwater.

A consensus of the best tailspinner anglers would reveal that they depend upon it most for fishing off points when the lake surface is fairly calm and visibility down into the water is very

good. When a wind blows and there is a chop on the surface, largemouth bass tend to move upward into shallow water where a tailspinner is difficult to fish.

Another super spot to try tailspinners—and to hook plenty of lunkers—is around submerged islands. A depth finder is necessary to locate these structures quickly and accurately. Almost invariably an island that lies beneath ten to fifteen feet of water and that is surrounded by much greater depth is a holding place for bass, as often as not including some of the biggest ones in the lake. That is doubly true if the island is moss-covered or has unseen vegetation growing from it. The way to fish these islands is to anchor nearby, or at one extreme end, but not directly over it. Then broadcast the entire island, retrieving with jig hops, allowing the lure to settle to the bottom each time.

Tom Mann of Alabama, who is a top tailspinner advocate, often uses what he calls a "ripping" method. He casts, allows the lure to sink to the bottom, takes up slack in the line, points the rod toward the lure, and then sharply lifts the rod to a vertical position—which "rips" the lure off the bottom. The next step is to let the lure sink back to the bottom as the tail blade turns, at which time most bass strike this kind of bait. All the time the line must be kept taut by turning the reel handle. Otherwise it may not be possible to feel the strike quickly enough, and the fish is lost. The fisherman should react to the smallest flick detectable on the line at any point during the retrieve.

At times just a straight, even retrieve, deep, will get results. If you feel a series of sharp

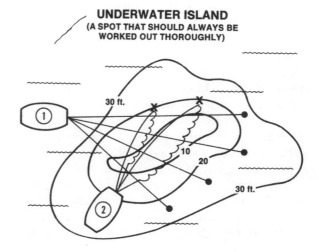

UNDERWATER ISLAND
(A SPOT THAT SHOULD ALWAYS BE WORKED OUT THOROUGHLY)

pecks, a bass is biting at the tail blade. Usually faster reeling or ripping will cause the bass to strike the body of the tailspinner and be hooked. Keep a tight line when a hooked fish jumps because this type of lure can be tossed free more easily than others.

The tailspinner is among the better lures in impoundments that contain smallmouth and spotted bass. It might also prove a valuable addition to the Great Lakes smallmouth angler's arsenal.

Although largemouth bass especially are considered to be a species of still, impounded waters, they do at times thrive in moving water —in currents, interconnecting narrows between lakes, in canals and drainage (or irrigation) waterways, even in the turbulent tailraces below

giant dams. Smallmouths frequent these places even more. One of the best possible lures to catch smallmouths or largemouths in these situations is the tailspinner.

Grubtail Fishing

Grubtail baits are so similar to jigs that fishing with grubtail baits is almost one and the same thing, with a few exceptions. These baits consist of a plastic body, molded in a spade-shape, as much like shrimptails as anything else, that fits onto jigging heads of various sizes. The spade-tails flip up and down when the lure is retrieved, or jigged, in a series of short hops. The grubs come in every color of the spectrum, are soft to

A grubtail bait fooled this bass on an Oklahoma reservoir.

the touch, and some are even scented or impregnated with a smell claimed to be fatal to fish. Whether scents or "tastes" built into any plastic lures have any fish catching (or even attracting) value is open to debate.

No matter; grubtails were first used in shallow salt water but can be effective on both largemouth and smallmouth bass of American reservoirs. Grubtails produce strikes in clearer water than some other lures and seem to work best just over the top and around coontail mossbeds. Try them also on clay or rocky points and on gravel shoals.

Grubtail experts tend to use the smaller sizes, ⅛ ounce and ¼ ounce, often two of these fished in tandem, on spinning rather than baitcasting tackle. They fish all types of underwater structures (see jigging). But grubtails will also catch bass that are schooling or chasing massed schools of shad in open water, as they do periodically on many lakes.

Chapter 6

SURFACE PLUGGING

Among the greatest dividends of springtime almost anywhere in America are those warm, still mornings when the landscape is drenched with dew, and mist blankets the waterways. At precisely such times a serious bass fisherman should be on the water as soon after daybreak as possible, if not well before. Such saturated mornings (and late afternoons to early evenings as well) are the magic times for surface pluggers.

During the past few decades, as we have already noted, largemouth bass fishing has radically changed. During this period the range of the species has been greatly expanded to every corner of the continent. At the turn of the century, the largemouth was confined to the generally shallow, lukewarm waters of the Southeast —surface plugger country. But today the bulk of bass fishing occurs in the giant artificial reservoirs that are scattered from coast to coast, and if the present trend continues, the largest largemouths of all are likely to come from California impoundments rather than from Florida, the natural home of the lunkers.

Because the giant reservoirs (no matter whether for hydroelectric power, flood protection, political pork barrel, or boondoggle) are deep, fishing techniques had to change. Bass anglers found they had to prospect deeper and deeper, at first with bottom-bumping plugs and lead-head jigs, then later with plastic worms, spinner baits, and crank baits. Nationwide, the old traditional bass fishing with surface lures has become a lost art—or almost lost, that is. Luckily there is still a good bit of shallow-water bass fishing left in this country, and the bass fisherman who ignores it is making a huge mistake. Nor is all of this water confined to the bayou and bottomland country of Dixie, although that region may contain the largest part of it.

No matter in what part of America you are fishing with surface plugs (top-water lures), casting accuracy is important. In some situations, it makes the difference between getting plenty of action or having none at all. During a trip to South Carolina's twin Santee-Cooper lakes some years ago, during midspring, the point was proved most dramatically.

At this time the biggest bass—the "hawgs"— were bedded far back beneath overhanging willows. Unless an angler could get his lure far back into the deepest shadows, into the "tunnels," there was no chance at all of a strike. That required proficiency both in sidearm and in backhand casting—as well as in being able to skip a lure across the surface in the same manner that a boy skips a rock. Even in the hands of some of the local Santee-Cooper experts, a percentage of lures cast were hung up on the willow limbs. But that was a small nuisance compared to the number of seven- and eight-pound lunkers that went onto the stringers.

Fishing surface plugs is neither a difficult nor a complicated technique. But it is more fascinating than any other and at least for me, far more suspenseful. The wooden or plastic lure is one that will not sink, either at rest or when retrieved. In theory, when a surface plug is retrieved, it should simulate some creature that is disabled or crippled and trying to reach a safe haven. Since bass are known to strike and feed on a great variety of both terrestrial and aquatic creatures in the water (from beetles, snakes, and ducklings to frogs and other bass), a top-water lure might suggest any or a combination of these. So you cast and retrieve to resemble some creature in bad trouble.

That may mean almost no retrieve at all. The basser tosses his top-water plug to a good target and allows it to rest there. For several minutes he may move it only so slightly as to send out

The Side Cast

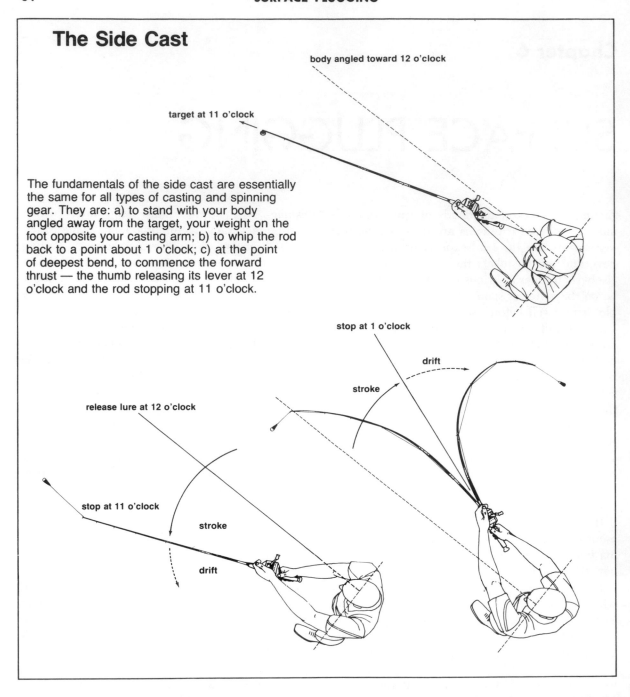

body angled toward 12 o'clock

target at 11 o'clock

The fundamentals of the side cast are essentially the same for all types of casting and spinning gear. They are: a) to stand with your body angled away from the target, your weight on the foot opposite your casting arm; b) to whip the rod back to a point about 1 o'clock; c) at the point of deepest bend, to commence the forward thrust — the thumb releasing its lever at 12 o'clock and the rod stopping at 11 o'clock.

stop at 1 o'clock

drift

stroke

release lure at 12 o'clock

stop at 11 o'clock

stroke

drift

small circles of water all around. Maybe you've seen a dying minnow or a bullfrog behave like this. It's tense and tedious business trying to provoke a strike this way, but, just often enough to hook a fisherman, it results in a sudden, explosive strike. On the other hand, even a very large bass may just surge up to the surface and inhale the bait. You had better set the hooks promptly and sharply after that.

Some surface plugs have blunt or notched heads to make them pop, sputter, or dart when the rod tip is flicked upward—motions that are meant to attract bass. Other top-water lures have propellers at one or both ends of the body to imitate a fluttering or injured small fish when the reel handle is turned. Still others, such as the long-popular Jitterbug, have a large concave metal face that makes the lure gurgle and wob-

A selection of typical surface plugs, all excellent for largemouth bass.

ble, somewhat like a swimming frog, when it is retrieved. But almost always with any or all of these designs (and there are many, many more we have not described here), the proper retrieve is a fairly slow, stop-and-go, erratic one.

It is a good idea to follow each cast closely in shallow water. Watch for signs of feeding or spawning bass, and cast the plug toward them. If there is a bulge or commotion in the water near any particular cast, but no strike, cast back in the same area again. Try making a slower, more tantalizing retrieve the second time, and if that fails, experiment with a fast retrieve on the third cast. The main thing is to make the surface lure seem to be a tempting, and easily available, morsel even for a not-so-hungry bass or an already well-fed bass.

There is another type of surface lure different enough from the floating-at-rest type to be given special mention. It is really a hybrid: a plug combined with an oversize, front-facing spinner designed to be reeled slowly and with a noisy sputter over the surface of the water. It will sink rapidly if not steadily reeled in. This sputter type of lure is useful only when bass are concentrated in shallow, usually very weedy areas punctuated with lily pads. When a bass does strike one of these surface spinners, it usually is a slashing and exciting attack.

Still another category of surface plug includes the ancient Zara Spook and the numerous imitations that have been sold for many years. These consist of plain, cigar-shaped, wooden, or plastic bodies with two sets of treble hooks, but no

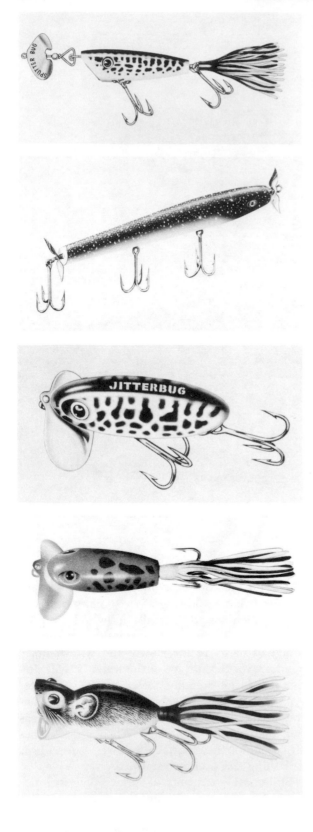

Typical surface plugs for bass.

spinners, dished heads, or anything else to impart action. The angler must make them perform entirely with his rod tip plus some body English. Zaras can be hopped, fluttered, jumped, or darted on the surface, any or all of these movements occurring during a single retrieve. Just shaking the rod tip from side to side while winding the reel slowly is a technique that causes the bass to smash the counterfeit, and the fisherman's pulse to pound.

One popular Zara technique is called walking the dog. In this case, you cast, take up line slack with the rod held low over the water, then raise the rod tip sharply over one shoulder. The lure will dart forward and to one side. Lower the rod tip, regain slack again, and raise the rod tip sharply over the opposite shoulder. And so on. On some days largemouths can't stand it and will charge up even from deep water to catch a walked dog. One additional tip: Zara-type surface plugs are heavy and fall noisily on the water, so cast beyond the target and retrieve the lure back directly over it.

A serious surface plugger can brush up on his accuracy long before the best top-water season begins. As mentioned earlier in the casting chapter, a couple of laundry baskets or hula hoops placed at random about a lawn make suitable practice targets whenever a caster has a few minutes to spare. Never worry about the next-door neighbor sneering at your efforts, because at the same time, indoors, he probably is putting golf balls into empty coffee cans.

Try Farm Ponds

For top-water fishing fans spring never seems to come fast enough—nor ever last long enough —especially in the vicinity of the more than two million farm and ranch ponds scattered across America. These were built for everything from land irrigation and water for livestock to recreation and improvement of the local water table. Eventually and by various means, largemouth bass have been stocked in most of them, and the fishing is usually very good. Some ponds seldom see a fisherman at all, and of course these are genuine bonanzas for the first angler who finds them. Normally the only ticket needed to fish these ponds is a courteous request of the landowner, most of whom will grant permission—

The surface spinner bait called Sputterfuss must be reeled rapidly over vegetation.

Some of the best surface plugging occurs where shallow, weedy water drops off suddenly to deeper water.

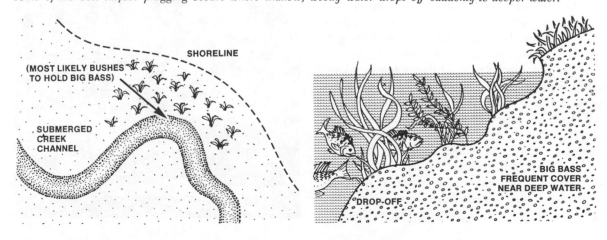

Angler Dick Kotis with a fine string of large bass taken from a farm pond.

Occasionally where the bottom is hard enough to permit it, farm ponds can be effectively fished by wading. By the time bass have moved into the shallow edges where they are susceptible to the surface lure, the water is also warm enough so that a wader can fish in comfort, even without hipboots. For this type of fishing I wear an old pair of tennis shoes and jeans and snap the stringer onto my belt.

The unfortunate part about surface plugging is that nationwide there is not nearly enough of it, and perhaps there never can be. Sadly, top-water fishing is a technique limited to those occasions when largemouths are in shallow water. In some places no deep water at all exists, as in natural lakes of the South, and in farm ponds. But mostly bass rise to shallows only when the water temperature hovers between sixty-five and seventy-five degrees. Occasionally at night, bass may also venture into surface-plug range even when the water is warmer than seventy-five degrees.

Nancy Williams hefts a fine bass caught on a surface plug as she was wading.

either for free or on payment of a nominal sum.

Most of the farm ponds have—or eventually will have—one thing in common: plenty of emergent and submerged vegetation. Therefore they are not the easiest places to fish, except for the surface plugger. So the clever bass angler's best bet for catching bass on top is to start getting acquainted with farm-pond owners.

For farm ponds I've found that a ten-foot-long cartop boat or floating tube are nearly as valuable as a tackle box full of top-water baits. At least half of these mini-impoundments are so densely fringed with vegetation that casting from shore is virtually impossible. But the small craft, light enough for me to carry on my shoulders (or to drag across dewy ground), makes it possible to fish in the patches of open water that are out of reach of an angler standing onshore.

But one thing is absolutely certain: No kind of bass fishing offers more excitement than surface plugging when it is possible. And even in the large reservoirs there are times, albeit too brief, when a floater is more deadly than a plastic worm or other lure dragged on the bottom. No wonder a few bass fishermen only venture onto the water during top-water time.

Tube Fishing

Bass fishing from tubes—or doughnuts or floats or belly boats or floater bubbles—has become increasingly popular everywhere, especially with surface pluggers and with fishermen in general on smaller lakes and ponds. Tubing and surface plugging go together perfectly. Once these devices were home-made from an old inner tube with a seat rigged in the center so a fisherman could sit there in the water and cast

Tube-fishing equipment: the inflatable tube (below), an angler sitting inside a tube (top right), and swim fins to propel the fisherman (bottom right).

conveniently all around. But now there are many good ones on the market, and they are a pleasure to use.

Fishing floats begin with a standard sixteen- or twenty-inch truck inner tube, which is placed inside a cover of tough material (usually canvas or vinyl-coated nylon) and then fully inflated. The cover protects the tube from punctures and also forms a saddle seat for the angler inside the hole. Wearing chest waders, the angler sits in the middle, legs in the water, with the covered tube forming an arm rest. Zippered waterproof pockets are sewn or bonded to the cover to hold tackle, lunch, a Thermos, and other items. Some deluxe pouches also include a sort of apron to cover the fisherman's lap (for fly casting) so that the coils of loose line do not fall in the water. Other tubes include an inflatable backrest for added comfort, and now there is available an attachment that permits installation of a depth sounder.

Besides the tube, a floating fisherman must have a means of propulsion, and there are two options. The simplest way of getting about is with a pair of snorkeler's swim fins attached to the feet. Just by raising the feet and kicking stiff-legged, as when swimming, the floater travels backward. Paddle-pushers—hinged fins made of plastic that strap onto the heels—provide the other kind of locomotion. Just by swinging the legs back and forth from the knees down, the paddle pushers move you forward or

A largemouth jumps as it tries to spit out a surface plug.

sideways and provide the greatest maneuverability of the two choices.

There are many good reasons for the expanding new interest in float fishing. Tubes make it possible to explore ponds, swamps, and sloughs that are either difficult or impossible to reach by boat. A tube opens up some scattered spots never fished seriously before. The whole outfit—tube, pump, fins, tackle—can be carried in a rucksack or daypack, on a trail bike or bicycle. Also there are some hard-core doughnut fishermen in the South who swear that the odds are doubled in favor of anybody fishing from a tube. They insist that tubes frighten fish far less than boats and motors, and that a tube fisherman, being alone, is a more quiet fisherman.

Cost is important, too. Today's typical, fully equipped bass boat (described in detail in Chapter 12) will cost an outdoorsman from forty to fifty times as much as the best tube outfit available. Of course, the boat owner has a vastly wider range and greater capacity. But the tuber is king of small, remote waters.

Sitting crotch-deep in cool water can become an uncomfortable chore during spring and autumn when the tuber will usually resort to long johns and woolen pants beneath his waders. But in summertime, when water temperatures reach seventy-five degrees and beyond, it may not be necessary to wear waders at all—just old cotton pants and tennis shoes. Incidentally, most veteran float fishermen prefer the rubber stocking type of wader worn inside oversize tennis shoes with an old pair of thick socks sandwiched in between.

The matter of safety must be considered, since a tube puncture is always possible. Too-old, worn-out inner tubes should not be used. Always carry a spare flotation device such as a water skier's belt worn around the waist, a U.S.C.G.-approved life-saving vest, or one of the cartridge instant-inflatables that can be carried in a pocket or clipped onto a jacket.

The big plus for every tube fisherman comes at the end of the day. Now there is no heavy boat to winch onto the trailer and no need to scrub it down. Not even a small canoe or a small craft waits to be hefted onto a cartop carrier. You simply step out of your doughnut, deflate, and toss it into the luggage compartment of your car. Then homeward bound to a fresh bass dinner.

Chapter 7

FISHING THE ARTIFICIAL WORM

Early in the 1970s a survey was made of about fifty of the top professional bass fishermen in America—the anglers who make a living at the sport. One question asked each man was which lure he would carry in his tackle box if he were limited to only that one. An overwhelming number selected the plastic worm.

That isn't any wonder in view of the fact that,

The artificial worm is probably the most effective single lure ever devised for bass.

of the thousands of bass lures built and sold, not one has been as successful as the plastic worm nationwide, or in fact anywhere that bass exist. Every year more bass are taken on plastic worms than on all other kinds of lures lumped together. An angler who hasn't used worms has not yet been bass fishing. At least he has not been catching as many or as big fish as he might.

A plastic worm is also the most versatile lure you can carry in a tackle box. This is one bait that can be fished successfully on the bottom, in very shallow water, or at any depth in between. The worm produces at any and all different retrieve speeds. There are more ways to rig a worm than could be catalogued in a modest library, and clever fishermen are likely to figure out more and still better ways. (For example, a worm can be rigged to be as weedless as any bait.) Worms are a lot less expensive to buy and use than any other artificial lures or natural baits.

It is difficult to explain why worms are so effective. They do not really resemble anything in nature except nightcrawlers, which are not aquatic and nowhere are an important part of a bass's diet. Plastic worms do look somewhat like leeches or lampreys, on which bass will feed, but which also are not really abundant in typical largemouth bass waters. Perhaps this is unimportant anyway. For whatever the reasons—shape, feel, "taste," or some particular color—bass have a harder time resisting worms than any other lures. Be thankful for that.

Of all the myriad ways to rig a worm—to affix it onto your hook or hooks—there are six or so old standbys, and in the course of a typical bass-fishing outing an angler might have need to try

Very large bass are especially susceptible to plastic worms.

three or four of these. No doubt the most confusing aspect of worming is the nomenclature. Different worm rigs may be named after some fisherman (possibly the originator), some lake, state, or part of the country. For example, there is the Underwood rig named after Lamar Underwood, former editor of *Outdoor Life* magazine and a serious bass fisherman. There is a Toho rig (for Lake Tohopekalika in Florida), as well as Texas, Carolina, and redneck rigs. To make the matter even more confusing, the same rig will have different names in different places. So an Oklahoma rig might be three or four different things, depending on who is using it. So here we will attempt to use the most common of the names and depend upon the illustrations to clear up any bewilderment. Keep in mind that no matter which name is used, rigging is the all-important factor in catching fish on the popular plastic worm.

The Texas Rig

Consider first the Texas rig, which may be the best for fishing medium to fairly deep water.

This one consists of a ¼-to-⅝-ounce torpedo- or cone-shaped slip sinker, a 4/0 or 5/0 single hook, and the plastic worm. The slip sinker's advantage over fixed-position weighted "jig" rigs is this: The slip sinker is free to slide up and down the line and does not interfere with the undulation of the worm. Because the sliding sinker is several feet up the line, a bass is not apt to feel any unnatural weight when he picks up the worm.

The slip sinker continues working for the fisherman even after his fish is hooked. Since it is not connected to the hook directly, the fish cannot use the added weight to throw out the worm in its fight to escape.

The hook's point should be inserted into the center of the worm's head and brought out about ½ inch below that point. Pull the hook shank into the worm until the eye is buried in the worm's head. The point of the hook should then be turned 180 degrees and buried in the body of the worm—rendering it weedless. If the plastic material is too tough, the hook may not penetrate properly into the bass's jaw when you set the hook.

For best action, keep the worm in as straight a line as possible. If the worm slides down the hook, stick a toothpick through it and the hook's eye. Snip off the toothpick where it emerges from the worm's body.

The Carolina Rig

Another deservedly popular worm rig probably originated on the Atlantic Coast and is most often called the Carolina rig. This one is excellent when used, in conjunction with a floating worm, for bass that are suspended between the bottom of the lake and the submerged tree tops. The sinker is placed on the line, and a small barrel swivel is attached. Next attach about twenty inches of line to the opposite end of the swivel. Knot on your hook and rig a floating worm similar to that used in the Texas rig. The floating worm will hover above the bottom as far as the extra line will allow.

There are two good methods to determine if bass are suspended. One would be to spot them on your depth sounder, since suspended fish usually will show up on the dial at whatever depth they might be holding. This will also reveal the

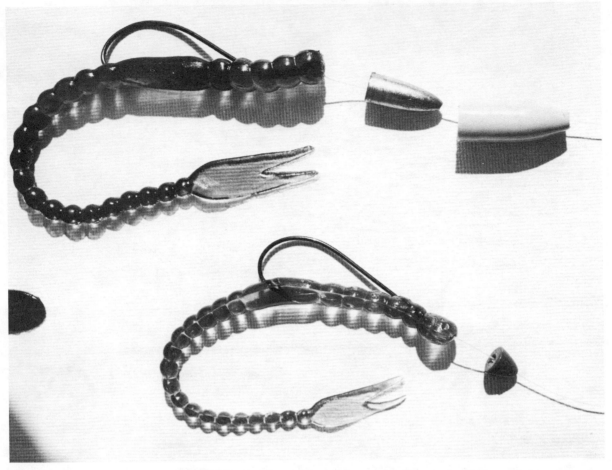

Close-up of two Texas worm rigs with sliding sinkers, showing how the hook is imbedded into the worm.

length of line to allow between the sinker and the worm.

Another way to detect suspended bass is to feel a strike as your worm is sinking. Assume you made a cast into eighteen feet of water, and after it fell fifteen feet you felt a strike—a good sign the bass are suspended. You might actually be pulling your worm under the fish unless you were rigged with the floating or Carolina rig.

Suspended bass can also be located in treetops if you detect a strike as your worm is being retrieved through a treetop. Just change to a very light sinker and try to swim the worm through the tree crowns. A floating worm works effectively in such a situation.

Weedless hook rigs are very important. A weedless hook does not have to penetrate the worm before sticking in the bass's jaw. This type of rig is for fishing shallow water or areas with very small amounts of cover or brush. When fishing very clear water, use a weedless hook plus a very light slip sinker on a light line. You do not need to strike as hard to set the hook with a weedless rig as with the Texas or Carolina rigs.

When worming first began to explode in popularity in the early 1960s, many worms were manufactured and sold prerigged—that is, with spinners and lead jig heads already attached and with weedless hooks molded into the worm body. Few of these were ever as effective as rigs devised later by ingenious anglers, such as the Texas and Carolina rigs, but often the prerigged weedless worms did work well. I used them (and still do) to great advantage.

The Jig-and-worm, or Jig-and-eel

Under certain conditions, the combination of a lead head jig with a plastic worm as the tail makes for the most successful of all kinds of

This lively largemouth was hooked on a jig-and-eel combination. Photo courtesy of Florida News Bureau.

worming. But first a fisherman has to find bass concentrated somewhere in fairly open water—water mostly free of vegetation or brush—as on sandbars or gravel bars, underwater mounds, and pebbly points. One good time and place I've found to use a jig-and-eel is at daybreak around the same bathing beaches, boat slips, docks, and pilings that will be swarming with people soon after the sun comes up. Bass move into these deserted spots to feed during darkness, but retreat again when the human activity begins. Any place where the lure will not hang up easily is a good target to try the jig-and-eel, since the hook is completely exposed. There is no reason, however, why an individual angler cannot solder a light wire weed guard onto his jig hooks.

Light tackle and light line can be used effectively with this rig, since it takes little effort to set the hook. Try a ¼-ounce jig head with a thin wire hook. In the event that you are snagged on the bottom, a steady, even pull on the line will usually straighten out the hook before the line breaks.

The jig-and-eel is another good rig for vertical jigging right beside and under the boat or along steep cliffs and banks, but usually after the fish have been pinpointed in a specific area by some other method.

All worm combinations or rigs are better fished slowly, erratically, with gentle lifting and twitching of the rod tip, than by fast retrieves. At times fish may seem to peck or only nibble at the worm, rather than try to swallow it. Often these nibbles may be from other species—say, bluegills, bullheads, and crappies—rather than bass. For these reasons worming can sometimes be too tedious, too tension-filled for some bass fishermen. Too often it is difficult to know—to judge—whether to strike back immediately (when a bass mouths the bait) or to allow the bass to run with a worm before striking. You can win or lose either way.

Most pro bass fishermen strike the instant they feel a tug on the line, but admit there are situations when a bass needs a moment or two to get the hook part of the worm rig in its mouth. One solution that helps to eliminate this problem, in fairly open water, is to run a monofilament line through the length of the worm and then to add a small trailer hook in the worm's tail. This will hook a lot of the short or hesitant strikers.

Ed Hutchins, an Ohio angler, has erased all

Worming demands all of an angler's attention. He must always be ready to pay out line—or strike—whenever a bass picks up the bait.

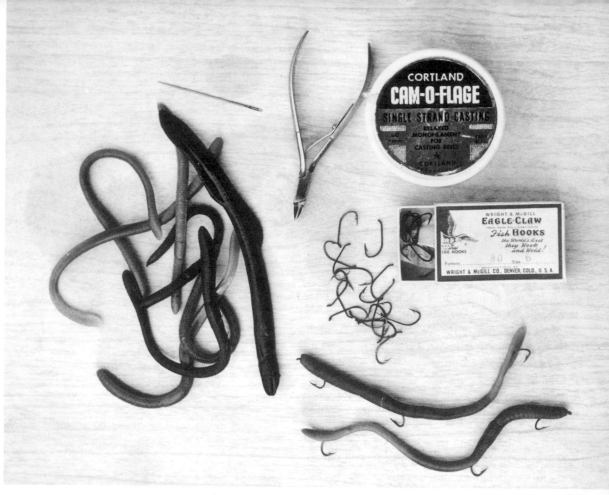

The Hutchins worm rig: the necessary rigging material (above), the finished worm (below), and a largemouth hooked on the tail hook of the worm (opposite). Photos by Stephen Maslowski.

forward, with only the curved parts exposed and the shanks hidden inside the worm. This rig has accounted for amazing catches in waters where the bass become sophisticated through heavy fishing pressure early in life. But, of course, the rig has its handicaps in snag-infested water.

Plastic-worm manufacturers have not allowed their imaginations to inhibit them, and there are almost as many different designs on tackle shelves as there are bass fishermen. Worms come in lengths from three inches to at least eighteen inches. Six inches or so is the most popular length across the country. Some are jelly-soft, limp, and limber. Others are stiff or coil-springy. Some float; others sink. Certain worms have coiled or twisted tails that continue to "work" (or uncoil) after a retrieve while the worm settles to the bottom.

Worms come in every color of the spectrum, including natural nightcrawler and clear, no color at all. The most popular hues are blue, purple, and black, not necessarily in that order and for no completely sound or proven reason. We will not discuss which color is best here because it probably boils down to personal preference more than anything else. In time science may learn why purple is better than black on Lake Blockbuster, but so far science is quiet.

Some plastic worms also are scented or impregnated with odors (or tastes), a popular device with a lot of anglers and manufacturers. The scents, surprisingly, are not always of an aquatic nature, but are of raspberry, grape, strawberry, and watermelon. In other words, these smell more like soda pop than bass bait. But as this is written in 1979, there is actually a new "sensational" bass-worm flavor rapidly growing in popularity. It is called marmalade of motor oil. Honest.

Speaking of strange worms, he is a wise angler who invests in a tackle box impervious to plastic worms, or rather to the chemical in the worms that corrodes a good many tackle-box materials. Short of that, worms should be carried in separate containers apart from other items in the tackle box.

One inexpensive item that should be in every wormer's kit is a small hook-sharpening stone. Every hook should be sharpened to a needle point before knotting it onto the line because a worm fisherman needs quick, sure penetration whenever he raises his rod tip to strike.

doubt about when to strike back at a tugging bass with a worm rig of his own creation. Hutchins buys the softest worms and with a sewing needle runs a section of seven- or eight-pound monofilament lengthwise through the center of the worm. To this monofilament he ties sharpened No. 6 hooks: One located in the tail, one in the head, and one just forward of the middle. The hooks are placed so as to be facing

Chapter 8

WEATHER AND WATER

Bass fishing, in one respect at least, is like any other kind of angling. No matter what the season, the basser is at the mercy of weather and water. He has no control over whether it will be hot and humid, cold and windy, whether the water will be gin clear or, while not muddy enough to plow, too thick to pour. The most accurate caster in the world, with the best available equipment and all the lures ever made in his tackle box, still has to cope with weather and water. Following are some ways to succeed despite the worst of it.

Fishing Grassy Water

One of the largemouth angler's greatest headaches is grass, a term that is used to include all types of both submerged and emergent vegetation, from smartweed and lotus to hyacinth, coontail, wild rice, and arrowroot. A little bit of the stuff is fine, and an accurate caster considers grass only a challenging part of the game. But some very good lakes are just vast salad bowls where the vegetation grows as thick as sauerkraut. Catching bass here is no easy matter, even when all other conditions are ideal.

A myriad of aquatic creatures live in grass (small fish, amphibians, snakes, beetles, crayfish, even bass fingerlings, to list a few), and these attract largemouths, at least many small-to-medium ones if not always the biggest. The shade and shelter also attract bass. So you have to deliver your lure close to where they are—which is often deep in the grassiest part.

The first advice is to be on the water promptly at dawn, since the first hour or so of daylight provides the best fishing. Second choice should be the last couple of hours before nightfall. Every grassy, weedy area has at least some

openings or channels (perhaps "runs" or "holes" kept open by muskrats, alligators, or boats) that are good places to fish top-water lures as described in Chapter 6. Obviously the short, accurate caster is going to have a great advantage here.

Barring a lot of openings in the vegetation, a surface-lure caster will have to concentrate his efforts around the fringes and edges of weedbeds. The best way to do this is to position the boat so that retrieves can be made parallel to edges, rather than at right angles away from

One of the bass fisherman's biggest challenges is water with dense vegetation. But such water can be conquered.

them. The parallel-to-cover retrieve gives any bass lurking in weedbeds a longer, closer look at the bait without exposing itself. Underwater observations in weedy bass waters in Florida (by scuba divers) have revealed that largemouth striking habits vary from day to day. So keep in mind that sometimes a bass will strike quickly, maybe even blindly at a lure cast close to it. On other days it may stalk the lure, swim behind it, and be far more deliberate in striking—if it strikes at all. There will be many instances when two, three, or more retrieves nearby are necessary to tempt a bass to strike.

Unfortunately there are times and places when fishing the fringes fails and a basser simply has to get his lure far back into the salad. This calls for a different selection of lures and proper tackle to match—in other words, weedless lures and a stout rod with a reel full of 12-pound to even 20-pound test line (if there are big bass known to be present in the lake).

Weedless lures are those with hook guards, usually of fine piano wire, or other devices that cover the hooks sufficiently to keep them from snagging on vegetation, but not enough to keep from hooking a fish when it strikes. Weedguards have been affixed to all kinds of lures, but by far the most effective are single-hook spoons, spinner baits, and plastic worms.

Some of the earliest of all bass lures were weedless because most bass fishing more than a generation ago took place in grassy, natural lakes rather than in large and deep dragon-shaped reservoirs. I'm speaking especially of the No. 3 Hawaiian Wiggler and Johnson Silver Minnow types, both of which are still successful and just may be the best lures today for fishing grass. Both slither snakelike through, over, and under the lushest vegetation without snagging and through the years have accounted for an astronomical number of bass.

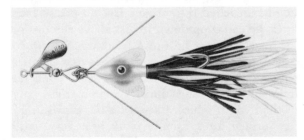

The Hawaiian Wiggler: a typical weedless lure with wire weed guard.

Worms and similar plastic lures fished with weedless hooks also can put largemouth bass on a stringer when manipulated properly in weeds. But there is more on all kinds of worming in Chapter 7.

The grassiest waters have to be fished from a boat, and probably one that is hand-propelled, because motors become fouled even worse than lures and also spook fish. The best technique is just to move boat or canoe gently along with a paddle. But a fisherman should consider wading in those fairly shallow, hard-bottomed lakes where the vegetation is not so dense that a fisherman becomes dismally enmeshed in greenery.

Many years ago at Florida's Lake Okeechobee I learned about a valuable technique that might be applicable to similar waters elsewhere. Okeechobee is shallow (the best bass water is between three and four feet deep) and subjected

Casting surface plugs as you wade is one good way to beat the hot days on weedy lakes.

Wading and towing the boat behind you is another way to cope with very weedy water.

to high winds around midday, so instead of al- lowing the boat to drift with the wind, my fishing guide and companion hit the water and tied the boat to his belt. Then we simply waded across the grassy shallows, which we were able to cast more thoroughly in this fashion. In addi- tion, wading was a refreshing alternative on that hot day, since we wore tennis shoes and swim- ming trunks rather than waders to plow through the weeds. It was a great and novel way to enjoy bass fishing.

Every bass fisherman eventually must learn to cope with weeds—because many bass waters are filled with them and *few* bass waters are com- pletely without them. Although some weeds grow in medium-depth water, most vegetation usually thrives in shallow areas and so much of this is potential surface-fishing water.

Vegetation begins to appear in springtime as soon as a combination of warming waters and sunshine stimulate their growth. There is a pe- riod then—sometimes for several weeks—when the stems extend upward but do not quite reach the surface and emerge. In many states this is also the period when bass spend the most time in the shallows, with water temperatures in the vicinity of seventy degrees. It is a superb time to be fishing.

An angler has three choices just before vegeta- tion has reached the surface. He can use surface lures, he can drop down to just above the tips of the vegetation, or he can fish bottom and try to make his retrieves between the heaviest patches of vegetation. All three work very well at different times, and during *some* periods any method will produce. Except for the proviso that the surface lures usually work best very early and very late in the day, it's necessary to try all methods to find the best combination for any given day.

The muddy water of early springtime doesn't rule out bass fishing. Make short casts where roily water blends into clear water.

Muddy Water

Late winter or early springtime produces a water condition over much of America that many bass fishermen dread, but that others anticipate with pleasure—muddy, murky, or at least seriously discolored water. I am not speaking here of industrial or domestic pollution, but rather of earth sediment (some of which is organic) that is the result of heavy rains and that will eventually settle out of the water.

Many southern largemouth fishermen who live where discolored water is a regular fact of bass fishing take it in stride and feel this may be the most productive time of the year. In fact, they seek out places where swollen or roily streams release a steady flow of nutrients into lakes that are otherwise clear. Bass often congregate in such areas to feed just before the spawning seasons begin. Also, the incoming water may be slightly warmer than deeper lake water, and this will also attract bass.

On many large impoundments where there is no vegetation along the shorelines and the wind has a wide sweep, wave action against the banks (especially of clay or shale) has a tendency to undercut and expose crayfish from their holes in a strip of turbulent, muddy shoreline water. Largemouths move in here to feed on what is a staple of their diets.

Murky water calls for short, accurate casts—say, from as short as twelve feet to not more than thirty feet, around brushpiles, deadfalls, and any kinds of stickups a fisherman can spot within casting range. If you make a short cast, you will waste less time retrieving a lure through unproductive water. As a rule of thumb, the water may be too muddy to fish if you cannot see the flashing blades of a spinner bait in ten inches to a foot of water.

If the water is warm enough and bass are gathered in shallows, a noisy surface plug may work very well in muddy water. But the consensus favorite is the spinner bait whose vibration or whine is attractive to fish that actually "hear" the lure before they see it. Many anglers believe that flourescent orange or lemon-yellow blades are more attractive than the standard silver or brass blades. But there is a sharp difference of opinion among experts on whether a fast or a slow retrieve is best.

Crank baits often score in muddy water where there are no visible targets such as sunken trees and brush. Worms also will hook fish, but roily water is one of the least suitable conditions in which to use them. Perhaps the best tip here is to fish most carefully the edges where muddy water from a freshet is being diluted into clear water anywhere on a lake.

Very Clear Water

When a bass fisherman is faced with alcohol-clear water where visibility is great, he has no alternative except to think light—light tackle, that is. Particularly on bright days, clear water is a signal to put away the old plug-casting rod and substitute a spinning outfit with less visible line, perhaps as fine as 4- or 6-pound test. Lures (jigs, grubtails, smaller-size crank baits) as tiny as ⅛ ounce and ¼ ounce are not too small. It is significant that all of these are deep-running, designed for deeper fishing, because ultraclear water rarely finds fish very near to the surface, unless there is thick grass.

Largemouth bass are very sensitive to light, and invariably search for shade in lieu of the underwater "dusk" that exists in muddy water. This may be the shade cast by dense vegetation, "islands" of lily pads, a submerged forest, or a steep cliffbank. Also patches of shade are longest and darkest when the sun is low, early in the morning and evening. In very clear water, it is a waste of valuable time to fish anywhere except in shaded or deep areas.

When casting in clear water, keep your boat well away from the target and rely on long casts. Sit down (rather than stand) while casting to make a lower silhouette. Many fishermen believe, probably correctly, that the shadow of a caster in a boat passing above bass in clear

Longer casts are necessary when waters are very clear and the sun is overhead.

water will frighten the fish out of the vicinity and out of striking. Maybe the best advice of all for fishing superclear water is to go fishing after dark when you can also go back to your heavier plug-casting tackle and heavier lures.

Hot and Humid Weather—Dog Days

Hot, unpleasant days occur every summer, and they are as exasperating as they are uncomfortable for the fisherman because bass seem to develop lockjaw. Maybe the best way to cope with that is to stay home and repair tackle or paint your boat. But if that seems unsatisfactory, there are a few ways you can—or might—score.

One obvious partial solution is to be on the water at dawn or preferably an hour or two before. This is the coolest and least uncomfortable period. It is also a strange and magic time when bass lakes (and the bass themselves) seem to come alive, if only briefly. You just might hook a couple of big ones with surface plugs fished slowly, gently, around weedbeds and shorelines. Or you might even try live bait such as minnows, lampreys, or crayfish fished around good

Very early morning just may be the best time to go fishing; this is especially true during dog days.

structure. Some mornings plastic worms may be deadly, too.

Since a good many mornings during dog days are still, without a ripple on the oily-calm water, a fisherman can well play a waiting game. While he tosses a surface plug to likely targets, he also should keep an eye on the lake all around. Watch for bulges or V-wakes near the surface, which may betray a bass chasing prey. Then cast toward the disturbance. This is also a time to watch for schools of shad cruising over a lake, because as often as not, bass may be near or underneath the shad.

But as surely as late summer is hot, there are brief periods when the heat spells break, and if an angler is ready to go fishing on brief notice, he can have plenty of action. These times occur just as a storm front or low-pressure weather system advances. Usually for just an hour or two, as thunderheads build and the storm breaks overhead, bass seem to go on feeding binges. If you are on the water you can catch them, often in shallow water, maybe even fill a stringer in no time at all. It has happened to me over and over again. I have been drenched in the process, but the fresh bass dinner later on was always worth it.

Unfortunately, the fishing following a storm (or a cold front anytime) is even poorer than it was before the front arrived. Bass simply seem to evaporate. Or at least I've never found anyone who could consistently catch bass anywhere just after a storm passed. But one fact seems certain: For a while after the passing of a storm bass retreat down into the heaviest cover they can find.

There may be an obvious explanation for this. Any heavy rain clears the atmosphere of dust and particles, making the sun seem extra brilliant. In other words, there is great light intensity on passage of a front, and being sensitive to light anyway, bass just escape to where it is less intense. That doesn't make catching them very easy.

One method, called flipping in California and doodlesocking in Oklahoma, works well enough at times to warrant a fisherman's trying it soon after a storm. This is vertical jigging—really, straight up and down into thick cover with plastic worms, jigs, spoons, or natural bait. Doing it correctly, which means very slowly, requires having the boat directly above the structure. At times it is necessary to allow the bait or lure to

The approach of a storm front seems to stimulate bass into striking with abandon.

lie right on the bottom for a moment before bringing it slowly, in steps, upward. Small lures usually are the ticket here.

Shallow Water

I have already addressed shallow-water fishing earlier in this *Bible*, but a few general tips remain. The shallower bass are located at any given time, the more widely scattered they are—and on the average easier to catch. Still there is the all-important matter of finding the best, most extensive, and often the least heavily fished shallows in any body of water.

Most flats are easy to see because they are close to or adjoin shorelines. Also they will be punctuated with vegetation, flooded brush, or both. The best way to fish these is to drift past or through with the breeze, on parallel paths if

Bass in deep water are hard to locate. But find one and you probably can catch a whole stringerful in the same place.

the shallows are extensive in area. Some entire lakes are shallow. If there is not enough breeze to drift you slowly and quietly, you may need a paddle or electric motor.

When drifting across vast shallow areas, watch especially for small, maybe insignificant-seeming depressions as you go. When you spot one, slip an anchor overboard nearby and then cast that spot thoroughly. It is another kind of structure that appeals to bass, often to the largest ones in that vicinity.

Explore even more carefully any shallows in

the center of a lake, because such spots are likely to be overlooked by most fishermen. Never fail to cast over these thoroughly with a variety of lures and retrieves. Or if such a shallow does not produce bass at one time of day, keep its location firmly in mind and return there at other periods. Eventually you will score.

Some shallows are best in mornings, others during twilight, simply because the sun strikes them at different angles and creates more shadow at one time of day than another. Middays tend to be poorest, wherever the shallow water. A very common mistake of bass fishermen is a restlessness that causes them to spend too much time cruising a lake and not enough time fishing it. However, when bass are in shallower depths, an angler may indeed have to spend at least a little more time exploring.

Fishing Deep Water

We have also already covered many techniques of deep-water fishing, but a few extra points should be made. Few bass fishermen know (and, of course, may not even care) how deep largemouths can and do go. Expert bassers who are on the water year round frequently find them between forty and forty-five feet deep, and they are known to dive down to one hundred feet. Largemouths far down strike very well, too, and one reasonable theory for this is that here they are not as much affected by wind, light intensity, temperature, atmospheric pressure, and any other variables that might motivate them on top.

One of America's most skilled and successful bass fishermen, Bill Dance, is convinced that the whole secret of deep-water fishing is finding and learning how to fish the channels. Channels are underwater highways as well as structures where bass congregate. When Dance locates a channel with the aid of a topo map and his depth finder, he then begins to cast a variety of lures—jig-and-eels, grubtails, spoon jigging, plastic worms, and crank baits—to the area by a number of different techniques. Often it takes quite a while and a good deal of probing along a long, serpentine channel to find bass, but when he does find a bass, Dance often can fill every snap on the stringer.

Dance also catches a lot of deep-water largemouths from trees standing totally submerged in a lake and unseen from above. Generally the bass are at one level in the tree and will not move far up or down to take a lure. So accuracy in getting the lure to a bass's level calls for counting the passes a level wind line guide makes from one side to the other of a reel. A single pass of line allows about eight feet of line out on an average bait casting reel.

Catching bass consistently in deep water isn't an easy matter. But it's a skill every serious basser must eventually master.

Chapter 9

FLY-RODDING FOR BASS

In the past too much has been written about the difficulty and problems of fly-fishing for bass, but not enough about the pleasures and numerous advantages. Bass bugging—casting small surface bugs or plugs—is a splendid, exciting sport. And to tell the truth, no hefty fly tackle is needed to cast hummingbird-size bass bugs. Today, hundred-pound tarpon and sailfish are being taken on fly rods once considered ideal for bass! Maybe that's why too many anglers were unconsciously turned off by bass fly-rodding. That heavy-gauge tackle just didn't fit the fish for real enjoyment.

However, if you choose to specialize in big southern bass and feel the need to power those hawgs out of dense cover, go ahead and use a 9- or 10-weight rod. But we submit that that is not where the charm of fly-rodding for bass really lies.

The Practical Fly Rod

A glass, bamboo, or graphite fly rod, 7½ to 8½ feet, is a practical outfit for bass bugging. The newer graphite rods are especially suitable because they are powerful and lightweight. The rod action should be such to cast an appropriate level or weight-forward fly line 25 to 50 feet. There are good reasons for using a line one weight heavier than the rod maker recommends, primarily because bass fishing is usually done at close ranges, with wind-resistant flies and limited false casting. A little heavier line works the rod more and the angler less.

If you expect to concentrate on bass with bass bugs and streamers, an 8-to-8½-foot rod for a 7-weight line is recommended. For small flies, stick with the No. 7 line, but use an 8 weight for flies larger than size 6.

An all-round rod for average-size bass is a System 6: It makes taking a 2-pounder a real thrill, and yet a truly big largemouth or smallmouth can be handily subdued with this tackle if you will play it carefully.

Reels to Do the Job

Two reel designs, single-action and automatic, are considered practical for bass. Most fly fishermen prefer the lighter, more versatile single-action reel. It is less trouble, more fun to play a fish on, and is usually far better for dealing with a fish that is strong enough to run for cover by taking line off the reel.

The automatic reel is twice as heavy. It is more mechanically complicated, lacks the versatility of a single-action design, and does not have the sensitive drag of a single-action reel. Thus if you hook a strong fish, you have to strip off line by hand to let it run or rely entirely on the leader's strength. There is also the hazard of accidentally pressing the trigger on an automatic and watching the fly rip off your rod guides.

Yet, some bass fishermen swear by an automatic reel. It allows casting with one hand and controlling the boat with a paddle in the other. When a fish is hooked, the automatic will zip up the slack line and maintain tension until the boat is maneuvered away from the cover. Then the paddle is put aside for two-handed fighting and landing of the bass.

The Best Fly Lines

Floating and Wet Tip Hi-D lines are the most useful in the majority of bass-seeking situations.

Most fly fishermen prefer the lighter, versatile, single-action reel.

The floating line is practical when fish are feeding on the surface or when you are casting over water three to five feet deep. A level floater works well for short casts and quite well with large, wind-resistant flies; but it does not allow for delicate presentations and long casts.

The special weight-forward *bass bug taper* developed by Scientific Anglers, is, perhaps, the ultimate bass-fishing fly line. Its design makes for trouble-free delivery of flies in all sizes. It casts well in the wind with heavy flies at short or long range with a minimum of false casting.

This line also allows a fly to be cast with extreme accuracy. Using a tight loop cast, the fly can be rifled low or high into the narrowest target paths—even exceeding the accuracy of an expert bait caster. Side-arm skip casting under and behind obstacles is duck soup; right- and left-curve casts behind stumps are breezes.

The same bass bug taper on a Wet Tip Hi-D line extends the depth range of your fishing. It casts well and can be used with all sorts of flies, from top-water divers and crippled minnow bugs to bottom-crawling eelworms, crayfish imitations, and spinner-fly combos. It is especially effective for fishing down to ten feet deep, because the tip sinks quickly. You don't have to wait and wait while the fly sinks on its own. By varying the speed of retrieve, rod angle, fly weight, and leader length, you can fish from top to bottom with very little effort.

For depth past ten feet, the Wet Head, Wet Belly, and full sinking Wet Cel Hi-Ds let you work a fly down to thirty or forty feet. However, fly-fishing at these depths for bass begins to become more work and less fun. Other methods, such as bait casting, are more practical and effective.

Leaders and Tippets

The final links in the tackle chain between you and the bass fly are the leader and its tippet. While they can be heavier and less invisible

The most efficient leader for bass fishing is, like the one shown here, knotless, tapered, and about 7½ feet long, including tippet.

than for trout, their design, lengths, and durability are indeed important.

The most efficient bass leader for a floating line is a knotless tapered leader, 7½ feet long, with a 12-to-24-inch tippet. The best taper design is usually identified as heavy butt, magnum butt, or salmon. All these are two to three thousandths larger in diameter than standard tapered leaders with similar-size tips.

A *knotless* taper is especially important. Hand-tied knotted leaders cause problems in most waters where bass are found. The knots hang and tangle in the heavy cover a bass may dive into when hooked; and they pick up algae and vegetation. Of course, you still have to tie the tippet to the leader, but by using a closely trimmed double surgeon's knot, the "knotty problem" is practically eliminated.

Leader tip and tippet should test from 6 to 15 pounds for most bass flies and fishing situations. Eight-pound is ideal for small-to-medium-size

flies (10 to 4) in fairly open water. For larger flies (2 to 3/0), a 10-to-15-pound test tippet will turn the fly over better and allow the hook to be set firmly without risking a breakoff.

Stronger tippets are called for when fishing really heavy cover. Bass are not polite. They will use every dirty trick in the book to foul your leader on underwater obstacles. A strong tippet increases your odds for holding and landing a good fish under these conditions. Always use the toughest, most durable tippet material you can find—not necessarily the smallest diameter-to-strength ratio, as this soft kind of tippet wears out very fast in bass cover.

How to Cast

Probably the best place to begin fly casting is on smooth-cut grass. Stand in the middle of an open space about eighty feet long. Lay the assembled outfit flat on the grass with the reel

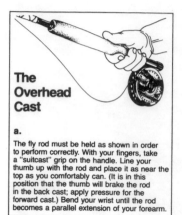

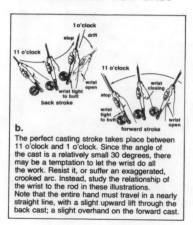

The Overhead Cast

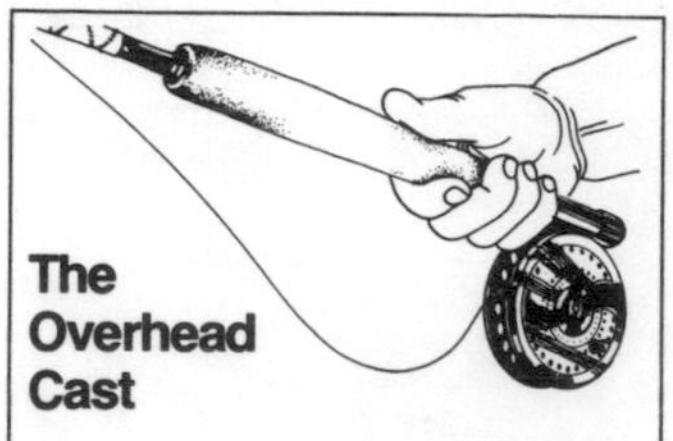

a.

The fly rod must be held as shown in order to perform correctly. With your fingers, take a "suitcast" grip on the handle. Line your thumb up with the rod and place it as near the top as you comfortably can. (It is in this position that the thumb will brake the rod in the back cast; apply pressure for the forward cast.) Bend your wrist until the rod becomes a parallel extension of your forearm.

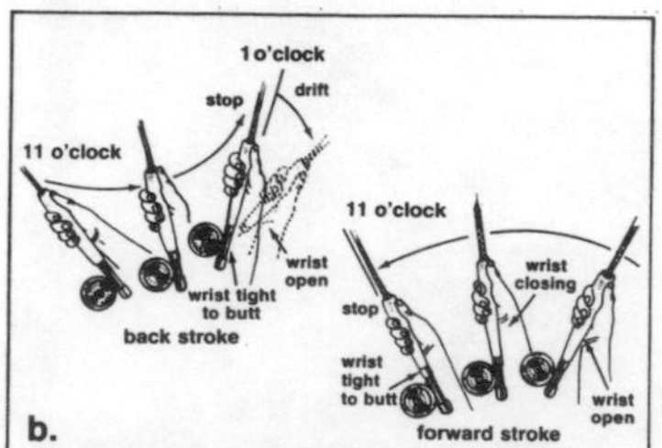

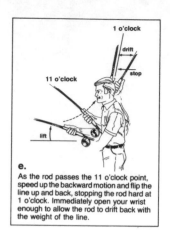

b.

The perfect casting stroke takes place between 11 o'clock and 1 o'clock. Since the angle of the cast is a relatively small 30 degrees, there may be a temptation to let the wrist do all the work. Resist it, or suffer an exaggerated, crooked arc. Instead, study the relationship of the wrist to the rod in these illustrations. Note that the entire hand must travel in a nearly straight line, with a slight upward lift through the back cast; a slight overhand on the forward cast.

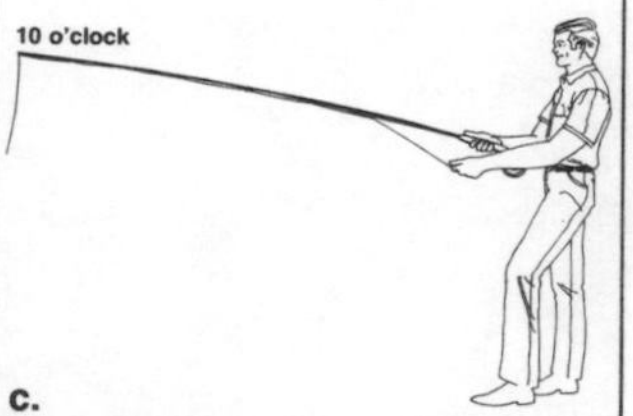

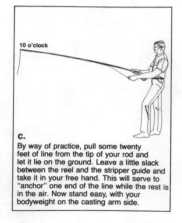

c.

By way of practice, pull some twenty feet of line from the tip of your rod and let it lie on the ground. Leave a little slack between the reel and the stripper guide and take it in your free hand. This will serve to "anchor" one end of the line while the rest is in the air. Now stand easy, with your bodyweight on the casting arm side.

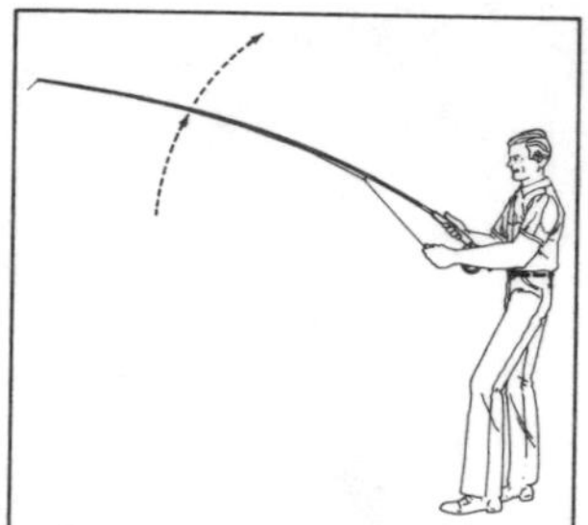

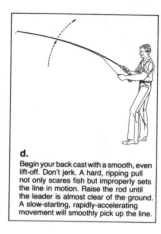

d.

Begin your back cast with a smooth, even lift-off. Don't jerk. A hard, ripping pull not only scares fish but improperly sets the line in motion. Raise the rod until the leader is almost clear of the ground. A slow-starting, rapidly-accelerating movement will smoothly pick up the line.

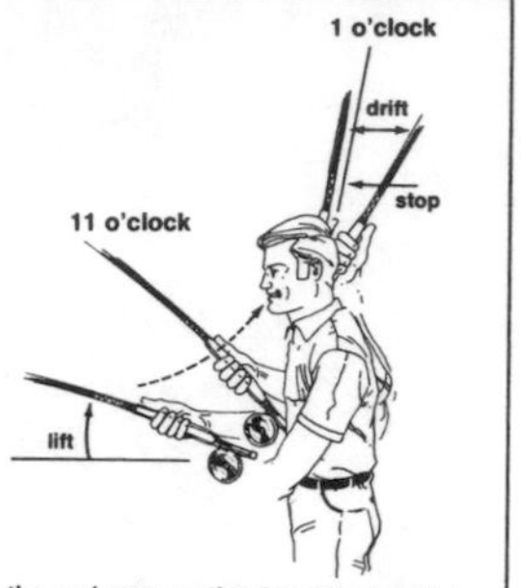

e.

As the rod passes the 11 o'clock point, speed up the backward motion and flip the line up and back, stopping the rod hard at 1 o'clock. Immediately open your wrist enough to allow the rod to drift back with the weight of the line.

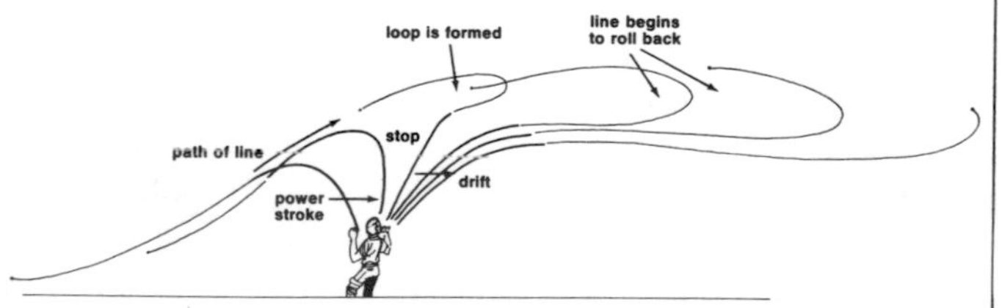

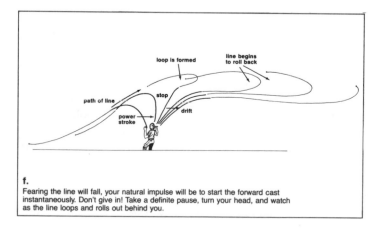

f.

Fearing the line will fall, your natural impulse will be to start the forward cast instantaneously. Don't give in! Take a definite pause, turn your head, and watch as the line loops and rolls out behind you.

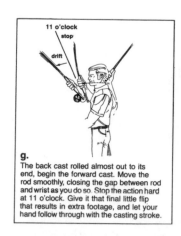

g.

The back cast rolled almost out to its end, begin the forward cast. Move the rod smoothly, closing the gap between rod and wrist as you do so. Stop the action hard at 11 o'clock. Give it that final little flip that results in extra footage, and let your hand follow through with the casting stroke.

handle up and walk away from it with the fly until you have pulled about thirty feet of line out of the guides.

Hold the rod pointed down the line toward the fly. Your grasp of the grip should be *firm* but not tight. Most good casters extend the thumb toward the tip on top of the grip—the side opposite the reel. Guides and reel should be down. Hold the line firmly in your left hand between the reel and the first guide.

Your feet should be separated a comfortable distance, both quartering to the right. In other words, instead of facing squarely toward the line stretched out on the grass, which is the direction in which you're going to cast, your feet should be at about forty-five degrees from it. (This is

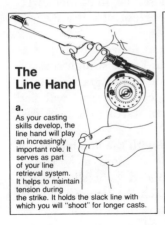

The Line Hand

a.

As your casting skills develop, the line hand will play an increasingly important role. It serves as part of your line retrieval system. It helps to maintain tension during the strike. It holds the slack line with which you will "shoot" for longer casts.

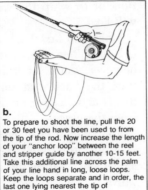

b.

To prepare to shoot the line, pull the 20 or 30 feet you have been used to from the tip of the rod. Now increase the length of your "anchor loop" between the reel and stripper guide by another 10-15 feet. Take this additional line across the palm of your line hand in long, loose loops. Keep the loops separate and in order, the last one lying nearest the tip of the fingers.

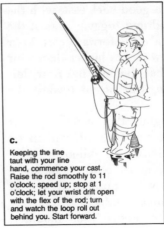

c.

Keeping the line taut with your line hand, commence your cast. Raise the rod smoothly to 11 o'clock; speed up; stop at 1 o'clock; let your wrist drift open with the flex of the rod; turn and watch the loop roll out behind you. Start forward.

d.

Stop hard at 11 o'clock. And just as you make that final flip of the rod, open the line hand. The momentum will pick up the slack and shoot it through the guides for that extra 10 or 15 feet.

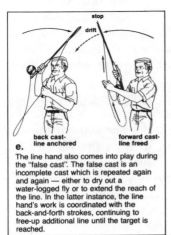

stop
drift

back cast- line anchored

forward cast- line freed

e.

The line hand also comes into play during the "false cast". The false cast is an incomplete cast which is repeated again and again — either to dry out a water-logged fly or to extend the reach of the line. In the latter instance, the line hand's work is coordinated with the back-and-forth strokes, continuing to free-up additional line until the target is reached.

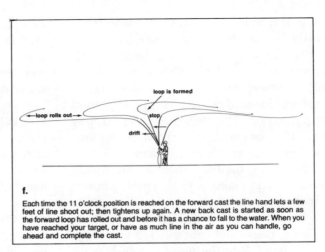

loop is formed

loop rolls out →

stop

drift →

f.

Each time the 11 o'clock position is reached on the forward cast the line hand lets a few feet of line shoot out; then tightens up again. A new back cast is started as soon as the forward loop has rolled out and before it has a chance to fall to the water. When you have reached your target, or have as much line in the air as you can handle, go ahead and complete the cast.

written on the assumption you're right-handed. A southpaw would reverse the angle.) You are about to make a back cast, and the reason for standing in this position is so you can watch the line over your right shoulder.

You are standing angled to the right, with your right elbow about three inches in front of your belly, forearm and rod pointed straight down the line. Your wrist will necessarily be bent down. It will remain in this position until the back cast is nearly made. Your left hand, holding the line, should be out toward the rod grip.

The back cast is made with the elbow and shoulder; the wrist remains locked in the position previously described. Start the line coming toward you on the grass by raising the elbow to lift the rod. The movement is up and back, accelerating smoothly and rapidly. *Hold the line firmly with your left hand; don't let any of it slip out through the guides.* As the rod approaches vertical, pull the line down sharply about a foot.

By the time the rod reaches the eleven-o'clock position, the line will be coming toward you in the air. Bring the shoulder into play to move the entire rod back about eighteen inches; at the same time, pivot the elbow until the rod is vertical, and stop dead. The stop is accomplished by tensing your forearm, wrist, and hand and then immediately relaxing.

The whole movement is brisk and continuous. Don't simply sweep the rod through the air; make it bend. Then permit the rod to tip back to one o'clock by bending the wrist. This doesn't contribute to the back cast, however, but puts the rod into position to start the forward cast. *If you have done everything properly, the line will fairly hiss out behind, passing above the rod tip, and straighten.* It will be parallel to the ground and as high above it as the rod tip at the conclusion of the backward movement. Watch it over your shoulder.

When you've made a good back cast, with the line out straight behind and tugging against the rod, you're ready to make the forward cast. Your right hand will be a few inches higher than your shoulder and somewhat behind it. Your left hand, holding the line, will be up toward the right shoulder.

Now without changing the angle of your wrist, bring the entire rod forward, still in its one-o'clock position. This is a full-arm movement by both shoulder and elbow, made somewhat as though you were pushing a weight along a shoulder-high table. Accelerate smoothly. Keep the reel above your shoulder; don't lower it.

As your arm approaches straight out in front, tip the rod forward to eleven o'clock by tipping your wrist and again come to a dead stop by tensing your arm muscles and then immediately relaxing. *Learning to stop dead at the end of back cast and forward cast is the most important part of fly casting.* The stop forces the tip over extremely fast, increasing the speed of the line. Simultaneously, lower your left hand—yes, it's still firmly holding the line—about a foot. Again, the entire rod arm makes a brisk, pushing movement, with the turn of the wrist coming at its conclusion. The rod stays in the same vertical plane, both back and ahead. Let the line straighten, then fall to the grass, at which point you lower the rod and arm as it does.

Practice, resting occasionally, until you can make both the back cast and the forward cast perfectly. Remember, the line must straighten behind in the back cast before you can make a good forward cast. This is why we suggested standing so you could watch it. There must always be a pause while the loop unfolds and the rod drifts back. At first, you'll have to watch to tell how long to give it; later, this timing will become completely automatic. You won't even have to think about it, much less watch. And, of course, with the same power, it takes the same length of line just as long to straighten in the back cast as it does in the forward cast.

False Casting

You are now ready to start false casting, so called because the fly doesn't touch the water (in this case, grass) on the forward cast. We false cast to work out more line, to change direction, or to whip the water out of a dry fly so it will float.

Make the first back and forward casts just as before. When the forward cast straightens out, however, don't let it fall to the grass. Instead, start the back cast immediately. You will find this is actually easier than starting the back cast from the grass.

Following a false cast, with the line higher out in front, the back cast is more a horizontal movement. Normally angled only slightly upward, it is made very much the same as the forward cast, save in the opposite direction.

Don't let the rod drift down farther than ten o'clock on the forward cast; start the line back as soon as it is straight. Watch your back cast until you can make it straighten properly every time, and until timing the necessary pause becomes automatic.

Now, the beginner's most common fault, next to waving his rod rather than accelerating it briskly, is to let line slip out through the guides at the start of both the back cast and the forward cast. Guard against this. If you hold the line *tightly* in your left hand and pull a little each time, as we advised, this won't occur.

Instead of attempting to cast farther and farther, continue practicing with 30 feet of line past the rod tip. Actually, these 30 feet, plus an 8-foot rod and a 7½-foot leader, make more than 45 feet. You'll seldom want to cast a bass bug that far. So you are already casting far enough to catch fish, and in the long run perfect control at this distance will do you far more good than straining to cast twice as far.

Actual Fly Fishing

At times bass are in the cover of fairly shallow water, and it is here that the fly rod becomes the deadliest of all methods with the least time wasted between casts. You can comb productive pockets without cranking in over barren water, as must be done with bait-casting and spinning lures.

Casting to bass usually involves "target shooting" to a prechosen spot. False casting is not necessary in most cases, nor is it practical with large, wind-resistant bass flies. Pick up the fly off the water, and with one back cast, place it in the

The fly rod is ideal for fishing smallmouth bass in shallow streams.

same spot or in a new one. The special bass bug taper line greatly enhances this one-cast presentation.

In order to place the fly accurately into prime cover spots, you should develop a tight-loop, high-line-speed delivery. A big, sloppy, slow-moving loop will not provide the reluctant bass flies with enough authority for a pinpoint cast. What's more, the wind, overhanging branches, and other gremlins will frustrate the big-loop caster.

By using mostly three-quarter to full sidearm casts, you will also keep the rolling line loop at the lowest angle and out of trouble. Your retrieves will be fairly short. This is especially true when using top-water bugs, which are seldom worked more than a few feet. Swimming or bot-

tom-crawling flies are worked farther, usually about half to three-quarter the distance back to the rod.

Two types of retrieves are particularly effective. The first is extremely slow to almost dead still. The other is a short, rapid, erratic retrieve.

The first retrieve suggests a helpless, vulnerable prey. Cast to or just beyond a pocket you think has a bass hiding in it. Then let the fly float rest or slowly sink without any animation or retrieve for thirty seconds to several minutes. Then work the fly just a little and very slowly at first. Most strikes come before or immediately after these initial moves.

The second retrieve suggests a crippled or escaping prey to the bass. Where the first method works on the bass's nerves and territorial rights, the second works on his response as a predator first to attack and kill, then to investigate. Make your cast and immediately begin a fast, erratic, showy retrieve. Also try "pounding" the same spot with many casts before moving on. This technique is especially effective in hard-fished or murky water. Retrieve the fly only a few feet, pick up, and cast back as fast as possible. Bass will often go into a frenzy after a dozen or more "pounding" casts.

Study and learn how the various natural food available to bass react in the water. Frogs, mice, little snakes, moths, aquatic insects, minnows, etc., have individual behavior characteristics you can mimic to draw strikes. So much of the charm in bugging for bass is playing master puppeteer.

The Approach

The best way to approach smallmouth bass cover is by wading quietly. However, this isn't always possible, due to deep water or an un-wadeable bottom. Where you can't wade, use a float tube and fins or a canoe. Any boat higher

Cast your bug toward the target, then gently pop or jiggle it to attract bass.

One good way to fly-fish around small lakes and ponds is from a light, maneuverable canoe.

or larger than a canoe will diminish your ability to sneak up on bass. Whatever craft you use, nothing beats the quiet efficiency of good paddle, pole, or oar work.

Wading will let you maintain absolute line- and fly-position control on a lake or river. The float tube is the second best method for control on a lake, because you can hold a fairly steady position with your swim fins. A canoe or boat should be used with a sea anchor when it's necessary to slow or stop the wind or current drift.

Here's another trick that pays off. When you find particularly good cover—a cypress stump, pad bed, or fallen tree—vary your approach and casting angles as much as 180 degrees. The best approach is not always the obvious one. A different approach is likely to produce more strikes because it hasn't been used by other anglers at that spot.

Inches Make the Difference

Successful fly-rodding for bass depends upon the ability to place and fish the fly within inches of an obstacle or surface spot. Therefore, pin-point casting is essential, and again, absolute fly control is a must.

You can complement your presentation by using snag guards on your bass flies. Then they

A selection of typical bass flies and bugs, most of which have soft bodies and texture.

can be cast or pulled into those critical "inch" areas without hangups or loss, and without spoiling a good spot by retrieving a snagged fly. An effective snag guard is formed by a stiff monofilament loop attached at the hook bend, extending below the hook point and up through the hook eye. It is simple and in no way affects the fly's action or hooking efficiency.

Thoughts on Bass Flies

Bass are susceptible to both imitative and attractor-type flies. Bass are especially interested in those that have a lot of action—either built in with materials like marabou and rubber hackle, or given to them by stripping, twitching, or jerking the fly line.

Fly texture or "feel" is best when it resembles the natural food that bass eat. A soft texture is

called for in most cases, particularly when flies are fished slowly or on subsurface retrieves. Most bass will quickly expel lures if they don't "feel" right.

If you retrieve a streamer or bug rapidly, bass usually strike viciously and are less apt to spit out the fly even if it is hard. They often hook themselves then, too. However, experience has proved that soft-textured flies consistently get more strikes and hook better than similar hard ones.

A useful selection of bass flies will run from sizes 8 to 3/0. Color patterns that imitate frogs, mice, crayfish, sculpins, minnows, shad, and aquatic and terrestrial insects are always needed. Unnatural colors are also productive: red, white, bright yellow, blue, purple; fluorescent red, yellow, green, and orange—in solid colors or combinations.

Bass are usually far less predictable than trout

and will favor different flies almost daily, even hourly, with little or no obvious reason. Therefore it's always wise to have a wide range of patterns and different hook sizes at hand.

Once you are really into bugging for bass, you will find there's something unique about bass flies. The hairbugs and poppers particularly have personalities all their own. It is easy to get attached to them. In fact, you may even "retire" those that have been especially good for you. And when you go over those old battle-scarred veterans, they will recall many an exciting memory.

Bass bugging is doubly absorbing because it can become a fascinating year-round pastime. On cold winter nights it is possible to spend profitable hours in basement workshops building and designing new bugs for next summer's use. Many companies sell kits or supplies for making bugs, but it isn't even necessary to buy elaborate materials. One of the best bugs I ever owned was fashioned from the cork of an empty bottle of Bourbon and from hackle feathers picked up in a chicken coop. Any bass fisherman who also hunts can easily save a few squirrel tails or bucktails and the skin from a pheasant or a grouse. Of course, any of these materials are also suitable for tying up a supply of streamer flies.

On cold winter nights a fly-rodder can make bass bugs in a home workshop.

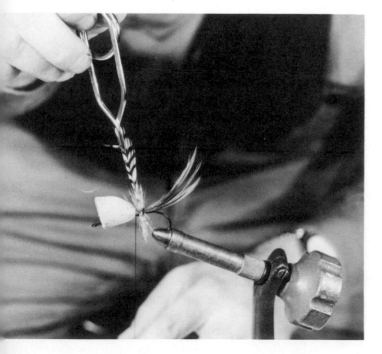

The body materials of today's bugs run from deer hair to cork to plastic, with an increasing trend to plastic, particularly in the bugs designed to imitate crippled minnows (bullet-shaped heads) or poppers (with dished-out heads to make a popping sound on the retrieve). The plastic bodies are far more durable, and most are easier to cast than cork and much easier than deer hair. The deer-hair bugs have a slight edge in northeastern (New England) smallmouth fishing, but the difficulty of casting and waterlogging are disadvantages.

Rubber-band legs have been added to some bugs. This would seem to be gilding the lily, but actually it has made the bugs more deadly in many situations.

Quite a number of weedless devices have been built into some bugs, and nearly all are valuable where vegetation is thick or where other sunken obstacles are numerous. The turned-up (rather than turned-down) hook is the best of these, but it does miss good strikes occasionally. A better hooker, but heavier and therefore slightly more difficult to cast, is the bug with a weed guard of fine piano wire. It's excellent for casting among pads, bonnets, or some of the smartweeds.

Still other fly-fishing lures are on tackle shelves today—everything from small spinners and spoons to "fly-rod size" editions of larger casting plugs. Again, nearly all of these will take bass, but few are really as suitable for fly rods as they are for the new light-spinning gear that handles them much better.

Bass Streamer Flies

Here follows a list of streamer flies and their dressing that a fly-tying bass fisherman can make at home. For most, only a few inexpensive materials are required. Others are a little more elaborate, but all are very effective. But by no means is this list complete.

Golden Dustman: Originated by, and one of the favorites of, Dr. James Henshall. He considered it best on dark days. Body: peacock herl. Hackle: golden yellow. Wings: bronze (from wild turkey if possible, but domestic turkey suitable). Tail: fibers from a golden-pheasant crest.

A selection of surface bass bugs, some homemade and some manufactured.

Irish Iron Blue Dun: A real antique among trout flies, but good for bass when tied as streamer on long-shanked hook. Tail: fibers of red feather from the breast of a golden pheasant. Body: fur from the belly of a muskrat ribbed with about five turns of silver tinsel. Hackle: dark gray. Wing: gray squirrel tail.

Shenandoah: Originated by smallmouth fishermen in the Blue Ridge Mountains region. Could be good elsewhere too. Wings: black bucktail or tail of black phase of gray squirrel. Tail: same. Body: black chenille tied fat. Head: black with a small wiggling disc attached. Tie on No. 4 or No. 6 long-shanked hook.

Black Dazzler: The same as Shenandoah except that the chenille body is not used. Instead cut some blue and clear cellophane strips about ¹⁄₁₆ inch wide. Tie these alternately along the full length of the body as you wind it with black silk. Strips should be crinkled and trimmed so that the projecting bits are about ⅜ inch long, forming a body that looks "bushy."

Hot Orange Marabou: A great pattern for roily water and midsummer stream fishing. Use No. 4 or No. 6 streamer hooks. Wings: bright orange-dyed marabou feathers topped with several strands of peacock herl. Body: a clear strip of cellophane wound until it's about three times the size of the hook shank. Shoulder: jungle cock.

Yellow Marabou: The same as Hot Orange Marabou except substitute yellow marabou.

Beltrami No. 13: A strange creation developed by George Herter and named after Beltrami County, Minnesota. It was meant for big brook trout, but it works well on brown trout and bass too. Body: oval silver tinsel. Hackle: about eight lengths of white rubber band tied on as a throat. Wing: barred orange topped off with black-bear hair. Head: coated with waterproof cement and covered with finely chopped-up black hair. Shoulder: flat plastic yellow and black eyes—or jungle cock.

Bumblepuppy: An old trout streamer designed by the legendary Theodore Gordon almost seventy years ago. Said to be a fine clear-water streamer. Tag: silver and red silk. Tail: Scarlet ibis, two mated feathers back to back. Butt: red or yellow chenille. Body: full with white silk chenille and ribbed with flat silver tinsel. Hackle: badger, large, long, and lots of it. Wings: strips of white swan or goose over white deer hair or goat hair. Sides: jungle cock. Head: black.

Smelt Marabou: A good one for New England and New Brunswick smallmouths. Wings: pale green marabou topped with two strands of peacock herl. Body: black and thin-ribbed with silver tinsel. Eye: jungle cock.

Mickey Finn: A well-known streamer developed by John Alden Knight. Head: black. Body: medium thick made of flat silver tinsel and ribbed with oval silver tinsel. Wing: a small bunch of yellow bucktail; then a medium bunch of red bucktail on top; then a medium bunch of yellow bucktail on top of all. Shoulder: jungle cock.

Warden's Worry: Head: black; red eye with white-painted center. Tail: a small section of red goosewing feather. Body: rear half flat silver tinsel; front half yellow seal fur-ribbed with gold tinsel. Wing: natural brown bucktail with several yellow polar-bear hairs tied on top. Shoulder: jungle cock. Hackle: yellow.

Chief Needabeh: Body: medium thick made of flat silver tinsel. Wing: four yellow neck hackles. Shoulder: jungle cock. Hackle: red.

Moose River: Body: thin of flat silver tinsel. Head: black. Wing: small bunch of white bucktail with peacock-eyed tail fibers tied above as a topping. Cheek: golden pheasant tippet.

Parmachene Belle: An old, old pattern. Head: black. Body: yellow chenille ribbed with flat silver tinsel. At rear of body put a ruff of peacock-eyed tail fibers. Wing: two white neck hackles tied between two red ones.

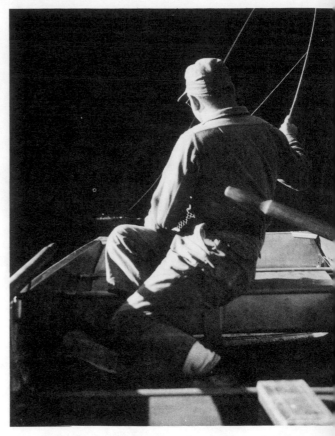

Fly-rodding for bass on a still pond at dusk can be one of fishing's greatest pleasures.

Shoulder: jungle cock. Hackle: one red and one white one tied together.

Red Angel: Developed for fishing West Virginia streams. Wing: angel hair dyed crimson tied long and sparse. Body: flat silver tinsel. Tail: black bear or squirrel hair. Head: black with black wiggling disc. Tie on No. 6 long-shanked hook.

Burlap Fly: A western pattern originated for steelheads by Wayne Buszek, but with splendid potential for bass. Tail: stiff bristle of deer hair tied to flair. Body: piece of burlap tied full. Hackle: soft grizzly. Wing: none.

Zebray: A surface bass bug rather than a streamer, designed by Art Kade of Sheboygan, Wisconsin, easy to tie. Tail: yellow Asian goat hair. Body: alternate black and white bars of bucktail deer hair, shaped wide at the rear or bend of the hook and tapered toward the front; the front end shaped deepest below the wings with a lift line to provide easy lifting from the water; body shallow above the hook to provide sufficient clearance for hooking fish. Wings: divided, spent wings of bright orange, Asian goat hair. Head: black silk waterproofed. Hook: hollow-point No. 4 Sproat with turned-down eye.

Golden Pheasant: An old English wet pattern that somehow, and with some revision into a streamer, will catch smallmouths in small rivers. Body: orange chenille with gold tinsel ribs tied medium fat. Tail: strands of black feather. Wing: two golden-pheasant feathers. Hackle: red.

Oriole: A streamer version of one of Dr. Henshall's favorite old patterns. Body: black chenille tied thin with gold tinsel ribbing. Tail: sliver of black feather above a thinner sliver of white feather. Hackle: black. Wings: two long white hackle feathers dyed bright orange; long golden pheasant feathers could be substituted. Use No. 6 long-shanked hook.

Chapter 10

GUARANTEED TECHNIQUES AND TIPS FOR TAKING BASS: II

Catching bass often involves more than just casting the right lures properly at the exact depth where the bass are located. It may also be a matter of escaping the heavy fishing pressure—or going when and where other anglers are absent. For example, that may mean fishing at night, fishing during the winter, getting far from the beaten tracks by camping or float-tripping on bass rivers. It may even mean reverting to old-time fishing methods that have been forgotten during the evolution to modern tackle. In other words, at times old tricks may be very good tricks.

Bass Fishing at Night

In many ways bass fishing's final frontier is the darkness of night. It is true that some great new reservoirs may be built in the future, or that bass may be stocked in exotic places far away. Also, super strains of bass may be developed by biologists. But aside from these possibilities, there are no new bass waters waiting to be discovered, and there are no new wildernesses to search for bass. Only nighttime remains relatively unexplored.

Fisheries scientists are not really familiar with the activities of bass at night, but there is great evidence that both largemouths and smallmouths are nocturnal, especially in shallower lakes. Both species certainly will strike lures and baits at night. And captive bass in aquaria will feed during darkness on the same minnows sharing their tank that they ignore in daytime.

Some of the best smallmouth bass fishing anywhere exists in western Lake Erie and Lake St. Clair, almost throughout the summer. But it is never better than at night for those few fishermen and local guides who are able to find the reefs and wrecks on which the fish are concentrated. These bass sometimes move en masse close to shorelines where they may be taken in fairly shallow water during the night.

Long before the advent of modern glass bassboats and powerful outboard motors, night fishing for largemouths was popular with some of the most serious bassers. They simply rowed or paddled out onto a weedy pond somewhere to cast weedless or surface lures. Even though the average human eye eventually adjusts to darkness and some limited vision is possible, this was fishing by "feel" more than by sight. Casting was at random, rather than toward targets. But a lot of bass, including big ones, were caught. And many of my own most exciting bass-fishing moments came when lunkers were hooked in the pitch black out beyond the boat.

For night fishing in weedy largemouth water, slightly heavier lines and stouter rods may be the best. It is a good idea for a night fisherman to be out on the water well before dusk so that his eyes can slowly, gradually adjust to the gathering gloom. There is still much to be learned about whether bass strike best during the dark or light of the moon. The actual fishing is easiest

For night fishing, all an angler needs (most of the time) are tennis shoes, headlamp, insect repellent, and a vest with many pockets.

during a full moon because the angler can better see what he is doing.

Some shallow places such as farm ponds and small meandering rivers can be fished by casting from shorelines or by wading. Several of the most successful night fishermen I know have developed special outfits for night fishing. These consist mostly of light khaki shirt and trousers, tennis shoes, a light vest with many pockets, a head lamp, and plenty of insect repellent. This outfit is good either for wading or for boat fishing. Since nearly all of this night fishing occurs in midsummer or when waters are warm, waders or hip boots are of little value. It's easier and more comfortable just to "wade wet."

A fisherman should always be familiar with the water he plans to wade at night. It is absolutely essential to make a reconnaissance in daylight—to check for sudden dropoffs or deep places. Even when a fisherman knows the water well, it is still wise to move slowly and cau-

tiously. To travel slowly is a safety precaution, but it will also spook fewer bass. In unfamiliar waters it's a good idea to use a wading staff, maybe just a big willow stick, to test frequently the depth ahead. Tubes also are effective.

Most night fishermen use casting rods, but there is room for debate here. Nowadays I use a fly rod and bass bugs exclusively—or almost without exception.

Even experts have occasional snarls and backlashes at night, and sometimes these are a headache to unravel. It's even worse for beginners, who often find bait casting troublesome after dark. Many of them give it up and thereby miss a world of lively sport just because casting is so complicated. But with a fly rod most of this is eliminated. I use heavy (ten-pound-test) leaders and make short casts. I pull line from the reel only as I need it—and do not leave excess coils hanging free, especially when I'm wading. Troubles and tangles just don't exist with this system. But more than anything else, I like bugging because it hooks more bass most of the time than casting with larger plugs.

After-dark anglers are far more in agreement on techniques than on tackle. Wading wherever it's possible is far better than boating, because a fisherman in the water is much less likely to alarm a bass (a largemouth especially) than a boat above—no noises like the rasp of an oarlock, of a paddle scraping the gunwale, or a thumping tackle box accompany a man wading.

The best technique is just about the simplest too. It's a case of using surface (or sometimes, in the case of plug casters, plugs that run very shallow when retrieved) lures just about as slowly as the angler's patience permits. It just isn't necessary to hurry a retrieve in this type of fishing. On the other hand, it is certainly true that underwater plugs can be very effective at night in open water.

Nearly any bass bug will work after dark. The frog imitations are deadly, and so are the spent-wing hair bugs. All the hair bugs are a little harder to cast accurately, though, and in areas of heavy vegetation this can be a problem. They also tend to sink quickly. Some bugs made with turned-up (rather than turned-down) hooks can be found on tackle shelves everywhere. Perhaps they actually were made for night bugging; in any case they're perfect for weedy waters or for ponds full of pads and bonnets.

In night bass bugging it is doubly necessary to have a floating fly line. All modern lines float well, but after extended use in ponds thick with algae, even the best begin to sink. So in this instance the extra reel and line I always carry are most valuable. I change lines as soon as the first one begins to sink.

To fish at night is certainly an angler's best weapon after dog days arrive. It gives relief from the heat as well as a chance to catch some fillets for the home freezer. It also is exciting beyond words when the bass are really striking.

Winter and Cold-weather Bass Fishing

It is true that a bass's metabolism slows down and that both largemouths and smallmouths school up when winter comes and water temperatures fall. But we also know that both species will strike when you can locate them; in fact,

Casting surface lures at night on a weedy pond in the Midwest results in plenty of action.

cold-weather fishing can be very, very worthwhile. The limiting factor seems to be how much cold the fisherman rather than the fish can stand.

We have already discussed the several techniques that score best when bass are deep and schooled: vertical spoon jigging, jigging, very deep-running plugs, and tail-spin-type lures. What is most important here is how to keep the fisherman warm and comfortable. No basser can concentrate on casting very long if he is slowly freezing.

Nowadays warm and windproof clothing is widely available, although at times with a hefty price tag. A fisherman should consider seriously garments designed for other sportsmen—skiers and snowmobilers—who also brave extreme cold. Start with warm, woolen, long underwear. Next, the insulated snowmobile suits and ski warmup suits are ideal; a person can sit down in these, be relatively inactive, and still remain warm. Any suit or jacket should have a parka, fur-lined if possible. Carry a knitted cap also, in case the parka hood becomes too warm.

When you are sitting down in a boat, feet also can be a problem, so wear insulated boots of the type used by snowmobilers. For running at high speed across open water, you might wear skier's goggles to protect your eyes and a scarf to protect your face. Some good knit caps also come down and cover all but the nose and eyes. But a fisherman's main problem will be in keeping his hands warm when casting.

One tip is to wrap metal parts of the rod handle and reel seat with tape so bare skin does not have to touch bare metal. This little precaution makes a lot of difference. Remember also that a right-handed plug caster can cast very well with his left hand inside a warm mitten, and vice versa. Mittens or gloves should have a waterproof exterior such as Goretex to keep the hand dry inside. A handwarmer or two in the pockets will come in handy when the casting hand begins to get numb.

One obvious way to operate in winter is to wait for those warmer, windless days when a bright, reflected sun, even in January, can make a man glad he is out fishing. Carry along a Thermos of hot tea, coffee, or cocoa, but forget the alcohol until the fishing is finished and you are home. It also helps a great deal, particularly when the action is slow, to get out on the bank, stretch, and walk around to restore circulation.

On cold days, a down jacket feels good out on the water.

There is a good bit of disagreement, though, about which winter weather is best. Many top anglers feel that the bright, clear days are not normally the best and that cloudy, still days are far better. Some splendid catches have been made during snow squalls when visibility was nearly zero. Summed up, the best time to go bass fishing in winter is the same as in any other season. Go whenever you have the chance.

Cane-poling, Skittering, or Flipjacking

Cane-poling for bass was once a widely practiced art. It means using a bamboo pole ten to fifteen feet long, without a reel, with a heavy line tied to the pole tip. In ponds and sloughs along the Eastern Seaboard it is known as skittering, and pork frogs were used for bait as often as spinners. One of the first artificial lures

Skittering with a cane pole is an old, old method that still accounts for a good number of bass in timbered places such as this.

ever manufactured—the Pfleuger tandem spinner—was made for cane-polers. One model came complete with luminous blades, a forerunner of the luminous lures used today by bait casters. Other popular baits and lures elsewhere were live crayfish, strips of pickled pork, and even the large, white-rubber nipples from baby's bottles with treble hooks concealed in the open end. When chugged slowly near the surface, the latter were especially deadly on midwestern waters—so deadly, in fact, that commercial fishermen used them to catch bass when it was still legal to market them.

Still another cane-poling lure was used long ago in shallow waters of the Deep South where alligators were abundant. Bass there have a habit of loitering in the alligator wallows, so inventive anglers cut imitation baby alligators from old black shoe leather and attached treble hooks to the feet. Years ago in Georgia's Okefenokee Swamp I saw an eight-pounder, among many others almost that heavy, taken on such a lure.

Cypress knee and old stump areas (where the timber was cut and the land flooded) were made to order for cane-poling, and they are worked in the following manner: Reaching out as far as possible with his pole, the cane-poler swings the lure (usually a bucktail spinner) and drops it gently beyond the target and then slowly draws it past the target—usually just fast enough to turn the spinner blades. If the target is a stump, he may completely circle it with his lure, and this is *really* an explosive trick if it can be managed.

Besides stump areas, cane-polers tease spinners around the fringes of weedbeds too. Where large areas are completely choked with pads and lotus bonnets, the angler poles right into the midst of them and then drops his spinner into tiny openings that may be only a foot or less in diameter. Then he just moves the lure up and down. When a bass strikes, and this happens often enough to make the hard work worthwhile, the fisherman immediately strong-arms it upward and swings it into the boat. If he is practiced, he can hook a bass and boat it in three seconds or less.

There is still another use for the cane pole in bass fishing, and although it's used widely now in southern reservoirs in late winter or early spring, it was probably first developed at Dix Dam in Kentucky right after that impoundment first filled with murky water. The tackle here is the same as in flipjacking, but the bait is a big gob of lively nightcrawlers, or a soft-shelled crayfish. Locally the technique is called jigging, but it isn't to be confused with jigging as we've described it elsewhere.

In this case the jigging fisherman travels slowly parallel to a steep and rocky shoreline, and at intervals he just dunks the gob of worms into the water—right up against shore or near sunken logs and tree trunks. The worm is jigged up and down a few times in each spot and then moved to another place. It does work effectively and it does catch big bass.

Not many fishermen try cane-poling anymore and only a very few may ever recall that it was ever done. But someday somewhere, cane-poling still might produce bass when all the plastic worms and spoon plugs fail.

Trolling

Trolling is far from a traditional method of catching bass, and until recent years very little

Trolling is not a traditional way to take bass, but it works well in some open lakes.

of it was ever done. But a combination of deep-living bass in southern reservoirs and dependable trolling motors with very slow speeds have developed trolling into quite an art. In Dale Hollow Lake, Kentucky, for example, a good portion of the largest smallmouths are taken by trolling.

Regular casting tackle is suitable for bass trolling. But a good medium-to-heavy spinning outfit with a ten-pound-test or twelve-pound-test line is fine in water free of snags.

Any lure can be trolled, but some are better than others. Many spinners tend to twist line badly, and it is necessary to use a keel a foot or two in front of them. Jigs are good because they are the easiest lures of all to get down deep enough. But for some reason those fishermen who spend the most time trolling and who have learned many tricks of the game prefer to troll with plugs. Many of the most popular trolling plugs are those that float when motionless because they become snagged less often; when they are snagged, just giving slack line will sometimes allow them to float upward.

The secret, of course, is to troll any lure right down on the bottom—actually to thump the bottom occasionally—a knack that is not easily learned. It's absolutely necessary, though. Here is a matter of "reading" the water, of estimating contours on the bottom by watching the contours on the surrounding shore, and then of trying to travel parallel to a contour rather than "against the grain." The latter results in snagged lures and usually nothing more. Depth finders are worth their weight in gold when trolling.

There are a few more important bits of advice for prospective trollers. Once you've caught bass trolling deep, keep coming back to that same spot. Second, carry a workable lure retriever in your tackle kit. And finally, troll as slowly as you can, using lures that have good action at these very slow speeds.

In a few northern waters fishermen troll shallow-running lures or streamer flies (sometimes several of them in tandem) at night along shore and across shallow underwater bars. There are times when this technique works marvelously.

Lead-line Fishing

One or two fishing-line companies have been manufacturing a line that has a lead core and is quite flexible. It is suitable both for trolling and for drifting. The idea of the lead core is to sink a lure more easily and more quickly.

I first used a lead-core line when trolling for landlocked salmon in New Brunswick several years ago. The line was used with a fly rod and a large-capacity fly reel. It worked so well that later I used the same technique when trolling—and eventually when just drifting over deep water with the wind—for walleyes. In the process I kept picking up more smallmouth bass than anything else.

Since I haven't given this any lengthy trial on bass alone, and since I don't even know anyone who has, it is unwise to go into much detail. It is very obvious, though, that here are a line and a drifting technique with great potential for any bass in medium to fairly deep water. The lead line makes it possible to feel your way better at any depth because it can be done on a much shorter line. In any case, this is basically unexplored territory, with good possibilities for success.

Float and Camping Trips

No special fishing techniques, other than those already described elsewhere, are involved in camping trips or in float trips on rivers, but both have important roles in catching more bass. Let's take float tripping first.

With modern boats, rafts, canoes, and outboard motors, today's fishermen have covered just about every square foot of fishing water that exists on bass lakes everywhere. Of course, some lakes are pounded harder than others, but all are fished to some extent. Today the only relatively undisturbed places remaining are on streams and rivers beyond easy walking distance from the highway bridges or in waters beyond the marinas and public docks where boats can be launched.

Float trips have provided me with good bass fishing, plus solitude and complete escape, even though I could hear occasionally the noise of traffic on busy U.S. highways nearby or the sound of a farmer's tractor in a hayfield. Most of these trips were on midwestern rivers—far from the bridges and popular fishing holes that other fishermen frequent. It's something that almost any angler in America can do at almost any time.

A good way to find solitude as well as good bass fishing is to take a float trip.

Except in a few regions such as the Ozarks and parts of the Southeast, float tripping for bass is a forgotten art, despite the fact that it is uncomplicated as well as productive. It's a chance too many fishermen miss to enjoy good sport, sometimes spectacular sport, only a few hours from home. Consider a trip that a friend and I made on a midwestern creek that passes almost through the state capital and that actually is heavily fished. Still we had high adventure; we caught fish and saw sections of the stream that few other sportsmen ever see.

We launched a canoe at a bridge just southeast of the city after making arrangements for a pickup the next afternoon where our river joined another. We carried plenty of tackle (that is possible when you're boating rather than wading), a small explorer tent, a cooler full of ice, a trotline, and even a seine to gather bait.

It was the most leisurely sort of trip downstream. During the morning I paddled while my friend cast into pockets and eddies along the way. In one stretch of water, where the paths along the banks had completely run out, he caught a pair of fat smallmouths and four rock bass. We ate them for lunch on a sandy bar—along with several ears of sweet corn apiece, which we purchased from a farmer along the way. This is topnotch agricultural country, and it is possible to buy anything from fresh eggs and frying chickens to fresh butter or carrots while traveling downstream.

That night we camped on a peninsula formed by a long bend in the river. While I built a fire my partner unfolded the seine and collected a bucketful of crayfish and hellgrammites for bait. At night, after dinner, we stretched the trotline across the river at a point just below a shallow riffle. Then we baited up with the crayfish Lew had collected. When we "ran" the trotline first thing in the morning, we found our breakfast in the form of two channel cats.

A river trip is an easy venture to organize. You simply get a boat, almost any sort of boat, collect the gear you need, and push off downstream. Nothing could be simpler. You can float for one day or for two weeks, depending on the time you have to spare or on the length of floatable water. First consideration, though, is the craft to use.

For two-man trips, I prefer a canoe because it's easier to handle, easier to move through dead water, and easier to carry over shallow places and deadfalls. I have an eighteen-foot canoe for larger, rocky streams and for longer trips. My thirteen-foot aluminum canoe is perfect for short trips on slow, mud-bottomed streams. It isn't wise, though, for beginners to take canoes on turbulent or dangerous waters. It isn't comfortable either.

In those regions where float tripping is popular, or even a business, professional outfitters invariably use long, sturdy, square-ended boats—johnboats, usually—because of their extreme safety and comfort. A fisherman can move around and stretch in most of them without turning the boat over. The johnboat is sluggish to handle in dead water, however, and it's completely out of the question for a fisherman who must depend on car-top delivery to and from the river. The most important requirement in *any* float boat is a shallow draft and fairly rugged construction. Until fairly recently all of them have been of wooden construction, but nowadays there are some splendid aluminum and Fiberglas models on the market.

It's always wise to check the distances to be traveled before starting downstream. On an average stream in mid-America, a party can cover ten miles per day rather easily. Figure on less if you want to stop frequently to fish—or more if the current is swift and the actual trip is more important than the fishing.

The best way to plan a trip is to use two cars with car-top carriers or boat trailers. Park one car at the end of the trip and drive to the starting point with the other. With two cars it's also possible to leapfrog from bridge to bridge, ending the trip whenever the mood strikes.

Float trippers can fish the back country with almost the same comforts and conveniences of an average fishing camp. Take a large tent, for example, and erect it each night on an air-conditioned (by nature) gravel bar. Safari cots are handy too. Take all the cooking utensils you need to make every meal a pleasant experience. While traveling, all this gear can be completely stored away with no trouble at all.

An enterprising traveler can almost live off the country while traveling downstream. Besides the bass he catches, fresh-water crayfish are delicious (and hard to tell from shrimp) when boiled and served like shrimp. Often it's no problem to gather frogs or catch a snapping turtle for soup. If the rivers run through limestone country there will be watercress for salad, and in springtime morel mushrooms grow along wooded banks. Look for white, button mushrooms in farm meadows during early fall. Other wild edibles a floater might find are cabbage palms, wild asparagus, any of the wild greens (dandelion, dock, lamb's quarter, mustard, horseradish, poke), walnuts, hickory nuts, and paw-paws; there's no end of them.

There are some precautions that every drifter should take. For instance, do not drink or use water from the rivers for cooking. If it's absolutely necessary boil it first and dissolve iodized tablets into it. Always carry an emergency kit containing first-aid materials, plenty of insect repellent, waterproof matches, lighter fluid (for starting a fire quickly), a flashlight, and, in the case of rubber or canvas boats, a patching kit.

Floating is made to order for bass fishermen who are limited to weekend fishing. This way they can escape the heavy concentration of anglers and boating fans on most impounded waters on those busy days. It's a good family activity too, and high adventure for small boys just learning to fish. It's also a good method to stay off the highways—and to use the weekend for unwinding rather than for developing *more* tensions.

But probably the best reward of all for the float tripper, no matter where he lives, is the new and lively brand of fishing in places that less adventuresome anglers seldom see. Since many streams even in highly developed states, are seldom fished in an entire summer, float tripping can be like discovering virgin bass waters—which it sometimes actually is.

Strange as it may sound, camping—either

Your parked recreational vehicle becomes your fishing camp. Spend evenings indoors repairing your tackle.

with tent or recreational vehicle—is another way to catch bass. Obviously it places an angler at water's edge at times when fish are striking; at the same time it saves a long drive from home. This is especially important for daybreak fishing. A camper can roll out of bed, brew a pot of coffee, and be casting with a minimum of effort and the maximum of sleep. In addition, camping is simply a wonderful experience that just goes hand in hand with fishing.

Thanks to the vast variety of fine camping gear that's available nowadays—everything from tents that "spring" open to effective insect repellents—it's possible to live outdoors inexpensively . . . and with all the comforts of home. I know families who spend almost the entire summer camping on various lakes while the husband commutes from work to camp. When vacation time comes, all pack and travel to Canada,

where they set up camp again on a good bass lake. The number of fish they catch in a season's time sounds almost fictional.

The new RVs, compact units on the road that open up into roomy living quarters, are made to order for a vagabonding fisherman. They are comfortable fishing camps wherever you park them. And no long drives in predawn chill are necessary to start a day of bass fishing.

Fishing from Shore

Many waters are best fished from shore or at least offer sport to fishermen who for one reason or another are shorebound. For example, a lot of water-supply reservoirs in the densely populated East and Midwest are big enough for boat fishing, but are off-limits because of antiquated regulations. So you try for bass from shore or not at all. Fortunately there are a good many ways to do it successfully.

Probably the most successful shore fisherman depends on natural baits. He casts a bait (nearly always a crayfish or a minnow) and tiny cork bobber, then lets the bait settle to the bottom. With the pickup bail on his spinning reel left open, a nibbling fish can easily run without detecting any abnormal drag such as a sinker or heavy bobber would give. (This no-drag result can be achieved with any spinning reel, open or closed-face.) It is telltale drag that causes fish to drop a bait before getting hooked.

The angler follows his fish by watching the tiny float. When it goes under for keeps he cranks the reel handle slightly to re-engage the drag on the line, then raises the rod sharply to set the hook in the fish's mouth. That's when the action starts.

If action does not come, he moves the bait slightly, in that way covering more water. Such a fisherman gets snagged on the bottom occasionally, and his toll in hooks is high. But he also gets more than his share of bass.

An alternative rig uses a tiny sliding float or a sliding plastic bubble manufactured mostly for spinning. With these, some snagging on the bottom can be eliminated, because they can be adjusted for a certain depth beyond which the bait is held suspended off the bottom. It's a good policy to avoid sinkers whenever possible.

Once you've logged some experience at bait fishing from shore, it's time to take a whirl at casting artificial lures. The average fisherman is surprised at how much this increases his catch. I feel there are fewer dull moments when I'm casting artificials, and I can't forget that the record books are full of trophies caught with artificials in the typical reservoirs.

There are many opportunities for tossing artificials from shore with a fly-casting outfit. Farm ponds and lakes with gradually sloping banks were made to order for bass bugging early and late in the day. But bass bugging is a slightly cumbersome technique for some shore fishing and requires more room than spinning or bait-casting gear, but it's deadly at times when bass can't resist striking at small lures "struggling" above them. Bass bugs are seldom effective, though, in water deeper than six feet.

The principle of bugging can be duplicated with spinning and bait-casting tackle. All you have to do is substitute floating bass plugs (wood- or plastic-bodied lures that usually resemble small fish) for the bugs. Cast and retrieve plugs in much the same way as for bugs. The secret to using any floating bait for bass is to fish it slowly and deliberately. Take plenty of time when retrieving; let the lure rest motionless at intervals. Make it behave like a critter in trouble.

Cover as much area as possible when casting for bass from shore.

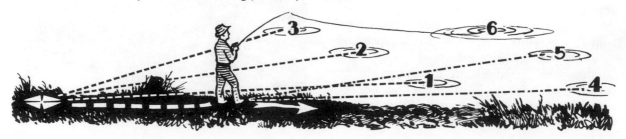

Your approach to shore fishing will depend a lot on whether you're mainly interested in relaxation or exercise. You can still-fish, walk the banks, or combine the two approaches. One technique that pays off handsomely is to walk the bank, concentrating on proven spots that you've turned up before.

When you walk the shore you're in a fine position to spot dropoffs, shoals, and sunken snags. An experienced shore walker will never pass up any of these spots for bass.

No matter what tackle or bait you use there's one trick that will help you to cover the most water from the shore: Make your first cast as nearly parallel to the shore as possible. Standing in the same spot, make the second, third—maybe even the fourth or fifth out from shore—like the spokes in a wheel. Then move forward fifteen or twenty feet and repeat the spokes-of-a-wheel pattern. If one spot looks good, concentrate there with several casts. Skip quickly over poor spots. For bass, a good spot is near "edge." It might be the edge of a weedbed, deadfall, dropoff, shoal, reef, channel, stump, or the edge of the lake itself.

A smart shore walker makes his casts so that he can retrieve parallel to the edges rather than perpendicular to them. Casting parallel to a fallen tree is an excellent example. Then the lure will pass a fish lurking anywhere under the trunk. A cast perpendicular to the trunk might fall out of sight of the fish.

There's also a knack to casting in weedbeds or other vegetation. Cast into any small openings, then retrieve as much as possible along the fringe of the vegetation. Use this method for both live bait and hardware.

When you walk the shore you inevitably have trouble with snagged lures, especially if you're casting along a rocky bank or a shore with many deadfalls. Often the difference between shore-fishing success and failure is to get the bait down close to the bottom where it is most likely to snag—but also most likely to catch fish. Particularly good in these places are the weedless spoons and the plugs that float when not in motion but dive deep when you retrieve them.

You may need several trips before you get the hang of it, but the ideal maneuver is to have the lure go almost to the bottom, then to reel it in

The bow-and-arrow, or slingshot, cast.

The flip cast.

just fast enough to maintain that same distance from the bottom throughout the retrieve. It will be a headache at first, but gradually it becomes almost automatic.

Some of the most productive sections are the hardest because they're full of brush. All but the most serious fishermen pass them by. However, the newest spinning gear make it possible for you to cast where there's practically no room at all. A few hours in the backyard and you'll master the bow-and-arrow cast and the flip cast.

The bow-and-arrow cast is the simplest. You merely grasp the lure between thumb and forefinger of your free hand, and bend the rod by drawing back the lure. (If you're using a bait-casting reel you keep the line from unwinding at this point by holding the thumb of your casting hand on the reel spool. With a spinning rig, release the reel's pickup mechanism, and then keep the line from unwinding by holding the line against the rod handle with the forefinger of your casting hand.) Aim the lure and let it go, and it will pull line out under gentle pressure of your thumb or forefinger. Be careful, of course, that you don't get the lure's hooks in your fingers.

For the flip cast, just poke the rod straight forward through an opening in lakeshore foliage. Allow the lure to hang six or eight inches below the rod tip. Now, with elbow action only, flip the lure first upward, then downward, and with the momentum obtained, flip it outward straight ahead. With just a little practice it's surprisingly easy. It's a good cast with crayfish and the heavier live baits.

Chapter 11

LIVE BAITS FOR BASS

Not too many bassers nowadays use live bait, because artificials serve very well. For those that do, however, live bait usually means minnows, crayfish, or nightcrawlers. These are effective sure enough, but a bass may tackle anything that moves, native to the water or not, and it's a wise bait fisherman who considers all the possibilities. The truth is that some of the lesser-known baits are the most effective. Here are some statistics on most of them.

Alewife: Also called killifish, the alewife is sometimes found landlocked in smallmouth lakes, although it is a saltwater species. They may migrate into freshwater coastal streams to spawn. Caught, kept, and hooked in the same manner as minnows, they make fair bait.

American brook lamprey: Found in the mud bottoms of streams, brook lampreys are harmless members of the family to which the parasitic sea lamprey belongs. In areas where brook lampreys occur they can be dug from the muck in fairly shallow water, a common digging implement being the hay fork. These tough and long-lasting baits can be hooked in various ways: through the tail so that the lamprey continues to swim freely; through one of the gill openings; or strung on the hook like a worm. They are especially favored for largemouth bass.

Australian cricket: Wingless cricket accidentally introduced into the United States. Good bait. Has been grown commercially.

Bee: Adult bees can be used for catching bass. More frequently, the grubs of bees, hornets, and wasps are used as bait. Use great care in handling.

Beetle larva: Beetle larvae, called grubs, make excellent bait for bass. One of the most popular of the grubs is the meal worm. Other grubs

can be dug from rotting logs and stumps, from beneath tree bark, grass roots, or manure piles. Best used for fishing through the ice.

Black-nosed dace: A small minnow common in cold, preferably fast-moving, waters. It is dark above and white below, with a dark stripe down the side; sometimes the dark line will appear to be yellow or tan, and the sides are often blotched. Maximum size, about three inches.

Blacknose shiner: One of the many shiners used as bait. See Golden shiner.

Bloodsucker: See Leech.

Brook lampreys are little-known, nonparasitic creatures that make excellent bass bait.

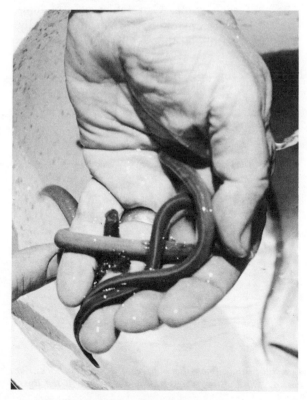

Blowfly maggot: These maggots, along with those of the housefly, the stable fly, and others, make excellent bait. They can be obtained by hanging out a piece of meat or dead animal and collecting the full-grown and fattened maggots that accumulate within about a week. If the meat or dead animal is hung up and a container placed beneath it the maggots will drop into it automatically. Frequently, such a container is filled with corn meal to dry and cleanse the maggots.

Bluntnose minnow: One of the most popular for pond propagation. Prominent spot at end of lateral line, just in front of caudal fin. Head is broad, blunt. Maximum size, about three inches.

Brassy minnow: A common bait minnow in the Midwest; found in creeks and ponds. It gets its name from the brassy color of the large scales along its sides.

Bream: Bluegill; the name also refers to one of the various shiners used for bait.

Brindled madtom: Madtoms are the smallest members of the catfishes; distinguished by continuation of adipose fin into caudal fin. Generally five inches or less in length. They prefer swift waters, and are frequently found under rocks. They have poison glands at the base of each spine. Can inflict painful injuries. Better bait for bass than is generally known. Durable on hook. Clip their spines for safety.

Bullfrog: Frogs, because they are lively and will attract a fish's attention, often catch fish where other baits fail. The leopard frog, the pickerel frog, and the green frog are favorites, although small bullfrogs also make good baits;

For still-fishing, hook the bullfrog through the back. For casting, the bullfrog should be hooked through the lips.

tadpoles, too, can take fish. You can catch the frogs by hand or with a scoop net; at night, blind them with a flashlight. They can be kept in a large wooden cage partly submerged in the water if you have provided them with rocks or pieces of wood for resting places. When you go fishing take them in a small container filled with damp grass and leaves.

Bullhead: Bullheads make good bait for bass when they are five inches or less in length. The horns on the pectoral and dorsal fins are generally clipped so that the bait is more attractive and less dangerous. Young bullheads can be seined from ponds and quiet backwaters and can be kept for long periods of time in bait buckets. They also live for a long time on the hook.

Caddis worm: Caddis worms, the larvae of small, winged insects belonging to the same order as the dobson fly (adult hellgrammite), live in the water and are generally encased in a portable protective sack made of sticks, leaves, stones, and other material that they cement together with a secretion from their mouths. Caddis worms can be caught by hand as they crawl about on the bottom. Removed from the case and strung on a hook, they are excellent bait for bass. Sometimes more than one can be used on a hook.

Carp: Carp are the largest members of the minnow family and were introduced to this country in the 1800s as a food and forage fish. Their closest relative, also an introduced species, is the goldfish. Both are good baits, but both are considered undesirable when placed in waters still free of them. State laws frequently ban the use of either goldfish or carp as bait.

Caseworm: See Caddis worm.

Catalpa worm: The catalpa worm is the caterpillar or larval stage of the sphinx moth. It sometimes reaches a length of three inches and can be found only on the catalpa tree, its sole source of food. These worms can be harvested by shaking the tree and picking up the worms that fall to the ground. You can keep them alive in a cage, feeding them catalpa leaves; or you can save them in corn meal in the refrigerator. They can be housed in ordinary coffee cans, provided they have leaves to eat. No holes need to be punched in the cans, as the empty space provides plenty of oxygen. They can be strung on the hook like a fishing worm, or the heads can be cut off and the soft body inside shucked from the skin, to make a possibly more appealing bait.

Caterpillar: Caterpillars are the larvae of butterflies and moths, and most of them can be used for bait. Smooth-skinned ones are better than those that are hairy or horned. Some of the hairy or spiny ones can sting.

Catfish: See Bullhead.

Chub: Chubs are stocky, hardy minnows with big heads and large scales. Generally caught in gravel-bottomed areas of creeks and large streams, they often reach a length of eight inches or more. They are sometimes caught on hook and line for sport. Small ones are excellent baits for bass.

Chub sucker: See Sucker.

Cicada: Cicadas (seventeen-year locusts) make good bait for bass during years of abundance. Actually, they are found in all years, but particularly at seventeen-year intervals.

Clipper: See Hellgrammite.

Cockroach: There are four common species of cockroaches: German, Oriental, American, and wood. The first three can be raised easily for bait or can be trapped by baiting them with raw or cooked vegetables. The containers in which they are kept should be tightly covered to prevent their escape, perhaps oiled near the top so that they cannot climb out. Make certain that the container holds an adequate supply of water. The entire roach is placed on the hook and is an excellent bait.

Common chub: See Chub.

Common shiner: See Golden shiner.

Common white sucker: See Sucker.

Conniption bug: See Hellgrammite.

Corn earworm: See European corn borer.

Crane fly: Also called gallinipper, crane flies are long-legged, extremely fragile flies whose water-dwelling larva, called leatherjacket and waterworm, make excellent bait for a variety of fish. The maggotlike larva, found under debris in streams, ponds, and lakes, has a tough skin and a small, hard head. Hook one or two through the head.

Crawdad or *crawfish:* See Crayfish.

Crawler: See Hellgrammite.

Crayfish: Also called craw, crab, crawdad, crawfish. The crayfish, which looks like a min-

iature lobster, is another excellent bait that bass cannot resist. A number of different species are found in swamps, brooks, streams, rivers, and lakes. They come out of hiding mostly at night, but during the day they can be caught by hand or with a small net under stones or in weedbeds. Minnow traps baited with dead fish or meat scraps will often catch them if the funnel openings are wide enough for them to enter. For a day's fishing you can keep them in damp weeds or moss in almost any container. The best crayfish for bait are those that have shed their hard shells and are soft and helpless. Tie these to a hook with fine thread and fish them for trout, black bass, walleyes, catfish, carp, and large panfish. To

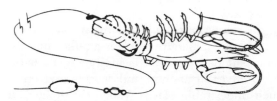

The best way to hook a live craw. Leaving hook point on top helps prevent hangups, while the slip-sinker rig lets skittish bass pick up craw without feeling resistance.

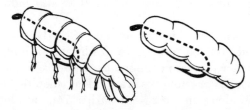

Crayfish tails, unpeeled (left) and peeled (right), are great bass catchers. Note how the entire hook is threaded through the tail.

use hard-shells, break off the large claws and hook them through the tail or back. The tail alone often makes a good bait. Frogs and crayfish require plenty of water and space, and it's not practical to try to raise them in small numbers. You can catch more than you need for yourself in most lakes or rivers.

Creek chub: See Chub.

Cricket: Catch crickets from under leaves and stones by hand or with a small net. Keep them in a box of grass on trips. For fishing, fine wire hooks are best. Run point under collar carefully so it doesn't kill the cricket. Good bait for bass. Two common species: gray and black. Easily grown.

Dace: See Black-nosed dace.

Damsel fly: See Nymph.

Darter: Also called Ohio log perch, sand pike, and zebra fish. Smallest members of perch family. Named because of habit of rapidly moving from place to place, then pausing. Found principally in and below currents. Catch on hook and line, or seine. Good bait.

Dewworm: See Nightcrawler.

Dobson fly: The adult stage of a hellgrammite.

Dragonfly: Dragonfly nymphs, often called perch bugs, ugly bugs, bass bugs; live in ponds, lakes, and quieter stream sections. They hide in mud, vegetation, and debris, where they can be caught in seines or dip nets. Bringing debris from bottom with rakes and examining for nymphs is also productive. Good bait for black bass.

Dung worm: Also called the stink worm or fecal earthworm, a manure worm is a rather uncommon bait because of its scarcity and its habitat. It lives in manure and sewage and other such undesirable places. When cut or hooked it gives off a yellowish liquid with a disagreeable odor. It is thinner than a regular earthworm, although it sometimes reaches a length of four or five inches. It is also more lively.

Earthworm: Earthworms are one of the best all-round live baits used in freshwater fishing. Whether they are common earthworms, nightcrawlers, or dung worms, they should be taken along on most fishing trips. You can dig them with a garden fork, grab the nightcrawlers when they emerge at night, or buy your worms from bait dealers. If you obtain your own, look for them in rich, moist soil. Worms can be kept for long periods in almost any large can or box filled with earth. For shorter periods or on the fishing grounds you can keep the worms in any small container filled with earth. But keep the worms out of the sun and rain. If kept for more than a week

The best method of hooking the earthworm is one that keeps the worm on the hook securely, yet allows it to wiggle freely.

or two the worms can be fed corn meal, bread crumbs, chicken mash, or other animal or vegetable matter mixed into the soil. When hooking the worms the best method is the one that keeps the worm on the hook securely, yet allows it to wiggle freely and to live the longest time. For trout, hook the worm under the sexual band or anywhere else near the center. In heavy weeds or when fishing on the bottom, the point and barb can be covered. When drifting the worm in fast, running water, the point and barb should be exposed. For bass, from one to six or so large worms can be used on a hook. Earthworms can be kept or raised almost anywhere, indoors or outdoors, and take up little space. If an angler just wants enough worms for himself and perhaps a friend or two, he can usually dig the worms in the spring of the year and keep them in boxes or cans throughout the fishing season. Just keep the soil moist by sprinkling some water into the containers every so often and feed the worms bread crumbs, chicken mash, ground oats, or almost any other vegetable or animal matter, small amounts of which can be mixed into the soil. You can also obtain special, prolific worms from tackle stores, bait dealers, or worm farms if you want to raise large quantities of them. From one hundred to three hundred of these worms can be used to start a colony in a large watertight box or metal container filled with rich soil. This container can be kept indoors in a cool spot, and after the worms are added the only attention it needs is occasional food and water to keep the soil moist. About a pound of corn meal to a half pound of vegetable shortening or lard can be mixed into the soil every two weeks or so. The larger the container, the more food should be added. The worms will breed, and you can remove the adult ones for bait at regular intervals. Outdoor pits can also be dug or constructed in a shady spot and filled with rich soil and manure or compost. Breeder worms can be added to this, and for best results the wormbed should be fenced with boards or concrete extending well below the surface to keep the worms inside. If organic materials are used for worm compost, wet thoroughly and turn daily until all heat is gone before stocking the worms. Best bed material is cottonseed meal, flue bran, or cotton

A variety of live baits can be used for either smallmouths or spotted bass in limestone streams such as this.

waste from gins. Add cottonseed meal if bed material is low in protein.

Eel: See American brook lamprey and eel.

European corn borer: Also called corn earworm, it is found on the leaves, husks, and tassels of corn during the summer months. During the fall and winter they can be taken from dry stalks. They make excellent bait both in summer and in winter. To keep them alive on the hook, it's best to hook them through the tough head or to tie them onto the hook with thread.

Fairy shrimp: A transparent, freshwater crustacean that grows to 1½ inches; found in streams, ponds, potholes in grass, weedbeds, and edges. They can be caught with a "drag" bucket of closely woven wire mesh, or seined. Excellent bait.

Fathead minnow: Also called blackhead minnow, they are among the most popular and the most easily raised minnows in ponds. They rarely exceed three inches in length and can be caught in many streams, ponds, and lakes.

Fidding: Method of harvesting earthworms by driving wooden stake into firm but moist ground and then running board or metal strip across staketop to develop a vibration in the ground. Within a few moments worms will be found lying on the ground surface.

Field mice: See Mouse.

Fish (as bait): Strips of fish, particularly belly meat, with the skins attached are trolled for bass occasionally.

Frog: See Bullfrog.

Gallinipper: See Crane fly.

Gall worm: Gall worms are the larvae of flies, moths, and wasps that cause the swellings called galls on the stems of plants. Gall worms are good wintertime bait and can be cut from the gall when other baits are not available.

Garden hackle or *garden worm:* Another name for earthworm.

Garter snake: See Snake.

Gizzard shad: Like the alewife, the gizzard shad is a member of the herring family. It is also used for bait.

Golden shiner: The golden shiner is one of the several species of shiners that make the finest of bass baits. Their bodies are compressed to form a sharp lid on the belly just behind the pelvic fin. Shiners are generally found in the shallower parts of lakes, ponds, and in slow-moving streams. They can be raised successfully in ponds for bass bait.

Goldfish: Species of minnow, *not* a carp. It is a successful minnow for bait production in ponds. Very prolific and hardy. Do not use *ornamental* goldfish for bait.

Grasshopper: Like crickets, grasshoppers can be caught in fields and gardens and can be kept for long periods of time in containers before actually using them on a fishing trip. They're hooked in much the same manner as crickets.

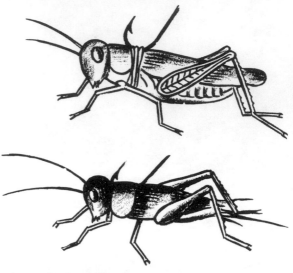

How to hook grasshoppers.

Grub: See Beetle.

Grubworm: Usually a whitish, thick-bodied larva of May beetle or June bug found in soil. Fair catfish and trout bait. See Beetle larva.

Harvest fly: Another name for cicada.

Hawk moth: A large, narrow-winged moth, the larvae of which live on tomato plants, tobacco plants, cotton plants, and other crops. The larva, like the catalpa worm, is an excellent bait.

Helldiver: Another name for Hellgrammite.

Hellgrammite: This popular water insect bait, also known by other names—such as alligator, water grampus, conniption bug, snipper, flip-flap, and helldiver, to name a few—is the larval form of the big, winged insect known as the dobson fly. It is black or dark brown with two sharp pincers, six legs, and numerous "appendages" on both sides of its long body. Hellgrammites live under rocks in the riffles of streams and rivers. They can be caught by

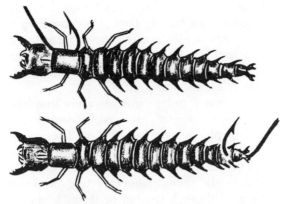

How to hook hellgrammites.

turning over the rocks and holding a wire screen or net below the rocks. Keep them in damp leaves or grass in a cool spot. They make a tough bait and can be hooked under the collar, in the tail, or turned inside out after cutting the head off. It's a great bait for spotted and smallmouth black bass, especially in rivers, but it will often take largemouth bass as well.

Hog sucker: See Sucker.

Horned chub or horneyhead chub: See Chub.

Horned dace: See Black-nosed dace.

Horned pout: See Bullhead.

June bug: See Beetle, Grubworm.

Katydid: Like grasshopper. Fish in same manner as cricket.

Lake emerald shiner: See Golden shiner.

Lamprey eels: See American brook lamprey.

Larva: Name used for the soft-bodied, immature stage of various insects, such as the grubs of beetles; maggots of flies; caterpillars of moths.

Leatherjacket: Another name for the larva of the crane fly.

Leech: There are many species of leeches (also called bloodsuckers), varying in size from less than an inch to several inches in length when stretched out. They belong to the same group as the earthworm, but most of them have a sucking disk at each end of the body and live by sucking blood from various animals. They can be caught in traps baited with blood or meat. Sometimes fishermen rub liver or bloody meat across their waders and then wade through a mucky pool where leeches will attach themselves to the waders. Leeches can live a long time without food, so can be easily kept in aquaria. They are very durable baits for bass.

Leopard frog: See Bullfrog.

Locust: See Cicada.

Maggot: See Blowfly maggot.

Manure worm: See Dung worm.

May fly: Also called Willow fly or Canadian soldier. Adult and immature May flies are important fish food. The immature or nymphal stage of May fly is often used as bait. Adults and nymphs are often copied in fly patterns and used by trout anglers. Nymphs are captured by scooping up muck and mud from the bottom of streams and pools, then draining mud away from the insects. They can be kept in aquaria where water is well aerated and the bottom covered with debris similar to that from which they were taken.

Meal worm: Large numbers of meal worms are easily raised in a large washtub or box filled with alternate layers of burlap and chicken mash or other grain meals. This container, which should be stocked initially with a few hundred meal worms, will need a sprinkling of water every day or so; you can add some raw carrots or potatoes to provide the necessary moisture. Keep the container covered with wire screen to prevent the meal worms and the adult beetles from escaping. Used for bass fishing through the ice. See Beetle larva.

Minnow: Most freshwater fish like minnows, and so they are a popular bait with anglers. There are many kinds, such as the bluntnose, fathead, and the various chubs, dace, and shiners. These small bait fish can be caught in most freshwater streams, lakes, and rivers with seines, drop nets, minnow traps, and tiny hooks baited with bread, dough, or bits of worm. They can also be bought from bait dealers. In minnow buckets, which keep the water cool and fresh, minnows will live for days if not too crowded. For longer periods keep them in "live boxes" submerged or floated in clean, cool water. Minnows from 1½ to 10 inches long are usually used for bait, depending on the size of fish sought. They can be hooked through both lips or the back for still-fishing and "sewed" on the hook for casting and trolling. Minnows can also be raised, but if you need only a small number

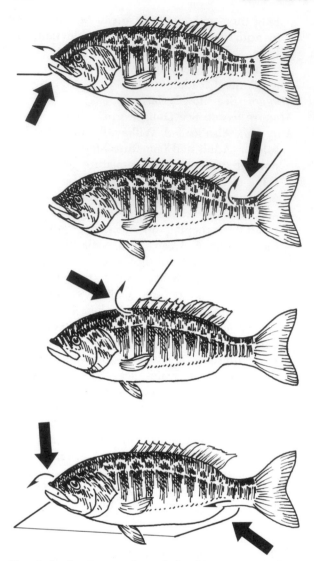

How to hook minnows, dace, chubs, shiners, or any other small fish used as bait.

during the fishing season it is cheaper and less trouble to buy them or seine them from a pond or a stream. To raise them in large quantities to supply several anglers or to raise them for sale, you need one or more ponds or tanks. Since there are many kinds of minnows that can be raised and since different methods are called for in different parts of the country, it is best to consult your state conservation or fish and game department for information on raising minnows in your area. They can supply the necessary literature on construction or selection of ponds, species, proper breeding, feeding, control of diseases, and handling.

Mouse: Both field mice and house mice can be used as bait for big bass. They are frequently tied onto the hook with wire or thread.

Muddler: See Sculpin.

Mud minnow: A small, hardy bait fish; lives a long time on a hook.

Newt: Newts and salamanders are amphibians, sometimes found near rocks and logs and damp places near the water. They must be grabbed by their heads or midsections because their tails break easily. They are cared for in the same manner as frogs and can be hooked through the tail or through one of the feet and used as bait. Also called waterdogs.

Nightcrawler: Nightcrawlers are the largest of the worms used for fishing, many reaching the length of ten inches. On warm, moist nights they come out and stretch across the surface of the ground, where, with the aid of a flashlight and a bit of dexterity, they can be caught. See Earthworm.

Nightwalker: See Nightcrawler.

Nymph: A name used for the immature stage of certain water insects. In these insects there are three stages of development—egg, nymph, and adult.

Peeler: Name of crayfish that can be peeled when hard shell loosens. See Crayfish.

Perch: See Yellow perch.

Perch bug: Name commonly used to refer to dragonfly nymphs. See Dragonfly.

Pickerel frog: See Bullfrog.

Pork rind: Although pork rind is used mostly with artificial lures, it is considered to be a natural bait. The rind can usually be purchased in a butcher shop that sells salt pork. All the fat should be scraped off the skin, and then a very sharp knife or razor blade is used to cut the rind into the desired shapes. After being cut, the strips should be put in a strong brine solution for two or three days. Then

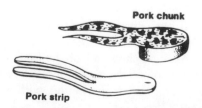

they can be removed and bleached by soaking in a dilute hydrochloric or acetic acid solution until they turn white. After this the strips can be packed in airtight jars containing a solution of 10 to 20 per cent formalin and a little glycerin. Another preservative is a solution of 1 per cent sodium benzoate in water. Or you can use ordinary rubbing alcohol or a heavy brine to preserve the rind until used. Pork rind can also be bought already made up in almost any tackle store.

Prawn: Small saltwater shrimp sometimes seined and used in freshwater fishing for bass.

Pupa: Pupa is the third stage in the development of insects that pass through the egg, larva, pupa, and adult stages of development. This is the resting stage, at which the insect is frequently used for wintertime fishing.

Rainworm: Another name for nightcrawler.

Redfin: Bait minnow. Popular in the Southeast.

Red horse: One of the members of the sucker family caught on hook and line when fully grown and used as bait while young.

Redworm: See Earthworm, English redworm.

River chub: See Chub.

River shiner: One of the shiners commonly used as bait. See Golden shiner.

Salamander: An amphibian similar to the newt.

Sculpin: Sculpin, or muddler, is a small bottom-dweller that has a rather large black head and permanently protruding pectoral fins. They resemble in general appearance small catfish and make good and hardy baits for bass. They can be taken from streams by turning over rocks and catching them as they wash down into a net.

Seventeen-year locust: See Cicada.

Sewn bait: A term applied to bait fish attached to spoons or spinners. Such rig is usually used in trolling.

Shiner: See Golden shiner.

Shrimp: A saltwater crustacean similar to the prawn, often used as bait for freshwater bass.

Silver chub: A common chub used for bait, also known as the Storer's chub.

Silverside: A long, thin minnow sometimes used for bait. This is also another name for the shiner minnow or friar. See Golden shiner.

Slug: The slug is a large, shell-less land snail, found under stones, logs, and in other damp places, especially gardens. Slugs can be used as bait for bass.

Smelt: Smelt are small fish found in lakes and are frequently used as bait for smallmouth bass.

The salamander is an important bass bait in some desert lakes of the Southwest.

Snail: The snail is sometimes used as bait after removal of its shell. See Slug.

Snake: Many of the smaller snakes such as garter snakes, green snakes, and small water snakes can be used as bait for larger carnivorous fish such as bass.

Snipper: Another name for the hellgrammite.

Soldier fly: A fly larva that feeds on organic matter. Those squirming masses of maggots found in outdoor privies are usually soldier flies. They can be grown in clean materials. About an inch in length, they are hardy and make excellent bait.

Sphinx moth: The adult stage of the catalpa worm.

Spottail shiner: Common shiner used as bait. See Golden shiner.

Spring lizard: See Newt.

Stone cat: See Brindled madtom.

Stone fly: The stone-fly nymph resembles the nymph of the May fly. They are found under rocks in swift water rather than in the mud and muck of stagnant water. Nymphs are used as bait for trout and are frequently copied in fly-pattern design. They are hooked underneath the collar, on wire hooks, or threaded on the hooks like a worm.

Stone pike: One of the common names for darter.

Stone roller: Minnow found in streams. Hardy on hook.

Striped dace: A dace often used for bait. See Black-nosed dace.

Sucker: The sucker is a bottom-feeding fish with thick, protrusible lips. There are several species, all of which may be used as bass bait when small.

Sunfish: Small sunfish, particularly with their spiny dorsal fins trimmed, are sometimes used as bass bait.

Tadpole: The tadpole is the immature, water-dwelling stage of the frog, sometimes good as bait. See Bullfrog.

Toad: Small toads, like frogs, are good bait on occasion. They are especially abundant near water during the dry season.

Tuffy: Another name for Fathead minnow.

Ugly bug: Another name for Dragonfly nymph.

Wasp: The larvae of wasps are good bait. See Bee.

Water dog: Another name for certain salamanders.

Water grampus: Another name for hellgrammite.

Water snake: See Snake.

Waterworm: Another name for the larva of the crane fly.

White sucker: Member of the sucker family. See Sucker.

Willow fly: See May fly.

Worm: See Earthworm.

Wriggler: Another name for the May-fly nymph.

Yellow meal worm: One of the meal worms used as bait. See Beetle larva.

Yellow perch: A small perch sometimes used as bait for larger fish, with the spiny dorsal fin often cut away to make the bait more attractive. Strips of perch belly with the fins attached are also used for trolling and skittering.

Zebra fish: Another name for darter.

How to Use Live Bait

There are so many potential and proven live baits that describing how to use all of them would require an entire library of information. There are some general points, however, that apply to nearly every type of live-bait dunking.

Since the only reason for using live bait instead of artificials is that live bait has an appeal and an "action" impossible to duplicate, live bait should be used in the freest and most unhampered manner possible. That means an absolute minimum of sinkers and bobbers, preferably none at all.

Probably the ideal live-bait tackle is a light or medium spinning outfit; with it, a crayfish, for example, can be hooked in the tail and cast, without sinker or float, exactly like a plug to a productive spot. The crayfish then swims to the bottom and behaves as a crayfish naturally would until a bass comes along and nails him. Now, the minute this happens the fisherman flips open the bail on his spinning reel and allows the bass to run with the bait with virtually no suspicious drag at all because the light line is pulling easily off the end of the spool. When the bass pauses to swallow the crayfish the angler closes the bail, gently gathers slack line, and then strikes. Another bass for the stringer.

This live-bait/spinning combination is equally good in lakes and running water. Critters like leeches, hellgrammites, and large grasshoppers as well as crayfish can be allowed to drift with the current in a completely genuine manner. Actually this is a deadly technique, particularly on a rising water level or when a stream is somewhat roily from rains.

Of course, there are times when it is impossible to do without a sinker or a float—either to get a bait closer to the bottom or to keep it from burrowing *into* the bottom. In that case, use the smallest and lightest sinker possible. Often a single split shot will do the job. Or when using a float, a small sliding, thumb-sized cork with a matchstick to fit in the core is enough. With this simple kind of float, it's easy to adjust lure depth. In any event, remember that the larger and more buoyant a float, the more "drag" is evident to a fish taking the bait.

It is not necessary to use large hooks in live-bait fishing, either. Only rarely is it necessary to use something larger than No. 8, and usually No. 10 is good enough. You can get much more mileage out of the bait, too, with a small fine-wire hook.

Too many bass fishermen cast a live bait and then allow it to soak for much too long in one small place. It is much better to move it often, to test different depths, to thump it along the bottom, and to toss it into likely "edge" just as you would a plug. And always try to keep a *fresh* bait on the hook. Nowadays it isn't difficult to carry a large supply of bait on any trip and to keep it lively for a long time, thanks to the many new containers and devices that are available. Several of these are illustrated elsewhere in this book.

A rig known as the Lindy is very effective for using minnow, nightcrawlers, and leeches over thick bottom moss and debris. This involves using an adjustable float that fastens to the line at some point between the bait and a swivel clip. The whole thing is cast and a walking-style slip sinker bounces along the bottom. But the bait floats free just above the bottom.

Live bait is most important for winter fishing —and essential in fishing through the ice. This may surprise some fishermen, but bass *can* be taken through the ice with some regularity. Strangely enough, ice-caught bass are usually big ones, and a former Ohio record largemouth was a nine-pounder taken in a frozen lake near Youngstown. Nor is it unusual to make good catches at other frozen lakes in the Midwest.

This is a good place to say something about pork baits—the pork strips, frogs, chunks, etc. Actually these have been in use almost as long as Americans have been bass fishing. Consider the few old-timers still living who once caught largemouth bass commercially for a living. For many years they would catch up to a hundred fish a day, every day, and nearly all on some sort of pork bait prepared at home on Sundays, their only days off.

Pork rind or skin has an undulating action in the water that was hard to match until the relatively recent development of the soft plastics. Chamois skin has a similar quality when soaked. Still, pork-rind and pork-fat baits that have been properly "cured" in brine have an interesting if not important role today. Probably bass fishermen will always depend on them. Although they are most often fished in combination with other lures, maybe with a weedless spoon or behind a June-bug spinner, pork strips and pork frogs are deadly when fished alone.

Try this someday when action is slow. Put a pork frog on a weedless hook and cast it into "islands" of lily pads. Then retrieve it erratically, in stop-and-go fashion, half over the pads and half between them. Stop altogether for several seconds, then jerk the bait hard. Pause again. The result is explosive.

Here is another possibility. Put a three-inch strip of pork on a bare hook and with a fly-casting outfit drift it into small pools and pockets. Let it sink to the bottom, then raise it and let it sink again. Raise and lower repeatedly. Sometimes you can catch bass, catfish, and panfish this way—and all without moving from the same spot. Try this method especially below low dams or along the "shelves" of limestone steams.

Any way you look at it, pork is an excellent bait in the hands of a fisherman who likes to experiment, for by doing so he will give his bait an action few bass have ever seen before.

Chapter 12

BASS BOATS AND OTHER ACCESSORIES

Next to his tackle, any bass fisherman's greatest need may be for some kind of watercraft to carry him safely across fishing water to the action. Some fishermen prefer not to own a boat outright, but depend on renting one wherever they happen to go fishing. There is a considerable economic advantage to this, which is offset, however, by the fact that the rental boats and motors available are not always what a fisherman needs or, to be honest, in the best of condition. So the most serious bassers will eventually buy a boat.

Almost any craft, from a frail canoe or inflatable raft to one of the electronic "bullets" so popular nowadays, can be used to cast for bass. Which one is best depends upon the kind of waters likely to be fished, but even more upon budget—how much the angler cares to spend. We also suspect that ego or "appearance" is involved more than a little. A fisherman might buy one of the huge bass boats for the same strange reason he buys a huge, gas-guzzling car, and never mind that it is no better (in fact, is far more unwieldy) than a compact. It is possible to invest as much as $12,000 (in 1979) or as little as $150 in a bass-fishing craft.

In any case, the ideal bass boat is, above all, transportable, either on car-top carriers (as are canoes or small aluminum rowboats) or on a low-slung trailer with a winch that matches the boat. Canoes, as noted earlier, are good for use on rivers and ponds, by one or two persons. They are light enough to pick up and portage to a marsh or swamp beyond the reach of a car. Glass canoes can actually be dragged over rough ground without undue damage to the finish.

A fisherman needs a more stable canoe, wider abeam and roomier, than the ones designed just for cruising or racing. In fact, he should try out any model before buying to be certain it is suitable for his use when casting. He might even consider one of the square-ended canoes to which a small gasoline or electric motor can be attached. There is no doubt that a canoe can carry a bass angler into places impossible to reach with heavier, less maneuverable watercraft.

The next step upward, and a sort of compromise, is a rowboat or johnboat, heavier and more stable than a canoe, but still far from the

For bass fishing, a canoe should have a wide beam, yet be easily transportable on car top.

A canoe, perhaps with a small motor, is a handy craft for fishing small streams and ponds. Photo by the Coleman Co.

Inexpensive handy carriers like these permit an angler to carry his boat or canoe on car top.

Light car-top boats like this are safe and ideal for casting in smaller bass lakes.

molded Fiberglas bass boat we will soon describe. Several generations of bass fishermen have had nothing more than a shallow-draft johnboat to play the game, and somehow they still caught bass. Admittedly they did not also have the great fishing pressure, nor the giant lakes of today to contend with. Nevertheless, the old-type two- or three-person rowboat is still an alternative for the bass fisherman who isn't in a hurry and who fishes mostly on small to medium waters. An aluminum johnboat of, say twelve feet, shallow draft, plus a ten- or fifteen-horsepower outboard is an extremely versatile, safe rig on lake or river for a fisherman who likes to do a lot of exploring.

Modern Bass Boats

No doubt the proliferating bass tournaments across America have had the most to do with the development of today's so-called bass boat. Depending on your viewpoint, these craft are either angry, glittering monstrosities that churn a lake into a noisy raceway or gorgeous mechanical marvels with bass-catching capability. Probably both assessments are correct. Until 1978, when the U. S. Coast Guard stepped in with tough manufacturing regulations, many bass boats also were unsafe at any speed. The situation is a little better now.

In length bass boats range from twelve feet to about eighteen feet. Most are designed for two (but occasionally for two plus a guide) fishermen who can cast either from swivel seats, front

The modern bass boat, equipped with swivel seats, is sleek, fast, and extremely stable as a casting platform.

A small boat like this one can carry a fisherman into narrow channels and many otherwise inaccessible bass hideouts.

and rear, or while standing up. The seats are comfortable and make casting convenient in any direction. Standing up, even on a gunwale, will not overturn the boat. Fishing from a bass boat can be pure pleasure.

The power is supplied by either an inboard or an outboard engine, usually with twice as much horsepower as is sensibly necessary. This is ex-

plained (by the pro-tournament competitors, at least) by the need to cover large areas of lake quickly—in order to spend more time fishing and less time cruising. Probably it works that way, too, but it also shatters the serenity of a lake for the majority of bass fishermen who care very little about tournaments.

Besides the main motor source, every bass

An electric trolling motor, operated by foot, leaves the fisherman free to concentrate on his casting.

boat also has an electric motor, a depth finder, a live well, a cooler, rod racks, a battery-operated anchor, a fire extinguisher, tackle storage areas, usually a water-temperature probe, an oxygen monitor, and a rack for marker buoys. How well all of these features are arranged in a boat will determine exactly how convenient it is to use. The electric motor, which must be charged nightly, is usually foot-operated by one person to maneuver the boat while all anglers aboard can cast without having to bother with paddles or oars.

A bass boat is expensive, and with a trailer to match, it may be the most expensive item (next to his own house) that a bass fisherman will ever own. So a new boat should be bought with extreme caution. There are a number of good, reliable, small-boat makers in the business, but there also have been many more fly-by-nighters.

It is therefore good advice at least to investigate the larger brand names.

Does the new boat have a warranty? Are other serious bass fishermen (besides the pros who are sponsored by boat companies and therefore naturally prejudiced) satisfied with the boat? Is the equipment in the boat situated for your convenience when fishing or is it just slapped in place? Can you give the boat a fishing trial before buying? Do you really need such a huge, heavy boat with such a large power plant? If you are out just to catch bass, rather than to impress, you might get along with a more modest outfit.

Depth Finders and Fish Locators

Electronic depth finders, some of which are fish spotters, come in so many varieties, degrees

Even an airboat can serve as a bass boat in weed-choked southern waters.

of sophistication, and price tags that properly describing them is nearly impossible. Some depth finders today are capable of bottom reading as far as one hundred feet down and with the boat breezing along at fifty miles per hour. These same instruments will "bleep" when they pass over a fish or a school of fish. Some units are portable to permit use on any boat; others are permanently mounted onto one bass boat, as a car radio in an auto dashboard. Depth finders have come a long way since Lo-k-tor introduced their "little green box" several years ago.

A locator's main function is to tell a fisherman how far down the bottom is and, to a surprising extent, what kind of bottom it is. With a depth finder, a topo map, and a small amount of experience, an angler can get an exact picture of the "terrain" that exists below him. That is a definite advantage when searching for bass.

There are a number of things to look for in a depth finder. Is the unit completely waterproof, even dampnessproof? Keep in mind that it must be able to withstand the beating of travel over rough, choppy water. Is it sensitive enough to pick up fishes and bottom features when traveling? Or must the boat be stopped? (This is a disadvantage.) Is the locator swivel-mounted to be seen from different points in the boat, and can you read the dial signals in bright sunlight? For the practical bass fisherman, a depth finder that works accurately to just fifty or sixty feet is of more value (and is probably less costly) than one that scans down one hundred feet deep. The former are bound to be more accurate.

Some bass-fishing fanatics with money to burn like to mount depth finders both fore and aft in their boats. Others have installed graph-type units (similar to those used on salt-water deep-

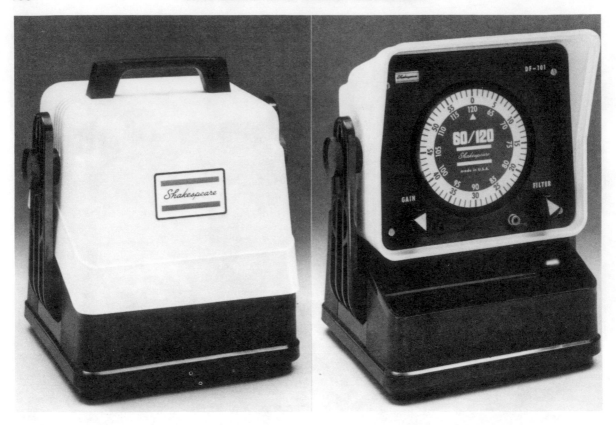

Portable depth finders and fish spotters are today almost standard equipment for serious bass fishermen.

sea boats) to draw pictures of the structures below. These are fascinating gadgets which can also keep a record of where fish were caught. Looking toward the future, bass boats soon may be equipped with miniature television scanners that reveal everything on the bottom, fish as well as cover, over a 360-degree radius from the boat.

Two kinds of water thermometers are available: one measures only surface temperature, and the other probes and reports temperatures at different depths. The latter is more valuable to a fisherman and indeed may be as important as a depth finder in pinpointing the level at which bass are most likely to be found. Another device with considerable value, especially in deep lakes, is a reliable oxygen monitor that reports the amount of oxygen at different depths, thereby indicating where bass are likely to be. Still another kind of meter, which measures the pH factor (acidity-alkalinity ratio) of the water, has been introduced. Recent investigations, still inconclusive, have shown that bass may be more active at certain pH levels than at others. So this is something to watch in the future.

For fishing in waters that contain big bass, a long-handled net can be invaluable.

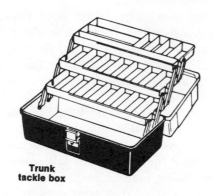

Trunk tackle box

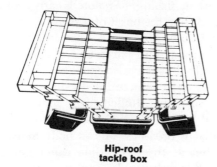

Hip-roof tackle box

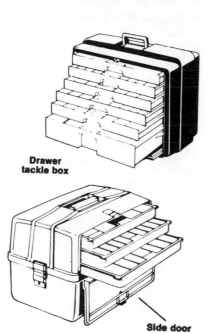

Drawer tackle box

Side door

Varieties of large and roomy tackle boxes available today.

A nighttime basser may want to install a soft-glow light in his boat for changing lures and such. Any fisherman's tackle box should be large enough to carry a larger number of lures than he originally expects to acquire or use, plus spare reels, repair tools, sinkers, a stringer, insect re-

pellent (keep this separate from the lures, though), suntan lotion, sunglasses, a knife, camera, film, and sundry other items. Look for a box that opens out so that all the contents are easily visible and extractable. A good safety feature, to keep from spilling everything onto a dock or in the water, is a handle that is upright for carrying only when the tackle box is closed and locked.

Traditionally most fisherman just wore old clothes not fit for anything else, but that has changed. The "uniform" of today's bass fisherman is a comfortable jump suit, or multipocket bass suit, of the type designed by top bass fisherman Dick Kotis of the Fred Arbogast Company. This is a one-piece cotton-polyester garment, loose-

A many-pocketed jump suit is practically a uniform for bass fishermen.

A poncho rolled up in a tackle box can be a lifesaver during sudden cold rainstorms.

fitting, for easy casting, with eight large, cargo pockets, including a pair in the short sleeves. There are also clip-on D-rings, front and back (to hold a net when wading). The machine-washable and permanent-press suit is pleated in the back to be bind-free.

An essential too often neglected by bass fishermen is a foul-weather suit that is completely protective, even in the worst downpour. Especially during the spring and fall seasons when the bass fishing may be best, weather is uncertain and unexpected precipitation is common. Besides that, fishing (as noted early) often is very fast during the onset of a storm front.

The best raingear for a boat fisherman is a two-piece pants and parka suit that is not only waterproof, but is also tough and durable enough to resist puncturing by hooks, fins, and other sharp points. Rolled up it could fit in the bottom of a tackle box. Goretex is a good material in that it breathes—allows body moisture to escape—but at the same time can repel a deluge. A full-length poncho can also protect a sitting bass fisherman, if it is made of reliably waterproof material.

Carrying a lot of equipment does not necessarily make the bass fisherman successful. But wise selection of the items an individual really needs can add much pleasure to the sport.

Chapter 13

BASS IN THE PAN

In some areas the black bass is known as the fish with the "muddy taste." Nothing could be more absurd *if* a bass fisherman keeps one important point in mind: Preparation for the table must begin the minute the fish is caught.

There are three ways to handle bass as they are caught—either alive on a stringer, in a live box, or in a portable refrigerator. The live box, or well, is by far the best alternative, and many boats come equipped with them. In a cooler the fish should be placed so that they do not slosh around in melting ice water. Lacking both a stringer and a cooler, soak a burlap bag and

One way to keep bass alive until ready to dress and eat is on a stringer with a safety-pin snap for each fish.

then wring it out as much as possible. Wrap the bass inside and place the bag in a shady place. Of course, this isn't so effective as the other methods.

When fishing is over, the bass should be cleaned immediately. From small fish, remove the scales, gills, fins, head, and entrails. Wipe the body cavity clean and dry. Fillet the larger bass—say, from 1½ pounds and upward. Avoid using water as much as possible in the cleaning; instead, sprinkle either the whole fish or the fillets with lemon juice. Water makes the flesh mushy, while lemon tends to "firm" it. If water is used, wipe the fish dry with a cloth before cooking or refrigerating.

If a "muddy" taste actually exists at all in bass of a certain lake, simply skin them.

Largemouths are "lean" or nonoily fish, and general cooking instructions are pretty much the same as for other such fish. It is most important not to overcook them, no matter what method is used. Overcooking always leaves bass very dry, flaky, and tasteless. No matter whether you fry, bake, or broil your bass, the best idea is first to subject the bass briefly to high heat to seal in flavors. After that reduce the heat, except in frying, in which case a bare six or seven minutes will take care of small pieces of fish.

Just as largemouths are unsophisticated fish, so should cooking them be uncomplicated. The flavor of bass is pleasant, and there is no reason unduly to disguise it.

FRIED BASS

Frying bass is as simple as heating a skillet of butter, bacon drippings, or peanut oil and then dropping salted and peppered pieces of bass into it. Three minutes or so on each side will do it. That's the most convenient and least compli-

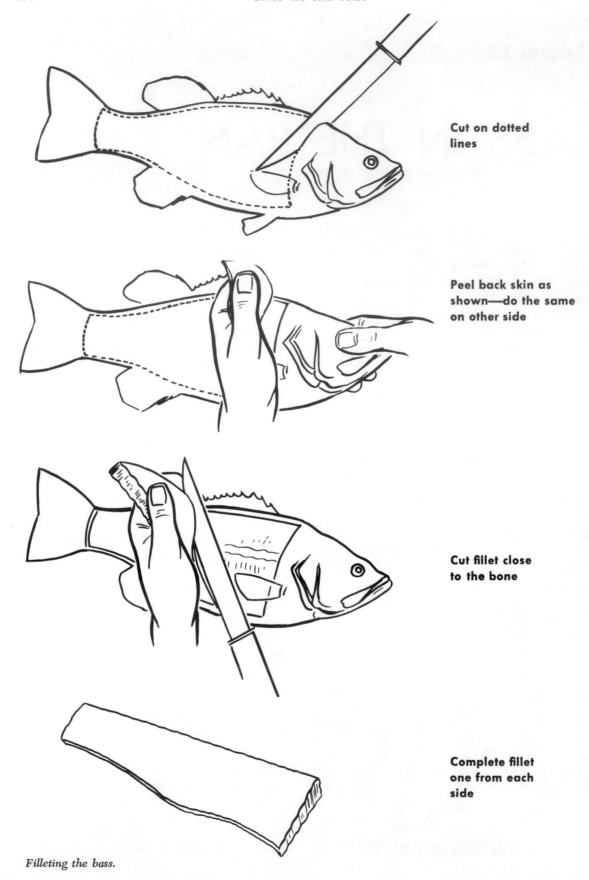

Cut on dotted
lines

Peel back skin as
shown—do the same
on other side

Cut fillet close
to the bone

Complete fillet
one from each
side

Filleting the bass.

The complete bass fisherman cooks his bass fresh out of the water.

cated of methods for cooking on the trail or in a light camp.

You can also roll the fish in a mixture of flour, yellow corn meal, and salt and pepper before frying. Still another alternative is to dip the fish in a batter of pancake flour, egg, milk, or beer, and a dash of chili powder and oregano before French-frying it in deep, hot peanut oil, until crisp and golden brown. Never allow fried fish to remain in the fat after cooking is finished.

GRILLED BASS

Clean a medium-to-large-size bass, but leave it whole. Split the fish and place it, flesh side down, on a grill from 10 to 12 inches above a bed of hot hardwood coals. After 10 minutes (for a 2-pounder) turn over and sprinkle with ½ teaspoon of monosodium glutamate, salt, and pepper on the flesh side. The bass will have a robust, somewhat smoky flavor. It should be served with potatoes baked in the coals.

Bass can be "grilled" at streamside just by spitting the pieces or whole fish on green willow sticks and holding them over the coals.

PLANKED BASS

Tack large fillets or split whole bass to a strip of clean, bleached driftwood with skin side to the wood. Prop the wood near the fire and brush the fish frequently with hot strips of bacon or bacon drippings as they broil. Baste also with lemon if it's available. Season with salt and pepper. This is a leisurely method of cooking that was designed for a warm midday on a wilderness pond.

POACHED BASS

Poaching is a convenient and delicious way to prepare small bass. Frying and baking small ones may result in bony, overcooked fish dinners. But poaching, which leaves the fish succulent and flaky, is the first step to a variety of tasty and nutritious meals that are not too difficult to prepare in a hurry. Following is a simple poaching method that is great for any bass.

4–6 small bass
2 tablespoons butter
2 tablespoons lemon juice
¼ teaspoon salt
dash pepper

Place an inch of water in a deep skillet (use a trivet on the bottom if available). Bring the water to a gentle boil. Arrange your fish on a piece of heavy-duty aluminum foil and turn up the edges of this wrap. Add butter, lemon juice, salt, and pepper. Place in the skillet, and cover. Cook gently for 10 to 15 minutes, or until the fish flakes with a fork. Then remove the skin and bones and flake the fish. Four cups of flaked fish will make about a pound.

Your poached fish can be served with a sauce or used to make a delicious casserole.

BASS AU GRATIN

This bass recipe is as delicious as it is unique. You will require the following ingredients:

2 tablespoons butter
2 tablespoons flour
1 cup milk
¾ cup grated Swiss or sharp Cheddar cheese
1 tablespoon Worcestershire sauce
2 cups flaked, cooked bass
salt and pepper, to taste

Melt the butter in a pan and blend in flour.

Gradually add the milk while constantly stirring. When the sauce thickens, pour in the cheese. After the cheese melts, add the Worcestershire sauce and fold in the flaked fish; season with salt and pepper. Heat the mixture completely through, and serve, possibly over noodles or wild rice.

BASS CASSEROLE

Here is a great way to use your poached, boned, skinned bass. Just skin and fillet the larger fish before poaching. Largemouth bass, especially, taste better when skinned. You will need:

2 cups cooked, flaked fish
1 (10½-oz.) can of condensed cream of mush-
   room soup
½ cup grated sharp Cheddar cheese
2 cups cooked rice
½ cup breadcrumbs

Preheat your oven to 350° F. Mix the first four ingredients together, and turn into a 1-quart buttered casserole. Sprinkle ½ cup breadcrumbs on top, and bake for 30 minutes.

BAKED BASS

Take a whole 3- or 4-pounder (or the fillets from several fish) and rub all surfaces with olive oil. Place in a well-buttered casserole, add a finely chopped onion and a half cup of tomato juice—and bake for 30 minutes in a 350° oven, basting frequently. Remove the fish, cover it with a creole sauce and buttered bread crumbs, and brown it under the broiler. Serve with rice and a green salad.

BOILED BASS

Place either fillets or whole fish in a clean cheesecloth bag. Place the bag in 2 quarts of boiling water to which 3 tablespoons of salt and 6 tablespoons of vinegar have been added. Poach for about 10 or 12 minutes and remove the bag gently. With a spatula lift the fish from the bag and transfer them to a serving plate. Cover with a hot fish sauce.

Hundreds of delicious fish sauces have been devised. Some are simple to make. Others are even available on grocery shelves. The easiest thing to do is to consult a cookbook. It's adven-

Large bass should be skinned and baked whole.

turesome eating—just as it's adventuresome business fishing for bass—anywhere.

Freezing Bass

The main problem with freezing most fish is that they will not keep very long, and bass are no exception to this. No matter how well the fish are prepared and wrapped, any kind of bass will lose taste and deteriorate after a few months in a freezer. Moisture is gradually withdrawn from the fillets in what is commonly called "freezer burn," leaving only dried fish behind. So plan to eat bass fairly soon after you freeze them, or else don't bother to freeze them at all. The following, however, is a freezing method used by Bob Stearns, capable boating editor of *Outdoor Life*. It's the best we've ever tried:

The sooner a fish is frozen after being caught,

Although bass are not the best of all table fish, a large-mouth fresh from cold water makes for a very tasty meal.

the better. Skin and fillet the bass, being careful to trim away all the "red meat" along the lateral line. That dark part tends to taste "strong." For freezing containers, collect enough thoroughly rinsed milk cartons or use the pop-top plastic cartons sold specifically for freezing foods. Also good are the throw-away cartons used for non-dairy whipped topping or for yogurt.

Place trimmed and rinsed fillets into the containers, but not too tightly. Next fill with water to within ½ inch or so of the top, making sure the fillets are completely covered. Immediately place the containers in the coldest setting until the packages are frozen. The success secret here is that the fillets are sealed in a block of ice, and moisture does not drain away.

However, great care must be used when thawing bass frozen in this manner. The fillets should not be allowed to soak in the melted ice water. Instead set the frozen block onto a strainer so that the melt water runs off immediately. Then pat the bass fillets dry and they are ready for any kind of cooking.

Chapter 14

THE SOUTHEAST

This is the most important and productive bass-fishing region in the world. An angler can find himself anywhere in the Southeast and practically never be more than a few minutes away from good bass waters—and from big bass. Following is a state-by-state list of the best and best-known bass waters.

Alabama

As with all states in the Cotton Belt, there's no shortage of bass fishing in Alabama—and most of it is good. The lineup of best fishing holes would run something like this: Eufaula (or Walter F. George) Reservoir near Eufaula: one of the best year-round largemouth lakes, it has produced several better than thirteen-pounders.

Columbia Reservoir downstream from Eufaula: small, but a good largemouth producer in spring. Demopolis Reservoir, near Demopolis and on forty-eight miles of Tombigbee and Black Warrior rivers in western Alabama. Bankhead Lake, near Gorgas and Hueytown: largemouth fishing can be excellent, especially in spring. Holt Reservoir, near Tuscaloosa: good largemouth fishing. Lake Jackson, near Coffeeville: good for largemouths in spring.

Miller's Ferry Lake near Camden: one of the state's best trophy lakes. Guntersville Reservoir, near Guntersville. Claiborne Lake, near Monroeville and Grove Hill. Yates Lake, near Tallassee. Lake Harding or Bartlett's Ferry Reservoir, near Phenix City: a feeder stream, Hallawakee Creek, produced world's-record redeye bass.

Wilson Reservoir, near Sheffield and Florence: good largemouth and smallmouth fishing. Lower part of Sipsey River from Grayson downstream to Lewis-Smith Reservoir: unsurpassed float

stream with spotted-bass fishing. Little River from DeSoto State Park downstream to Highway 35 west of Blanche: good for floating. Tallapoosa River, near Embry, downstream 250 miles to its juncture with Coosa River. Cahaba River, east of Birmingham downstream to Centerville: good for spotted bass.

More information is available from the Alabama Division of Fish and Game, 64 North Union, Montgomery, AL 36104.

Arkansas

This is another of the great bass-fishing states. Float tripping such beautiful rivers as the White and the North Fork has always been popular among bass fans, but fishing can be phenomenal in the large reservoirs. Norfork Lake near Mountain Home has long been a hot spot. At times Bull Shoals, on the Missouri border, has been even better for trophy fishing. Lakes Hamilton and Catherine near Hot Springs are reliable. The truth is that it is hard to go wrong in finding a bass lake in Arkansas.

Upper Table Rock Lake near Eureka Springs: tops for largemouths and spotted bass. Greer's Ferry Reservoir, near Heber Springs: good for all bass species. Lake Greason, near Kirby: good for all species. Lake Ouachita, near Hot Springs: mostly for largemouths. Nimrod Reservoir, near Plainview: largemouths. Lake Atkins, south of Atkins. Arkansas River and Pine Bluff Lake, near Pine Bluff: largemouths. Lower White River from Clarendon downstream. Millwood Reservoir, near Ashdown: perhaps the hot spot in the state for large average bass. DeGray Reservoir, near Arkadelphia. Lake Conway, near Little Rock. Gilham Reservoir, near DeQueen: large-

The rod bends as bass rolls on surface just before jumping.

mouths and smallmouths. Diecks Reservoir, near DeQueen. Lake Overcup, near Morrillton. Blue Mountain Reservoir, near Booneville: now in renovation, but should be good for largemouths when completed.

More information is available from the Arkansas Game and Fish Commission, Game and Fish Commission Building, Little Rock, AR 72201.

Florida

Florida is so choked, literally, with good bass waters that even cataloguing them is next to impossible. An angler just cannot go too far wrong in this state; besides the good fishing everywhere, there are adequate accommodations in every community and on every bit of choice fishing water.

The major hot spot of northwestern Florida is Apalachicola River below Jim Woodruff Dam, near Chattahoochee. The Ochlockonee River and Lake Talquin turn up some excellent bass in June. Try noisy top-water plugs, underwater weedless, and live shiners.

South Florida

Some of southern Florida's best bass fishing is on the northwestern corner of Lake Okeechobee, out of Glades County; try weedless spoons, popping bugs, and other top-water lures. Tamiami Canal region, between Miami and Tampa, is always good. For other sections of Okeechobee, small bass hit well on natural baits or fly-rod lures. Big bass do better on live shiners. All canals and Lake Trafford will produce bass.

Central Florida

Bass will take live, dark minnows at night in

This heavy bass was hooked in the thick weeds of a northern Florida lake.

Lake Weir, and standard shiners do well in the Withlacoochee River between the Rutland Bridge, near Bushnell, and Ross Bridge, between Ocala and Hernando. Bass in Lake Kissimmee and Kissimmee River will be hitting hard on spoons and live shiners. Lake Pierce bass seem to go for live bait at any time, with deep-running lures in the early morning. Don't overlook Fisheating Creek and the phosphate pits around Mulberry, south of Lakeland. Tiny canals around Lake Wilmington in Indian River County will produce small-to-medium-size bass. Try Lake Istokpoga in Highlands County between Lakeland and Lake Okeechobee. Medium bass will take any artificial that resembles a live shiner, as well as small popping bugs and shallow-running spoons.

Northeast Florida

Bass will hit spoons in Doctors Lake, near Green Cove Springs, in Crescent Lake, near Crescent City. Fly fishing is good in Suwannee River, especially around the rivermouth. Santa Fe Lake and River will produce big bass. St. Johns River, near Orange Park, will turn up fine early-morning catches. If you like to fish a new wilderness area, find the limestone sink known as California Lake, in South Dixie County, which is productive in June.

Oklawaha River from Silver Springs downstream to Rodman Reservoir. Many pro anglers consider this the top largemouth waterway in Florida or anywhere. St. Johns River in the Palatka, Sanford, and Cocoa area will be especially good in March and April. Most are medium and very large; some real trophies, especially in the Palatka and Astor areas. Lake Seminole, near Chattahoochee, is a top producer of largemouths. Lake Jackson, near Tallahassee, is another great one, especially in the spring. Lakes Harris and Griffin, near Leesburg: good in winter and early spring, but heavily fished. Orange Lake and Lake Lochloosa, near Gainesville, have a few lunker bass but are full of vegetation. Lake Kerr and Salt Springs Run, near Silver Springs and Salt Springs. Salt Springs Campground is ideally located between the two and many big bass are brought in there. Lake Tohopekaliga, near Kissimmee, is always a fine bet for hooking a hawg. Withlacoochee River in the Dunnelion area. Sandhill ponds of Ocala National Forest, near Ocala, Salt Springs, Palatka, and Leesburg. The Clermont chain of lakes near Clermont. Homosassa River, near Homosassa Springs. Crystal River, near Crystal River, produces some top bass fishing in late February and early March.

There are many hundreds more bass waters in Florida, and listing all is not practical. More information is available from Florida Game and Freshwater Fish Commission, Farris Bryant Building, Tallahassee, FL 32304.

Georgia

Here is another state with more excellent bass fishing than can be listed. In the middle section of the state erosion is so great that some streams continually run red with silt, but there are fine bass waters both to the north and the south. The world's record largemouth came from a backwater pond, a former oxbow of the Ocmulgee River near Valdosta in the southern portion.

John Oney nets bass for Dave Hickman on a central Florida lake. The fish was hooked on a surface plug.

Although it has known poor years during periods of drought, there is no doubt but that the vast, strange, six-hundred-square-mile Okefenokee Swamp is the state's most interesting bass-fishing hole. A lonely and soggy region where the earth "trembles," nearly all of Okefenokee's open-water areas contain largemouths. This is not a place to fish or to explore alone, but with a guide it's possible to cast the canals and lakes, the winding waterways and alligator holes in safety. If fishing is slow, the scenery and the abundance of wildlife are far more than enough to make up for it. There is also excellent bass fishing in the St. Mary's and the more celebrated Suwannee rivers that drain the swamp. Guides for both swamp and river fishing can be contacted at Folkston, Fargo, or Waycross.

Walter F. George Reservoir, near Fort Gaines: excellent for largemouths and spotted bass, especially early, often for lunker bass above ten pounds. Clark Hill Reservoir, near Clark Hill, South Carolina. Altoona Reservoir, near Cartersville: at times among the best largemouth lakes. Hartwell Reservoir, near Hartwell: often good for largemouths and spotted bass, excellent for striped bass and white-bass hybrids. Blue Ridge Reservoir, near Blue Ridge: good smallmouth fishing. Chatuge Reservoir, near Hiwassee: a fair to very good smallmouth lake. Jackson Lake, near Covington, could be the most consistent largemouth lake in Georgia. Lake Sidney Lanier, near Gainesville, has a spotted-bass lake in the lower section and good largemouth fishing in the upper. Nottely Reservoir, near Blairsville. Patrick's Fishing Paradise, near Tifton, is a commercial bass lake. (Many lakes, small in size, charge modest fees.) Lake Seminole near Bainbridge: very good largemouth lake, often producing bass above five or six pounds. West Point Reservoir near LaGrange. Lake Sinclair near Milledgeville. Carter's Lake near Calhoun: a reservoir with good redeye-bass fishing. Chattahoochee River below George Reservoir: a very good largemouth-bass stream. Flint River near Thomaston (north end) and from Newton to Bainbridge (south end). Altamaha River and Ocmulgee River.

More information is available from the Georgia Department of Natural Resources, 270 Washington Street SW, Atlanta, GA 30334.

Kentucky

Every season is bass-fishing time in Kentucky, with many types of fishing conditions to suit any angler. At one time only the warmer months attracted anglers to this state. However, the impoundment of many major lakes, augmented by more than fourteen thousand miles of running water and over one hundred thousand farm ponds, has lured fishermen from everywhere to the fine year-round facilities offered here.

Fall fishing in Kentucky is excellent in streams and lakes. When cooler weather arrives bass begin to strike in all lakes and streams. Winter bass fishing is good, even on very cold days. In the spring, of course, fishing breaks out all over. Bass are on a rampage during this three- or four-month period.

Kentucky Lake, with adjacent huge Barkley Lake in the western part of the state, is the largest man-made lake in the world. It is comparatively shallow and offers good year-round fishing. All three species of black bass may be taken from these waters. Facilities around this lake are excellent.

Lake Cumberland, another of the giant Kentucky lakes, is 105 miles long and lies wholly in Kentucky. A deep lake, its bass population is very high.

Dale Hollow lies in the extreme south-central section of the state and has long been known for the huge smallmouth bass caught there. Burnen River from Akersville downstream to Brown Ford on Highway 98: about thirty miles or three days of floating water for smallmouth bass. South Fork of Kentucky River from Booneville downstream to Beattyville: twelve-mile float for all bass species, depending on season. Barren River Reservoir near Buckhorn. Dewey Reservoir near Prestonburg. Nolin River Reservoir near Sweden: largemouths, smallmouths, an excellent reservoir during spring. Rough River Reservoir near Madrid: largemouths and smallmouths.

More information is available from the Kentucky Department of Fish and Wildlife Resources, Frankfort, KY 40601.

Louisiana

The state has approximately 8,000 miles of freshwater rivers, and, although all contain bass,

Fishing around cypress knees in the weedy lakes of the Southeast calls for accurate casting.

many are lightly fished. Since many of the main river systems—the Mississippi, Red, Atchafalaya, Ouachita, Sabine, and Pearl—flow at a higher level (inside dikes and levees) than their drainage plains, they form numerous bayous, lagoons, and oxbows, all full of bass. There is actually more bass-fishing water in Louisiana than anyone could explore. Much of it exists so deep in remote, swampy sections of the state that it is practically virgin.

Trees, shrubbery, and vines close in on these dark waters and lend an air of what might be called brooding mystery. Cypress trees, trailing moss, stand in the shallows. Their roots spread, forming underwater hiding places and obstacles, and grotesque "knees" thrust their rounded tops above the surface. Tupelo gums, pines, palmettos, and other growths crowd the water's edge.

Straddling Louisiana and Texas, Caddo Lake (northwest of Shreveport), long noted for its bass, is an excellent example of the lonely, haunting swamp lake. Some other Louisiana largemouth waters are located at Sabine Refuge Freshwater Pools near Hackberry. Penchant, southwest of Houma; Chicot, north of Ville Platte; Claiborne, ten miles southeast of Homer; D'Arbonne, southeast of Farmersville; Nantachie, southeast of Verda; Vernon, near Anacco; False River, near New Roads; St. John, north of Ferriday; Spring Bayou, near Marksville; Turkey Creek, west of Wisner; Indian Creek, west of LeCompte; Bistineau, near Minden; Old River, east of Innis; Bussey, near Bastrop; Bundicks, northwest of Dry Creek; and Toledo Bend, located along the Louisiana/Texas border (Logansport-Leesville) (see Texas).

More information is available from the Louisiana Department of Wildlife and Fisheries, 400 Royal Street, New Orleans, LA 70130.

Mississippi

Within Mississippi boundaries are many U. S. Corps of Engineers lakes, but old Ross Barnett Reservoir is probably the best bet for heavy largemouth bass, probably because of the constant year-round water level maintained in its 33,000 acres. Other worthwhile destinations for a basser are: Grenada Reservoir, near Grenada, for largemouths and spotted bass. Sardis Reservoir, near Sardis; Pickwick Reservoir, near Luka, for all bass species. Okatibbee Reservoir, near Meridan: excellent for largemouth bass. Enid Reservoir, near Enid: an excellent largemouth lake with some spotted bass. Archusa Reservoir, near Quitman. Little Black Creek Reservoir, near Purvis. Maynor Creek Reservoir, near Waynesboro; Lake Lamar Bruce, near Tupelo; Chotard Lake, north of Vicksburg; Bogue Homa Lake, near Laurel.

More information is available from the Mississippi Game and Fish Commission, Box 451, Jackson, MS 39205.

North Carolina

The overall good angling of the state's coastal region is enhanced by the freshwater streams, lakes, and sounds nearby. Spring and autumn offer the best bass fishing.

One of the top fishing grounds anywhere is freshwater Currituck Sound, dividing the mainland from the Outer Banks. Largemouth bass are taken with plugs, bugs, flies—on anything. Information regarding boats and guide service is available at Currituck Village, on N. C. Highway 34; Coinjock, on U. S. Route 158 and the Inland Waterway, and nearby Waterlily; Poplar Branch, just off U. S. Route 158; and Point Harbor on the southern tip of the Currituck Peninsula.

Just across the Wright Memorial Bridge from Point Harbor in the Kitty Hawk-Nags Head area are many freshwater ponds that yield good catches of largemouth bass. This section also may be reached by U. S. Route 64 (free ferry at Alligator River), which crosses Croatan Sound to Roanoke Island and Manteo by the Umstead Memorial Bridge.

Along U. S. Route 264 is Lake Mattamuskeet, the largest natural freshwater lake in North Carolina, where largemouth bass fishing is unexcelled (a special permit, obtainable from Refuge Headquarters, New Holland, is required). Information: Refuge Manager, New Holland, North Carolina 27715.

John H. Kerr Reservoir near Clarksville, Virginia, may be North Carolina's prime water for large bass. Lake Fontana, near Lake Fontana

Dam Village and Cherokee, has largemouths and smallmouths. Currituck Sound, near Currituck: excellent for largemouth bass by boat or by wading. Lower reaches of major coastal rivers such as the Chowan, Pamlico, and Neuse usually provide excellent spring fishing for largemouth bass. North Carolina is also an excellent farm-pond state, with small impoundments scattered everywhere. More information is available from the North Carolina Wildlife Resources Commission, Raleigh, N.C. 27611.

Oklahoma

Once one of the most bone-dry states of all, Oklahoma is a bass-fisherman's paradise because today the state contains almost 450,000 acres of impounded waters, with more in prospect for the future. Bass fishing here is a year-round proposition—and it has become big business too.

Not long ago a visiting sportsman would have had trouble finding suitable accommodations in Oklahoma, but that also has changed. Nowadays there are excellent resorts, cottages, boat docks, and bait shops around every major lake. In addition, the state park bureau has installed a system of inns and resorts designed for outdoor families. Result: smooth sailing for bass fishermen.

One of Oklahoma's largest bodies of water is Texoma Lake, located midway between Oklahoma City and Dallas, a reservoir of 100,000 acres where the largemouths grow to prodigious size. Except for seasonal high winds, which can keep fishermen off the lake, this is one of America's great bass-fishing holes.

Located in picturesque Cookson Hills northeast of Tulsa, Tenkiller Lake is little more than one tenth the size of Texoma—but the growth rates of Tenkiller's bass rank with the fastest anywhere. Tenkiller is an extraordinary place to prospect for big bass. As around other Oklahoma lakes, accommodations are available.

Although the big reservoirs absorb about 95 per cent of the bass-fishing pressure, there are other possibilities—such as the beautiful Illinois (below Tenkiller) and Kiamichi rivers, where float trips are highly recommended. Long stretches of these rivers are seldom disturbed, and the bass are unsophisticated. Oklahoma also can brag of over one hundred thousand farm and ranch ponds; nearly all contain bass.

Eufaula Reservoir, near Eufaula, is among the largest largemouth lakes in the Southeast, red hot in the spring. Fort Gibson Reservoir, near McBride: largemouths, but tough, tricky to fish. Oologah Reservoir, near Oologah; Wister Reservoir, near Victor; Hugo Reservoir in southeastern Oklahoma; Eucho Reservoir, near Jay, and Lake Spavinaw, both water-supply reservoirs, have great potential for very large bass. Broken Bow Reservoir, in southeastern Oklahoma, is popular for its "schooling" largemouth bass. Grand Reservoir near Grove; Pine Creek Reservoir, in southeastern Oklahoma, has largemouths. Robert S. Kerr Reservoir, in east-central Oklahoma, has good largemouths. Webber Fall Reservoir, near Muskogee; Fort Cobb Reservoir, near Fort Cobb, and Lake Thunderbird, excellent for tube fishing, near Norman. More information is available from the Oklahoma Department of Wildlife Conservation, 1801 North Lincoln, Oklahoma City, OK 73105.

South Carolina

This state, with a foothold in the mountains and a beachhead on the Atlantic, contains more varied bass fishing than native anglers manage to use in a year's time. Much good water lies untried and untested from year to year. A good example is the maze of moss-hung waterways and tributary streams in the lowlands from Charleston to Georgetown. An angler with a cartop boat or canoe could spend season after season exploring these places deep in the boondocks and seldom see another fisherman. A bit of good advice to any visiting fisherman would be to contact the local game wardens here. All are friendly, helpful, and know the region well.

Most local fishermen concentrate on the big reservoirs of the state. The largest and most productive of these is the Santee-Cooper Reservoir, which flooded 170,000 acres of Santee River swamps to form two giant lakes—Moultrie and Marion. Bass fishing is great in both, but especially in stump- and tree-filled Marion. Plenty of accommodations around Moncks Corners and Manning. Information is available from Santee-Cooper Country, Box 12, Santee, SC 29142.

Other South Carolina reservoirs include Catawba-Wateree, 26,160 acres near Camden; Lake Murray, 50,800 acres near Columbia; Clarks Hill Lake, 78,500 acres near Aiken; and Lake Greenwood, 11,800 acres near Greenwood.

South Carolina's rivers are greatly neglected by fishermen, though all have bass. Also, most are fine for leisurely float tripping. Here are some excellent rivers to try: Edisto, Combahee, Santee, Wateree, Witheree, Salkehatchie, Ashepoo, Cooper, Black, Waccamaw, Pee Dee, Little Pee Dee, and Congaree. To these, add the thousands of farm ponds where many bragging-size largemouths are taken every year.

Lake Hartwell and 25,000-acre Keowee-Toxaway Reservoir have good largemouth bass. The latter is especially productive in late winter.

More information is available from the South Carolina Wildlife Department, Box 167, Columbia, SC 29202.

Tennessee

This is a state of widely contrasting waters—from giant reservoirs to shallow, eerie earthquake ponds such as Reelfoot Lake, but except for the cold mountain streams in between, few waters do not contain bass. All three species of bass live in Tennessee waters, the largemouth being the most common black bass in ponds and lakes. Some larger, slower rivers also provide largemouth fishing from March to November. Originally the smallmouth was almost exclusively a stream fish in Tennessee, but with the impoundment of smallmouth streams into lakes, the species has adapted well. The smallmouth is found in many streams throughout that part of Tennessee east of Kentucky Lake. Other good streams are found in middle Tennessee. Among the eastern Tennessee stream providing better smallmouth fishing are the Powell and Clinch rivers, above Norris Lake; Holston River; Little River; and several smaller streams in Monroe County. The larger streams on the Cumberland Plateau also support some smallmouth. In middle Tennessee almost every clean stream that flows the year round is inhabited by smallmouth. Among the better ones are Elk, Upper Duck, Caney Fork, Collins, Stones, Harpeth, and Buffalo rivers, plus many of their tributaries.

For larger smallmouth, some weighing from five to ten pounds, the fisherman should go to Dale Hollow and Center Hill lakes, which have produced many outstanding fish. The best smallmouth fishing, on either streams or lakes, is during the spring and fall months.

The Kentucky or spotted bass is less abundant than the others. It is fairly common in clearer streams of western Tennessee, such as headwaters of the Obion, Hatchie, Loosahatchie, and Wolf rivers. Harpeth River in middle Tennessee also has this species.

A list of major lakes follows: Chickamauga Lake, on the Tennessee River near Chattanooga, covers 34,500 acres; largemouths are predominant. Cherokee Lake, a storage lake on the Holston River, near Morristown, covers 31,000 acres of excellent bass water. Douglas Lake, on the French Broad River, covers 31,000 acres near Dandridge; principal fish is the largemouth. Fort Loudoun Lake, on the main channel of the Tennessee, covers 14,500 acres. Great Falls Lake (Rock Island), located on Caney Fork River near McMinnville, has 2,270 acres.

Hales Bar Lake, on the main channel of the Tennessee below Chattanooga. Kentucky Lake, which extends from near the Mississippi state line entirely across Tennessee to Gilbertsville, Kentucky, a distance of 184 miles, covers 158,300 acres and has a ragged shoreline of 2,380 miles. It covers more area and has a longer shoreline than any other man-made lake in the United States; excellent bass water. Norris Lake, first of the TVA-created lakes, is located north of Knoxville, is easily accessible, and is fished for bass year-round. Pickwick Lake extends 53 miles on the Tennessee from the dam at Pickwick Landing to Wilson Dam in Alabama: largemouth bass are the chief attractions.

Watts Bar Lake covers 38,000 acres and is 74 miles of largemouth bass fishing. Fontana Lake, in a wooded mountain region on the Little Tennessee, 68 miles from Knoxville, has smallmouths. Dale Hollow Lake covers 40,000 acres and provides some of the best sustained bass fishing in Tennessee. Reelfoot Lake: during a great earthquake of 1812, forest lands sank beneath the surface and the Mississippi River poured in, bringing almost every variety of fish known to inland waters. This later became known as Reelfoot Lake. Many of the submerged trees died, and the resultant stumps formed one of the finest natural fish hatcheries in the world. The lake has largemouth bass along with 27 other species.

Center Hill Lake, a 40,000-acre impoundment on the Caney Fork River, near Smithville, has largemouths. South Holston Lake is a good bass lake near Bristol. Watauga Lake covers 6,400 acres, in Cherokee National Forest, near Elizabethton. Parksville Lake, between Ocoee and Ducktown, has 1,900 acres. Davy Crockett Lake contains 900 acres and is located near Greeneville, on the Nolichucky River. Cheatham Lake, just west of Nashville, has numerous boat docks and other facilities. Old Hickory Reservoir covers 25,000 acres on the Cumberland River, east of Nashville. Woods Reservoir is located near Estill Spring. Boone Lake: good bass water in the northeastern corner of the state. Fort Patrick Henry Lake: good bass near Kingsport on South Fork of Holston River. Bedford Lake, Bedford County, 47 acres, is noted for large bass; two largemouths weighing more than 13 pounds each have been taken here. Brown's Creek Lake, in the Natchez Trace Forest, covers 167 acres. Burgess Falls Lake, White and Putnam counties, is noted for big largemouth bass in the lake and smallmouths below the dam.

More information is available from Tennessee Wildlife Resources, Ellington Agricultural Center, Nashville, TN 37220.

Virginia

Back Bay, in Princess Anne County, near Virginia Beach, is Virginia's best water for bass in great numbers. Here 25,000 acres of locked-up fresh water provide unique largemouth fishing. Spring and fall months are best. Nonresidents should first make arrangements at Back Bay through local guides.

Sheltered behind the Outer Banks, Back Bay is southeast of Norfolk. From there take State Highway 165 to State 615, which joins other state and county routes leading to several improved marinas and launching areas. Motels, campgrounds, and restaurants are in adequate supply throughout the region.

Largemouths are common in many brackish rivers at tidewater. Among these are Chickahominy River, James River, Appomattox Creek, Mattaponi Creek, Piscataway Creek, and Piankatank and Pamunkey rivers. But the trophy largemouth fishing in Virginia is probably in the 51,000-acre Kerr or Buggs Island Reservoir, near Clarksville.

Bass fishermen favor Claytor Lake, near Pulaski, because largemouth, smallmouth, and spotted bass are found in this 4,500-acre reservoir. Facilities are available at Claytor State Park.

Good bass fishing exists in other reservoirs of the state: Chickahominy in New Kent County, Carvins Cove in Roanoke County, South Holston Reservoir in Washington County, Philpott Reservoir in Patrick (3,370 acres), Lake Jackson in Prince William County, and Lake Cahoon and Lake Prince in Nansemond County. Chickahominy, southeast of Richmond, is particularly good in June or at night later on.

Smallmouths are found in all of the larger rivers in the Piedmont and mountain sections. The best smallmouth waters are the James, Shenandoah (both forks), Holston, Rappanhannock, Jackson, Back Creek, Cowpasture River, Maury River, and Little River.

Fisherman Don Williams hefts a fine bass taken while he was wading in Lake Kissimmee, Florida.

More information is available from the Virginia Commission of Game and Fisheries, 4010 West Broad Street, Box 11104, Richmond, VA 23230.

West Virginia

Some good bass fishing survives in West Virginia despite a serious pollution problem from coal strip mining. Flowing northeast through the eastern panhandle are the Cacapon River and the South Branch of the Potomac River, two good smallmouth steams. Once the Shenandoah and the North Branch of the Potomac were also in this category, but both suffer from pollution. Through Clay and Braxton counties of central West Virginia winds the Elk River, another top-notch bass producer.

Another smallmouth river is the New River, which originates in Virginia and rushes northward across the state. Long stretches of this river are far from highways and deep in rocky gorges.

Perhaps the loveliest of all West Virginia rivers is the Greenbrier, good for floating in a canoe as well as for wading. Downstream from Marlinton is good bass water. The river flows alternately through lush bluegrass valleys, through rhododendron jungles, and through rocky hemlock canyons. The entire setting of Greenbrier County is beautiful. For fly fishermen who like background and atmosphere with their sport, this region is hard to beat.

There isn't too much lake fishing for bass in West Virginia. The best producer is 1,000-acre Bluestone Lake near Hinton, a flood-control reservoir on the New River, mostly in Summers County.

Other bass possibilities are: Plum Orchard Lake in Fayette County. South Fork of Hughes River, in Ritchie County, for spotted bass. East Lynn Lake in Wayne County. Sutton Reservoir near Sutton; Tygart River Reservoir near Grafton; and Ohio River along Route 2 from New-Martinsville to Point Pleasant, for largemouths, smallmouths, and spotted bass. All bass fishing in the West Virginia part of the Ohio River is improving as pollution-control measures begin to work. Summersville Reservoir near Summersville.

More information is available from the West Virginia Department of Natural Resources, Charleston, WV 25305.

Chapter 15

THE MIDWEST

Except for the Southeast, the land of the largest bass and the most bass, a fisherman's best bet may be the Midwest. This is a fertile region, generally, with both natural and man-made waters. The man-made waters, usually large water-supply reservoirs, are located close to centers of population. And natural waters become more numerous the farther north you travel.

This is also the region of the Great Lakes, which contain the very best smallmouth fishing holes. Smallmouths grow larger in a few southern reservoirs, but in quantity of bass, the Great Lakes are unsurpassed.

So in the Midwest, an angler is never far from good bass-fishing waters, and in no other region are facilities so numerous. That includes everything from motels to tackle shops, bait stores and boat docks, to the thousands of outfitters or camp owners from Missouri to Minnesota who cater to bass fishermen.

Illinois

An agricultural state, Illinois is extremely level in terrain and fairly well endowed with bass-fishing waters. The best fishing occurs in lakes, and there are accommodations near all of these —if not on the lake itself, in the adjacent communities. Here follows a list of the most important bass waters.

Probably the largest largemouths are found in five lakes of southern Illinois: Lake-of-Egypt, Crab Orchard, Devil's Kitchen, Rend, and Little Grassy. Other largemouth waters include: Belly Deep Slough; Sagashkee Slough, south of Willow Springs; Tampier Slough, northwest of Orland Park in Cook County; Grass Lake, east of Spring Grove; and Deep Lake, northeast of Lake Villa. Lake Shelbyville, near Shelbyville; Carlyle Lake, northeast of Carlyle; Evergreen Lake, near Bloomington; Argyle Lake, near Colchester; Lake Story, near Galesburg; Lake Springfield, south of Springfield; Sanchris Lake, west of Kincaid; Lake Jacksonville, southeast of Jacksonville; Ramsey Lake, northwest of Ramsey; Greenville City Lake, northeast of Greenville; Lincoln Trail Lake, south of Marshall; Otter Lake, west of Girard; Gillespie New City Lake, near Gillespie; Red Hills State Lake, northeast of Sumner; Dolan Lake, southeast of McLeansboro; Dale Lake, northwest of Johnsonville; Randolph County Lake, near Chester; Baldwin Lake, north of Baldwin; Kinkaid Lake, northwest of Murphysboro; Mermet Lake, west of Mermet; Atwood public-access at county road bridges; West Okaw River. Mississippi River Pool 13, north of Fulton; Prairie Creek-Kankakee River, northwest of Wilmington; Forked Creek-Kankakee River, northeast of Wilmington; and Kankakee River in Will County near Wilmington, are all smallmouth waters.

More information is available from the Illinois Department of Conservation, 602 State Office Building, Springfield, IL 62706.

Indiana

Somehow the Hoosier state escapes recognition as a good bass-fishing state, although the northern portion is full of good bass waters. These are natural lakes scooped out by glaciers in prehistoric times. Elsewhere in the state, artificial lakes take up the slack.

Several of Indiana's streams have great potential for float tripping, and on the Tippecanoe, at least, outfitters have facilities for visiting fisher-

Casting for bass at dawn on a midwestern lake is likely to result in plenty of action.

men. Even though it is quite often roily, the Wabash is good for floating too.

Monroe Lake, near Bloomington, is the state's largest and best for big bass. But lunkers are occasionally caught in coal strip pit lakes of the South. Other worthwhile waters are: Versailles Reservoir, near Versailles: all bass. West Boggs Creek, near Loogootee; Monroe Reservoir, near Bloomington; Reservoir 26, near Dugger; Lake James, near Angola: largemouth bass, smallmouth bass. Willow Slough, near Morocco; Bruce Lake, near Rochester; Lake Maxinkuckee, near Culver; Cataract Reservoir, near Cloverdale; Mansfield Reservoir, near Ferndale; Hardy Lake, near Austin: all for largemouth bass.

More information is available from the Indiana Department of Natural Resources, 308 State Office Building, Indianapolis IN 46204.

Iowa

This fertile state contains 15,000 miles of fishable streams, 45,000 acres of natural lakes, and 3,500 acres of state-owned artificial lakes, plus countless gravel pits, oxbow lakes, small reservoirs, and farm ponds—nearly all of which contain bass. The state has provided and developed across sites and boat-launching facilities to supplement private installations at all major bodies of water. Iowa is not a great bass-fishing state, but is a very good one.

Consider first the natural lakes of Iowa. Spirit Lake in Dickinson County, 5,684 acres, has clear, open water with generally well-defined shores. Numerous small lakes and sloughs connected to it provide spawning areas and food sources for bass. West Okoboji, Dickinson County, 3,939 acres; Clear Lake, Cerro Gordo County; Storm Lake, Buena Vista County; East Okoboji, Dickinson County; and Lost Island Lake, Palo Alto County, are among the largest. Other natural lakes are Trumbull, Silver, West Swan, Tuttle, Blackhawk, Five Island, North Twin, Center, Marble, Geode, Little Spirit, Swan, Twelve Mile, Ingham, Little Wall, Crystal, Prairie Rose, and Cornelia. All have largemouths and a few also contain smallmouths. West Okoboji boasts the state's largest smallmouths.

Although bass fishing in the Mississippi above Iowa (in Minnesota) is excellent, it is only spotty in the pools and backwaters of Iowa's navigation dams and locks. But the following rivers are good for bass, and some have float-tripping potential: Upper Iowa, Turkey, Volga, Little Turkey, Yellow, Wapsipinicon, Maquoketa, Big and Little Cedar, Raccoon, Skunk, and East Fork of Des Moines.

A few small artificial lakes are distributed over the state, all with bass. The best oxbow lakes are Manawa, near Council Bluffs; Blue; Brown's, and Odessa, near Wapello.

More information is available from the Iowa Conservation Commission, State Office Building, Des Moines, IA 50319.

Kansas

Flat, often dry Kansas depends on artificial impoundments for bass fishing because of great fluctuations in river water levels. Here is a list of the best lakes.

Glen Elder Reservoir (also called Waconda Lake), near Beloit; Norton Reservoir, near Norton; Webster Reservoir, near Stockton; Melvern Reservoir, near Melvern; Tuttle Creek Reservoir, near Manhattan; Perry Reservoir, near Perry; Fall River Reservoir, near Fall River; Milford Reservoir, near Junction City; Wilson Reservoir, between Russell and Salina; all contain largemouths. Fall River Lake also has spotted bass.

More information is available from the Kansas Fish and Game Commission, Box 1028, Pratt, KS 67124.

Michigan

Michigan was attracting fishermen before many other territories were attracting settlers. The state has been in the holiday business since before the War Between the States, thanks to its jack-pine woodlands, its lakes scooped out by glaciers, its beaches and waterways, and most of all its splendid fishing.

Still one region—the Upper Peninsula—is outstanding. It's a chunk of real estate free from hay fever, the size of Massachusetts, Rhode Island, Connecticut, and Delaware combined. It separates Lake Superior from Lake Michigan and Lake Huron, and contains 4,303 inland lakes, 12,406 miles of streams, and 1,723 miles of shoreline on the Great Lakes, all of which have bass.

The first tourists came to the first resort on the UP by horse and carriage from St. Ignace to jewel-like Brevoort Lake. Accommodations now are more modern, but the lake is as lovely as ever. And it still has bass. Farther west are Millecoquins and Millekokia lakes, both providing good fishing, as do dozens of other lakes in the vicinity. Still farther west are the Manistique lakes.

Near the Mackinac Straits, Mackinac County includes a number of islands—Mackinac, Bois Blanc, and Les Cheneaux. The waters around Bois Blanc have plenty of bass, and it is hard to match the smallmouth fishing around the Cheneaux Archipelago. North of Mackinac and farthest east of the UP counties is Chippewa, with 294 miles of rocky, broken, Great Lakes shoreline, 169 lakes, and 800 miles of streams, most of which contain bass.

Offshore and to the east is Drummond Island, surrounded by some of the most fertile fishing water for smallmouths. Neebish and Sugar islands are also situated in the center of good fishing waters.

Trout Lake has good angling and so has Caribou Lake, near Raber. The state park near Brimley has splendid facilities for public camping. Luce County on Lake Superior boasts about 571 inland lakes and 658 miles of streams. Some of the best fishing occurs in the Manistique Lakes, but this is country that an adventurous basser with a car-top boat or trailer can explore much farther. West along Lake Superior is Alger County and the spectacular Pictured Rocks country. A quick tabulation shows 81 miles of Lake Superior shoreline, 253 lakes, and 699 miles of stream, more water than exists altogether in many states. Specific places to find bass are the Au Train River, Au Train, Trout, Long, Ready, and Lost lakes.

Largest lake in Marquette County is Michigamme, good for bass. Ives and Independence lakes, near Big Bay, are hot spots, as are Goose, Teal, Bass, Kawbowgam, Deer, Silver, Mountain, and Pine lakes. There is excellent fishing for bass in the Princeton, Gwinn, and Little system of lakes. Budget-priced accommodations are available at most lakes, with a public camp site located on the nearby 333,000-acre Escanaba Game Area.

Baraga County includes Keweenaw and Huron bays of Lake Superior. Best bass fishing is in Vermillac, King, Drummond, Ned, Fence, and Cliff lakes. In Houghton County, Portage Lake, near Chassell, is good. There is also excellent bassing in Perch, Bob, Otter, Gerald, Roland, Rice, Norway, and Mud lakes.

Keeweenaw County is almost surrounded by Lake Superior but nonetheless contains 125 lakes and 275 miles of streams. Lac la Belle is a fine producer of bass. So are Fanny Hooe, Manganese, Breakfast, and Schlatter lakes.

In Ontonagon County the best of the bass fishing is in Lake of the Clouds, Gogebic, Mirror, and Bond lakes, waters that produce all summer long, since they remain cool, even during dog days. There are 1,200 miles of streams and 488 named lakes in Gogebic County. In June there's fast fishing in lakes like Tamarack, Duck, Crooked, Sucker, Cisco, and Lac Vieux Desert. Gogebic Lake, an especially fine resort and cottage area, but with public campgrounds, is fine for bass.

Iron County has 528 lakes, 902 miles of streams, and bass fishing in power-dam reservoirs on the Paint and Michigamme rivers near Crystal Falls. Public camp grounds are on Fortune, Chicaugon, and Runkel lakes.

Another good fishing area is located around Iron River in Sunset and Pickerel lakes. In Dickinson County fishermen can find bass in the Hamilton lakes, around Loretto, and Lake Antoine. In Menominee County, the Big Cedar River at times has fine smallmouth fishing, and good bass can be found in the small lakes east of Stephenson and Ingalls.

Escanaba is well known for Big and Little Bay de Noc, both of which contain smallmouths. Boats, motors, guides, and all sorts of accommodations are available out of Escanaba, Gladstone, Rapid River, Stonington, Nahma, Sac Bay, Garden, and Fairport.

Lower Michigan has over 3,000 miles of shoreline along four Great Lakes alone, plus 30 major river systems, with bass fishing that rates very high. Within easy reach of Detroit and the other motor cities are Gun and Thornapple lakes, in Barry County; Black and Spring lakes, in Ottowa County. The Irish Hills lakes have good fishing early in the spring. Smallmouth fishing in Lake St. Clair, between Lake Erie and Lake Huron, is excellent. Two lake "areas," the first extending from Lapeer and near Flint to Hillsdale and Coldwater, and the second from near Greenville to the Indiana line, contain bass.

The northern part of Michigan's Lower Peninsula has hundreds of bass lakes such as Clam, Elk, and Torch lakes, in Antrim County; Big Platte Lake, in Benzie County; Black, Burt, and Millet lakes and Indian River, in Cheboygan County; Elk Lake, in Grand Traverse County; Torch Lake, in Kalkaska County; Lake Leelanau, in Leelanau County; Hamlin and Pere Marquette lakes, in Mason County; Bear Lake, in Muskegon County; Pentwater Lake, in Oceana County; Houghton and Higgins lakes; Grand Lake, in Presque Isle County; Lake Avalon, in Montmorency County; and Lake Margrethe, near Grayling.

The Muskegon, Manistee, and Au Sable rivers are known as top-notch trout streams, but the lower reaches contain smallmouths.

More information is available from the Michigan Department of Natural Resources, Mason Building, Lansing, MI 48926.

Minnesota

It is nearly impossible to list all the bass possibilities in this land of sky-blue waters. Equally difficult is the task of selecting Minnesota's *best* bass-fishing waters—but probably the nod must go to the Mississippi River for its full length, but mostly upstream from the Twin Cities. It contains unlimited bass fishing, and to get the details, simply stop in any tackle store or contact any crossroads "expert" along the way.

There is also premium bass fishing in lakes of the Quetico-Superior wilderness along the border near Ely. Basswood Lake is great in springtime, through the summer. Typical of these is McNaught Lake (actually in Ontario), near Ely. This Quetico-Superior country is completely roadless and wild. To fish there is to go by canoe. Outfitters can completely arrange trips of any length or duration. They rent everything from canoes and car-top carriers, to tents, food for a planned daily menu, sleeping bags, utensils, and even waterproof route maps of the country. There's great adventure here as well as great bass fishing.

Other lakes most often considered among the best in Minnesota include Bad Medicine, Brule,

East Bearskin, Greenwood, Little Vermilion, Loon, Rainy, Saganaga, and Turtle, all in the northern half of the state. The following is a list of regions with at least fair bass fishing (grouped according to general locality): Grand Marais, Gunflint Trail, Ely; Tower, Whiteface River; Alden Lake, Cloquet, Cotton; Central Lakes, Finland, Two Harbors, Hibbing; Virginia; Biwabik, Deer River; Grand Rapids; Nashwauk, International Falls; Little Fork, Cook, Baudette; Lake of the Woods; Northwest Angle, Red Lake; Blackduck, Bemidji; Cass Lake, Leech Lake; Hackensack, Brainard; Whitefish Lake Chain; Emily, Little Falls; Motley, Bay Lake; Deerwood; Aitken; Mille Lacs Lake, McGregor; Arlton, Moose Lake; Barnum, Park Rapids, Detroit Lakes, Fergus Falls; Pelican Rapids; Henning, Alexandria; Glenwood; Osakis, Appleton; Ortonville; Morris, Willmar; Litchfield; Hutchinson, Paynesville; Richmond; St. Cloud, Annandale; Buffalo, Pine City; Mora, Cambridge; Princeton; Elk River, Center City; Forest Lake, White Bear Lake, Redwing; Wabash; Winona, Fairbault; Mankato; New Ulm.

More information is available from the Minnesota Department of Natural Resources, 301 Centennial Building, St. Paul, MN 55155.

Missouri

Bass fishing is traditional in Missouri, which isn't hard to explain when you consider the abundance of fine waters—impounded and flowing—especially in the Ozark region, which includes that portion of Missouri south of the Missouri River. In this area alone, there are about 16,000 miles of streams and 100,000 acres of impounded waters.

In a resort area in the northern part of the hill country is Lake of the Ozarks. Its coves, peninsulas, and rocky outcrops form a shoreline of 1,372 miles—one of the longest in the United States. Fish caught in its 60,000 acres of water include largemouth black bass, and smallmouths, in the rocky coves. Lake Taneycomo in Taney County, with Branson, Hollister, Forsyth, and Rockaway Beach on its shoreline, has recreational facilities and a number of fine Ozark streams in the immediate vicinity. Created by a dam in Arkansas, Norfork Lake backs up into Missouri for about eight miles.

In the southeastern area of the Ozarks, Lake Wappapello attracts bass fishermen. Clearwater Dam, on the Black River in Reynolds County, has created Lake Clearwater. Bull Shoals Lake extends into Ozark and Taney counties of Missouri and has an area of 45,000 acres. The lake replaces the portion of White River below Lake Taneycomo. About 15,000 acres of coves, arms, and deep water lie in Missouri, including some of the best bass areas.

In northern Missouri, Thousand Hills Lake, near Kirksville, and Lake Paho, in Mercer County, offer fine bass fishing, as do smaller lakes and farm ponds above the Missouri River. Year in and year out, Table Rock Lake, and specifically James River Arm, is Missouri's top spot for trophy largemouths. The state record of almost 14 pounds was caught here in 1961.

The water systems of the White, Eleven Point, Current, Black, Gasconade, Meramec, and St. Francis rivers are the major Ozark bass streams. The numerous springs of this region, coupled with vast areas of forest, make these waters ideal for smallmouth bass.

Float-trip fishing, which originated in the Missouri Ozarks at the turn of the century, is still popular. This unique method of going after fish attracts fishermen from everywhere. You can float for a half day or a week—commercial guides who do all the paddling, campmaking, and cooking are available. But if you are an experienced river man, you can float the streams yourself. There are some twenty-five popular float streams in the Missouri Ozarks, and they're all cold and clear, curving and bent back on themselves. Rapids and "white water" give way to long, deep pools, and bold rock cliffs are succeeded by gently sloping gravel bars. The scenery is the equal of any in the nation, and you can drift along at the current's speed all day long and still be near where you started that morning.

Where a number of boats are necessary for a large float-trip party, a "commissary" boat—loaded with camp and cooking gear—is provided. The "commissary" crew works out a schedule whereby it will have the lunch camp set up in advance of your arrival; at dusk tents and overnight camp will be ready when fishing is done.

All the fisherman needs to bring along is his tackle. Outfitters usually supply the camp equipment, food, and other essentials. The cost per person for a float trip averages about twenty-five dollars to sixty dollars per day, but for exact costs and information write to outfitters.

The major Ozark streams on which floats are conducted, or on which experienced fishermen float themselves, are as follows: Beaver Creek, Big Piney River, Big River, Black River, Bourbeuse River, Bryant Creek, Courtois Creek, Crooked Creek, Current River, Dry Creek, Eleven Points River, Elk River, Flat Creek, Gasconade River, Huzzah Creek, Indian Creek, Jacks Fork, James River, Kings River, Long Creek, Meramec River, Niangua River, North Fork (White River), Osage Fork, Osage River, St. Francis River, Swan Creek, and White River.

The individual taking a float trip should keep the calendar in mind when making plans, so that appropriate clothing will be available. The weather likely will be rather cool at night during spring and fall months. Also, spring rains can suddenly roil rivers and make them unfishable.

More information is available from the Missouri Department of Conservation, Box 180, Jefferson City, MO 65101.

Nebraska

Nebraska, one of the drier plains states, is far from a great bass-fishing state. Still there is considerable bass water but comparatively few bass fishermen—and those few enjoy good sport in semiprivacy. Some of the best waters are Medicine Creek Reservoir, north of Cambridge; Harlan Reservoir, at Republican City; Long Lake, south of Valentine; and Hord State Lake, near Central City.

The sandpits and bayous on the North Loup River in the Brewster area have consistent fishing. Wellfleet State Lake at Wellfleet is a good bet. So are the lakes of the Valentine Waterfowl Refuge, twenty miles south of Valentine. There are two hundred or more farm ponds in Dawes and Sioux counties in the area north of U. S. Route 20, between Chadron and the Wyoming border, most of which contain bass.

Other public bass lakes are Red Deer south of Valentine; Smith State Lake, south of Rushville; and Lewis and Clark Lake in the Santee area. Count on some bass fishing in the following pay lakes: Rays Valley lakes, Pleasure lakes, and

Hartford lakes, near Valley; Linoma Beach Lake, near Ashland; Venice lakes and Platteview lakes, near Venice.

More information is available from the Nebraska Game and Parks Commission, Box 30370, Lincoln, NE 68503.

North Dakota

Bass fishing in this prairie state is very spotty and unpredictable. Nearly all waters are shallow and cold and are subject both to roiliness until late summer and to winter kills. The following is a list of lakes that contain or once contained bass. It isn't a recommendation to fish any of them. Frequently no accommodations exist nearby.

Lake Odland, Cedar Lake, North Lemmon Lake, Raleigh Reservoir, Dickinson Reservoir, Benet Lake, Heart Butte Reservoir, Danzig Reservoir, Welk Lake, Bald Hill Reservoir, Lake Elsie, Homme Dam, Kadrmas Lake, and Lake Illo. Lake Nelson in Oliver County may be the most consistent for medium largemouths.

More information is available from the North Dakota Game and Fish Department, 2121 Lovett, Bismarck, ND 58501.

A smallmouth is netted from Lake Erie near Ohio's Bass Islands.

Ohio

It is hard to imagine, when passing through Ohio on high-speed turnpikes, that this is even a fair bass-fishing state. Success is good despite the most intensive farming, industrialization, and heavy population. Ohio ranks fifth in population, but only thirty-sixth in size. There are ten million resident fishermen.

Today there is ten times the amount of impounded water that existed originally, thanks to a network of lakes built for flood control, recreation, water supply, industrial supply, or a combination of these. There is a good network of rivers, too, but far too many of these have been badly, unnecessarily polluted.

Here follows a list of Ohio's public fishing lakes. Accommodations of all types exist on or very near every one of them. Detailed maps of most are available (from the Division of Wildlife), which show underwater contours, stump areas, channels, locations of roads, docks, concessions, and launching sites.

Adams Lake (Adams County), Allen Lake (Hardin County), Atwood Lake (Carroll and Tuscarawas counties), Bass Islands Area (Ottawa County). The latter is among the best smallmouth areas in America. Best time is May or June, but actually good all summer; Put-in-Bay and Sandusky are centers of operations. Bellevue Reservoirs 1, 2, 3, and 4 (Huron County), Bellevue Reservoir 5 (Huron County), Berlin Reservoir (Stark, Mahoning, and Portage counties), Blue Rock (Muskingum County), Brush Lake (Champaign County), Buckeye Lake (Fairfield, Perry, and Licking counties): good in early spring. Burr Oak Lake (Morgan and Athens counties), Caldwell, Stewart Hollow Lakes (Ross County), Charles Mill Reservoir (Richland and Ashland counties). Chippewa Lake (Medina County), Clearfork Reservoir (Morrow and Richland counties), Clendening Lake (Harrison County), Clouse Lake (Perry County), Clyde City Reservoir (Sandusky County), and Cowan Lake (Clinton County).

Decker Lake (Miami County), Delaware Reservoir (Delaware County): very *good* fishing and not too heavily fished by bass anglers. Delta Lake (Fulton County), East Harbor (Ottawa County): excellent in May but slumps thereafter. Echo Lake (Miami County), Erie Lake (Ottawa and Erie counties), Findlay Reservoir (Hancock County), Findley Forest Lake (Lorain County), Forked Run Lake (Meigs County), Grant Lake (Brown County), Guilford Lake (Columbiana County), Hargus Creek (Pickaway County), Harrison Lake (Fulton County), Hocking Lake (Hocking County), Hoover Reservoir (Franklin and Delaware counties), and Hope Lake (Vinton County): good camping area here. Hosterman Lake (Clark County), Indian Lake (Logan County): good in April and May. Jackson Lake (Jackson County), Jefferson Lake (Jefferson County), Kelley's Island area (Erie County).

Kiser Lake (Champaign County), Knox Lake (Knox County), Lake Park (Mahoning County), Leesville Lake (Carroll County), Loramie Lake (Shelby and Auglaize counties), Lost Creek Reservoir (Allen County), Madison Lake (Madison County), Metzger Lake (Allen County), Milton Lake (Mahoning County), Mogadore Reservoir (Portage County), Mosquito Reservoir (Trumbull County): excellent spring bass fishing in large stump areas. Mount Gilead Lakes (Morrow County), Neers Pond (Champaign County), Nettle Lake (Williams County), Nimisila Reservoir (Summit County), Oxbow Lake (Defiance County), Piedmont Lake (Belmont, Guernsey, and Harrison counties), Pine Lake (Ross County), Pleasant Hill Reservoir (Richland and Ashland counties), Portage lakes (Summit County), Punderson Lake (Geauga County), Pymatuning Reservoir (Ashtabula County), Richwood Lake (Union County), Rocky Fork Lake (Highland County), and Roosevelt Lake (Scioto County).

Sandusky Bay area (Ottawa, Erie, and Sandusky counties), Schoonover Lake (Allen County), Seneca Lake (Guernsey and Noble counties), Spring Valley (Greene and Warren counties), St. Mary's Lake (Mercer County), Stonelick Lake (Clermont County), Swift Run Lake (Miami County), Tappan Lake (Harrison County), Van Buren Lake (Hancock County), Van Wert Reservoir (Van Wert County), Vesuvius Lake (Lawrence County), Veto Lake (Washington County), White Lake (Pike County), and Zepernick Lake (Columbiana County).

Ohio's best bass streams include the following: in northeastern Ohio, Maumee River (especially Maumee Rapids above Toledo area) for smallmouths; Tiffin, Auglaize, and Blanchard rivers, Sandusky River from Old Fort to Upper Sandusky, Huron and Vermilion rivers, near Norwalk, in early spring. In northwestern Ohio, best bets are the Grand River (Ashtabula County) and the Chagrin in Geauga County. The Grand can be float-tripped.

Central Ohio is probably Ohio's best region for stream smallmouth fishing. Good waters include Big and Little Darby, Big Walnut, Whetstone, Deer, and Blacklick creeks. Also the Olentangy and Licking rivers. Kokosing and Mohican rivers are possible float-trip rivers, with a few camp sites along the way.

In southeastern Ohio the Muskingum River, plus tributary Wills Creek, and Tuscarawas and Walhonding rivers, have bass fishing. Add also Leading Creek and Shade River, in Meigs County; Symmes and Indian Guyan creeks, in Lawrence County; Hocking River, above Athens. In southwestern Ohio best bets are Stonelick Creek, East Fork of Little Miami River, Todd Fork, White Oak Creek, Caesar Creek, Rattlesnake Creek, Compton Creek, Rocky Fork Creek below Rocky Fork Lake, Sunfish Creek (for spotted bass) in Pike County, and Paint Creek.

More information is available from the Ohio Division of Wildlife, 1500 Dublin Road, Columbus, OH 43212.

South Dakota

Although not a great bass-fishing state, some lakes exist in the eastern third of the state. Bass also live in several Black Hills lakes, but the fishing is poor and the bass seldom grow to a desirable size. For practical purposes there is no stream fishing. A list of state lakes would include

Lake Traverse, Clear Lake, Roy Lake, Elm Lake, Pickerel Lake, Enemy Swim, Cottonwood Lake, Pelican Lake, Lake Louise, Lake Byron, Lake Poinsett, Lake Madison, Marindahl Lake, Fort Randall Reservoir, and Angostura Reservoir. Roy Lake might be the best bet of a poor lot.

More information is available from the South Dakota Department of Game and Fish, State Office Building, Pierre, SD 57501.

Wisconsin

Any bass angler is lucky to find himself in Wisconsin—a beautiful pine, balsam, and birch state, containing 8,676 lakes and enough waterways to stretch around the earth. Bass are almost everywhere.

There are all kinds of lakes—deep ones like Big Green, which drops off 300 feet; big ones like Winnebago, with its 137,708 surface acres; small, clear "kettle" lakes located in terminal moraines; and lakes with rocky shorelines and gravel bottoms. Virtually all contain bass.

Maps showing size, depths, bars, weedbeds, and principal roads are available for about 800 lakes. They can be obtained from the Department of Natural Resources and are certainly worthwhile.

Far too little emphasis has been placed on Wisconsin's wonderful streams, many of which are great for float tripping. The Chippewa is excellent, as is the entire Chippewa Flowage-Hayward lakes region. So are the Flambeau, the Wisconsin, the Fox, Wolf, Black, St. Croix, and the Namakagon. Autumn floating may mean carrying across shallow riffles, but it is a productive, magnificent experience when weather and the color are at their best. The Mississippi River from La Crosse to Red Wing, Minnesota, is also outstanding bass water.

For large smallmouths, anglers might consider the lower Wisconsin River above Prairie du Chien. But better by far is the Door Peninsula and Washington Island. Lake Michigan and Green Bay waters here are good in spring and again in October. The biggest largemouths seem to be in the backwater sloughs of the Mississippi, pools 8 and 9, from Lake Onalaska to Lynxville.

A stringer of largemouth bass taken in a midwestern farm pond. Photo by Stephen Maslowski.

A list of northern Wisconsin counties with the greastest number of good bass lakes would include Ashland, Barron, Bayfield, Burnett, Chippewa, Dane, Douglas, Florence, Fond du Lac, Forest, Iron, Juneau, Langlade, Lincoln, Marathon, Marinette, Marquette, Oconto, Oneida, Polk, Portage, Price, Rusk, St. Croix, Sawyer, Sheboygan, Taylor, and Vilas.

More information is available from the Wisconsin Department of Natural Resources, Box 450, Madison, WI 53701.

Chapter 16

THE NORTHEAST

Although half of the sportsmen of America live in this small region, not one who ever buys a fishing license is very far from fair bass-fishing waters. That is even true for residents of Long Island, Philadelphia, or Baltimore. Most waters of the East are heavily fished, of course, but still a good bass fisherman can stir up enough action to make a fishing trip worthwhile.

Not all waters of the East are heavily fished, though; remote waters still remain in parts of New York, Pennsylvania, and New England. A few streams, especially, are not subject to heavy pressure at all—and these are places on which a serious bass angler should concentrate.

Connecticut

This state isn't a promised land for bass fishermen, because it's extremely crowded, fishing waters aren't too plentiful, and fishing pressure is heavy. There's also the ugly matter of pollution in may streams that would otherwise contain good fishing.

A fairly complete list of the best bass-fishing waters would include the following: Wood Creek Pond and Toby Pond, near Norfolk; Wononkapook Pond, south of Wononskopomuc, and Mudge Pond (for largemouths), below Wononkapook, in the Berkshires; Tyler Pond, west of Goshen; Spectacle Lakes and Hatch Pond, east of Kent; Lake Waramaug, near New Preston; Bantam Lake, between Bantam and Lakeside; Black Rock Pond, southwest of Thomaston; Winnemaug Lake, near Watertown; Big Candlewood Lake (largest in the state with 6,000 acres), near Brookfield; Zoar Lake, at Sheldon; Trumbull Reservoir and Beardsley Park Pond, near Bridgeport; Black Pond and Beseck Lake, near Meriden; Cedar Swamp Pond, south of Bristol; Highland Lake, southwest of Winsted; Shenipsit Lake, between Tolland and Ellington; Bolton Notch Pond and Willimantic Reservoir, near Bolton; Wamgumbaug Lake and Columbia Lake, near Willimantic; the group of ponds north of Colchester; Terramuggus and Pocotopaug lakes, above East Hampton; Shaw, Pickerel, Basham, and Moodus Reservoir, near Hartford; Gardner's Lake, west of Norwich; Powers, Pataganset, and Rogers lakes; Mashapaug, northeast of Stafford Springs; Roseland and Alexander lakes, near Putnam; Quandsick Reservoir; Long Pond, between Old Mystic and North Stonington. Moodus Reservoir annually produces the largest bass in the state.

More information is available from the Fish and Wildlife Unit, Department of Environmental Protection, 165 Capitol Avenue, Hartford, CT 06115.

Delaware

Only a very limited amount of bass fishing is available in Delaware. The ponds of the Delamarva Peninsula are described in the Maryland section of this chapter. The state owns twenty-six public ponds that contain bass. Also worthwhile are Nanticoke River, especially the upper reaches between Seaford and Woodland, for largemouths and smallmouths; Red Mill Pond, near Nassau, for largemouths in spring; and Noxontown Pond near Middletown, where state-record largemouth bass have been taken.

More information is available from the Delaware Division of Wildlife, Edward Tatnall Building, Dover, DE 19901.

A fisherman plays bass on a damp morning on a lake in Maine.

Maine

Half a century ago there were no bass in Maine, but today smallmouths are well established in over three hundred lakes. They're more than established, really, because now Maine must rank with the best smallmouth fishing regions in America. Not only are the bronzebacks plentiful, but also a few six-pounders are taken each year to add a flavor of trophy collecting.

Bass fishing here begins in June, is excellent all through the month, and although it falls off, it remains fairly good all through the summer. The premium fishing is with fly rod and bugs in early June. Later live bait or jigging are recommended. In August, trolling is often very successful.

Sebago Lake, Long Lake, and Oxford County region: Sebago, the second largest lake in Maine, is the center of a region that en-

compasses a great part of southern Maine. During the summer there is fine bass fishing here.

To the north, connected to Sebago by the beautiful Songo River, is Long Lake. In the same region are Brandy Pond, Highland Lake, Woods Pond, Crystal Lake, Thomas Pond, Lake Pennesseewassee, and Moose Pond. A few miles to the west of Sebago is Peabody Pond and Hancock Pond. Toward the east is Panther Pond and Little Sebago. Toward the northwest is beautiful Lake Kezar, a jewel of a lake, nestled in the foothills of the White Mountains. South of Sebago, in York County, lie Bunganut, Crystal, Kennebunk, and Mousam.

Kennebec lakes region furnishes excellent smallmouth-bass fishing in the spring. It includes Cobbosseecontee, Maranacook, Little Cobbosseecontee, and Annabessacook Lakes. Nearby, near Wayne, are Androscoggin and Pocasset lakes. A long chain of smaller lakes affording very fine bass fishing extends through the towns of Readfield, Fayette, and Mount Vernon.

Big Lake, near Princeton; St. Croix River, near Princeton; East Grand Lake, near Forrest City; Spednick Lake, near Forrest City; and Pocimoonshine Lake, near Alexander, all have good smallmouth-bass fishing.

It cannot be overemphasized how well suited Maine is for handling the visiting bass fisherman. For example, there are over 3,000 skilled guides available, license fees are reasonable, and the country is very beautiful.

More information is available from the Maine Department of Inland Fisheries and Game, State Office Building, Augusta, ME 04330.

Maryland

This state has great fishing pressure, but still contains fair bass waters. The Potomac, which flows from Hancock to Washington, D.C., is one. A list of Maryland's principal bass waters follows. Liberty Reservoir, in north-central Maryland, contains large bass, but no outboards are allowed. Deep Creek Lake, 3,900 acres near Thayersville, has a good bass population, but they are hard to catch; this is a good "challenge" lake for the most serious anglers.

Herrington Lake, near Oakland; Tridelphia Reservoir, near Brighton; Pretty Boy Reservoir, near Hereford; Loch Raven Reservoir, near Towson (has bass that are sometimes hard to catch, but a few lunkers are taken by jigging); Conowingo Dam, near Conowingo; Garland Lake, near Denton; Linchester Lake, near Preston; Smithville Lake, near Smithville; Wye Pond, near Wye Mills.

The following rivers contain smallmouths: Casselman River, near Grantsville: Savage River, near Bloomington; Beaver Creek, near Hagerstown; Octoraro Creek, near Richardsmere; and Deer Creek, in Harford County.

Also, on the Delamarva Peninsula (which separates Chesapeake Bay from the Atlantic and which includes parts of Delaware and Virginia as well as Maryland) are about fifty ponds, which range from public to semiprivate to private. Most offer fair to good bass fishing, especially bass bugging, in settings with a southern accent. Motors not allowed on most of these. Boats are available for rent on a few.

More information is available from the Maryland Department of Natural Resources, Tawes State Office Building, Annapolis, MD 21401.

Massachusetts

This is another densely populated state with some fishing waters but with only fair bass fishing at best. The best often is in privately owned ponds, many of which can be entered by contacting the owner and/or paying a small fee. Many rivers are too polluted for bass fishing. The best bass lake with both largemouths and smallmouths is 25,000 acre Quabbin Reservoir, near Hardwick.

Berkshire County has more than the state average amount of bass water. Best spots are Lake Potoosuc and Richmond Pond. Other bass waters include: Hoosac Reservoir; Garfield Lake, east of Great Barrington; Otis Reservoir and Big Pond, just to the north; Lake Mahkeenac; Greenwater, Yokum, Center, and Goose ponds, southeast of Lee; Ashmere Lake, near Dalton; Burnett Pond, east of Adams; Lake Wickapoag and other small ponds in Worcester County; Quinsigamond Lake, near Worcester; and ponds of Myles Standish State Forest near Plymouth.

Cheshire Reservoir, near Cheshire: largemouths. Mashpee-Wakeby Pond, near Mashpee: smallmouths. Congamond Lake, near Southwick: largemouths, smallmouths. Quaboag Pond, near Brookfield: largemouths. Concord River, between Concord and Billerica: largemouths. Monponsett lakes, near Bridgewater: largemouths. Long Pond, near Lakeville: smallmouths.

More information is available from the Massachusetts Division of Fisheries and Game, 100 Cambridge Street, Boston, MA 02202.

New Hampshire

Cool, green, and beautiful, New Hampshire's lofty mountains, rolling hills, valleys, and pasturelands form a scenic setting for a hundred lakes and bass ponds, plus miles of brooks and rivers. Deep forests of mixed conifers and hardwoods help to condition both air and water, maintaining good temperatures for fishing.

In the White Mountains zone, the Connecticut River along the western boundary has smallmouths. So do Armington Lake, near Piermont; Upper and Lower Baker ponds, near Orford; Burns Pond, near Whitefield; and Tarleton Lake, near Piermont.

Stretching across the state, just south of the White Mountains, lies a belt of lakes and ponds from Sunapee and Mascoma on the west, to Ossipee and Province Lake on the east. The four largest lakes in this section—Winnisquam, Sunapee, Winnipesaukee, and Squam—all have bass.

Following is a list of bass waters in the central part of the state: Blaisdell Lake, Bradley Lake, Cooks Pond, Crescent Lake, Crystal Lake, Grafton Pond, Great East Lake, Guiena Pond, Halfmoon Lake, Highland Lake, Kanasatka Lake, Kezar Lake, Knights Pond, Knowles Pond, Kolemook Lake, Kusumpe Pond, Lovell Lake, Mirror Lake, Perkins Pond, Places Pond (Sunset Lake), Post Pond, Province Lake, Rust Pond, Silver Lake, Waukewan Lake, Webster Lake, Whitton Pond, Wickwas Pond, and Winona Lake.

A list of southern New Hampshire bass waters includes: Ashuelot Pond, Ayers Pond, Beaver Lake, Bow Lake, Chesham Pond, Cole Pond (Crescent Lake), Connecticut River (lower part), Contoocook Lake, Contoocook River, Country Pond, Crooked Pond, Frost Pond, Gilmore Pond, Gould Pond, Gregg Lake, Halfmoon Pond, Harvey Lake, Haunted Lake, Highland Lake, Hubbard Pond, Hunts Pond, Island Pond (near Atkinson), Island Pond (near Washington), Jenness Pond, Massabesic Lake, Massasecum Lake, Mendums Pond, Merrimack River, North River Pond, Northwood Lake, Norway Pond, Otter Lake, Pawtuckaway Lake, Phillips Pond, Pleasant Pond, Robinson Pond, Shattuck Pond, Spofford Lake, Suncook lakes, Thorndike Pond, Willard Pond, Willey ponds, and Winnipocket Lake.

More information is available from the New Hampshire Fish and Game Department, 34 Bridge St., Concord, NH 03301.

most from every acre or foot of inland fishing water. Most of its ponds and lakes contain as many fishermen as fish. Still, a good bass angler can find sport here by trying new methods and new lures, and often by fishing at night.

The largest natural lake in the state is Hopatcong, a few miles northwest of Dover. Cottages and resorts, docks and amusement parks virtually consume its entire forty-mile shoreline. But several eight-pound bass have been taken, nearly all after dark.

Most of Jersey's lakes and ponds are located in Sussex, Morris, Warren, and Passaic counties, much of this land being state-owned. Culvers, Owassa, and Kittatinny lakes, and Swartswood Lake in Swartswood State Park, contain bass. So does the Wallkill River (eastern Sussex County) and Lake Mohawk at Sparta.

There is smallmouth fishing in the Delaware River from the northwestern corner of New Jersey to Philipsburg, with good wading most of the way. Greenwood Lake in Passaic County has bass, as do Ramapo Lake; Pompton lakes; the Pompton River; Musconetcong Lake, above Stanhope; Budd Lake, between Hackettstown and Netcong; Mountain Lake, in the Jenny Jump State Forest.

The southern half of New Jersey is flat, and nearly all of its slow-moving rivers that are not polluted contain bass. The Millstone River and Cranberry Brook east of Princeton are good. Also, many streams that drain into Delaware Bay have largemouths in the brackish fringes where fresh water joins the salt, such as the Navesink near Red Bank; Manasquan, Toms River, and its branches. Mullica and Wading rivers, north of Atlantic City; Great Egg and Tuckahoe rivers, upstream from Somers Point; Maurice River, downstream from Millville; Cohansey Creek, outside of Bridgeton; Salem Creek, above Salem; and Oldmans Creek, above Harrisonville.

More information is available from the New Jersey Division of Fish and Game, Labor and Industry Building, Trenton, NJ 08625.

New Jersey

Through the years, because of a high and always expanding population, New Jersey has been in the unenviable position of squeezing the

New York

New York is a picturesque state for fishing, no matter whether in the glens and tilled valleys of the Finger Lakes region, in the green and blue

Thousand Islands, or in the cool and lonely Adirondacks. There is bass-fishing variety here, and there is an abundance of water, but the competition for it sometimes is keen.

Close to New York City, there is some bass fishing in the Catskills. Smallmouths can be had in the Delaware River, from Deposit to Port Jervis. The lower East Branch of the Delaware has bass, and so does the lower Neversink River.

The Adirondack highlands include some lakes and ponds with bass. Lake Champlain has better-than-average smallmouth fishing. Lake George may be the best bass spot in the state. Sacandaga Reservoir on the Hudson and Sacandaga rivers constitute one of the best bets in the East for a trophy-hunting bass. Above Riparius is Schroon Lake with smallmouths. There is scattered smallmouth fishing in the Saranac lakes region, but it is much better in Long Lake, a widening in the Raquette River.

The St. Lawrence Valley contains some of the best smallmouth waters in the East. Fishing is fastest in the Thousand Islands area and then westward into Lake Ontario beyond Cape Vincent. Watertown is an access point to the Thousand Islands. So are Alexandria Bay and Clayton. Good smallmouth fishing is in Black Lake; the Indian, Oswegatchie, Grass and Raquette rivers, near Massena; the St. Regis, near Hogansburg; the Salmon, near Malone; and Chazy River, which flows into Lake Champlain.

Western New York has many bass waters too. Besides Lake Ontario and Lake Erie, consider the Finger lakes: Skaneateles, Otisco, Owasco, Cayuga, Seneca, Keuka, Canadaigua, Honeoye, Canadice, and Conesus. Cayuga, Canandaigua, and Honeoye are the best, however. Much trolling for bass is done in the Finger lakes.

Lake Oneida near Oneida has smallmouths, and Delta Reservoir near Rome has bass. Add Canadarago Lake near Richfield Springs and Otsego Lake at Cooperstown for smallmouths.

The Niagara River, from Buffalo past Niagara Falls to Lake Ontario, is good for smallmouths. Chautauqua Lake has both largemouths and smallmouths. River anglers in western New York frequent the Allegheny, near Olean and Salamanca; and the Tioga, Canisteo, and Cohocton, in the general vicinity of Corning. The Genesee is a good bass river in Allegheny County; float tripping is a possibility.

More information is available from the New York Division of Fish and Wildlife, 50 Wolf Road, Albany, NY 12201.

Pennsylvania

By any standards Pennsylvania is a fine bass-fishing state. Though suburban development, industrial expansion, and pollution have damaged or completely destroyed many waters, a bass fisherman can still find much pure water. And perhaps the pollution picture shows some signs of improvement.

Pennsylvania has picturesque bass rivers excellent for float tripping. Consider, for example, typical three-day floats on four rivers—the Allegheny, the Juniata, the North Branch of the Susquehanna, and the Delaware—which any basser can make.

The Allegheny trip begins at Warren, with a first night's camp at Tidioute. President is a good place to camp the second night. The trip ends at Franklin, about sixty-six miles downstream—good smallmouth fishing all the way.

The Juniata trip begins at Ryde, above Lewistown, and runs downstream to Granville for the first night's camp. Muskrat Spring near Mexico is fine for a second camp, and during the second day's run you will find some of the hottest bass fishing in the state. The float ends at Amity Hall.

The Susquehanna River winds alternately through fertile farm country and between high palisades that make it accessible for long stretches only by boat. A three-day North Branch trip can begin at Sayre, with a first-night stopover at Towanda. The second-night camp can be at Wyalusing; the trip concludes at Mehoopany.

A typical Delaware River float trip can begin at Tighe's Boat Livery above Narrowsburg. The first and second night's camp can be made at Masthope and Pond Eddy. The float ends near Milford.

Even in a lifetime of fishing, a fisherman couldn't adequately explore all the tributaries of these four float-trip rivers. In many cases, the tributaries have even better-looking bass waters that the main streams. One specific example is the Raystown Branch of the Juniata, which would excite any bass fisherman in the world. It's about fifty airline miles from Bedford (on the Pennsylvania Turnpike) to Huntington, but it must be at least three times that mileage because of stream meandering.

Pennsylvania's best bass lake is Raystown Lake, an 8,300 acre impoundment in Huntingdon County, which has an abundance of structure under the surface. Other worthwhile spots are Pymatuning and Allegheny reservoirs, in the Northwest; Beaver Run, Loyalhanna, and Conemaugh reservoirs, east of Pittsburgh; and Shenango Reservoir, near Sharon.

More information is available from the Pennsylvania Fish Commission, Box 1673, Harrisburg, PA 17120.

Rhode Island

This state has very limited bass fishing. The best is available in small ponds, where permission to fish must be obtained. There are a few "company" ponds and reservoirs built primarily for power- or water-supply purposes. Nearly all of these are open to fishing too.

One spot is worth special mention: 1,040-acre Worden Pond. It is a bowl-shaped natural lake no more than 6½ feet deep, often murky, devoid of the structures bass fishermen seek. But it can be a hot spot, especially in springtime. More information is available from the Rhode Island Department of Natural Resources, 83 Park Street, Providence, RI 02903.

Vermont

This scenically attractive state contains good bass fishing in spite of its proximity to the eastern centers of population. In fact it is invaded by thousands of out-of-state anglers every year, and many of them have at least fair success. A bass fisherman's best bet is in early October, when the smallmouths seem to be the most active. There is little fishing pressure then, and the color and atmosphere of autumn are magnificent.

Some of the best Vermont fishing is in border waters—Lake Champlain on the west and the Connecticut River on the east. Both have small-

Smallmouth bass are established in many New England lakes and furnish fast action in springtime.

mouths. The Missisquoi River, from Richford to Swanton, has smallmouths, and below Swanton, largemouths begin to appear. Lake Carmi, east of Franklin, and Fairfield Pond, northeast of St. Albans, also have bass.

Add also these waters for bass, mostly smallmouths: the lower reaches of the Lamoille and Winooski rivers; Hinesburg Pond, near Hinesburg; Shelburne Pond, east of Shelburne; Hosmer ponds, near Lowell; Seymour Lake, near Morgan; Wallis Lake, near Averill; Lake Groton, between Groton and Marshfield; Fairlee and Morey lakes, near Ely; the West River, between West Drummerston and Brattleboro; Little Otter Creek, near Lake Champlain; and Bomoseen, Hortonia, and St. Catherine lakes, in Rutland County.

More information is available from the Vermont Department of Environmental Conservation, Montpelier, VT 05602.

Chapter 17

THE SOUTHWEST

Traditionally an arid region, it is impossible to drive very far through the Southwest today without encountering an abundance of boats and trailers. There are two reasons: Many giant reservoirs were built during the past half century, and there is good fishing in all of them. And although nothing like these lakes ever existed in original bass range, largemouths are thriving in nearly all these waters. Bass fishing, in fact, is extremely good.

Arizona

Arizona's bass fishing can be grouped into two major areas: the Salt and Colorado River lakes, and four individual lakes—Carl Pleasant, San Carlos, Bartlett, and Horseshoe. The Salt River chain of lakes in east-central Arizona is formed by a series of dams on the Salt River. Starting at Phoenix and going east, the lakes are: Saguaro, Canyon, Apache, and Roosevelt. Boats and camping facilities are available at all of them. Roosevelt is considered to be the best producer of large bass, with Apache (a smallmouth lake) second. Canyon and Saguaro have become playgrounds for water-sports enthusiasts, but manage to produce a good many largemouths.

The Colorado River lakes begin at the lower end of the Grand Canyon, where the largest and most famous, Lake Mead, is formed by Hoover (Boulder) Dam at Boulder City. The bass fishing at Lake Mead is well known, and in some seasons it ranks with the best. The next lake downstream is Lake Mohave, with the distinction of being excellent for both black bass and rainbow trout. Toward the lower end of the lake the water is not so cold, and boasts the best fishing for bass.

Between lakes Mohave and Havasu is a swampy area where the river meanders and forms a large pool of shallow fishing water. Topock Swamp produces very good bass fishing, although the water supply to it is somewhat uncertain. Lake Havasu itself is an excellent bass producer.

Between Lake Havasu and Imperial Dam near Yuma are a number of small lakes not well known, but that furnish good bass fishing. Among these are Cibola, Ferguson, and Martinez lakes. The final lake on the river is Mittry Lake, just outside Yuma.

Alamo Lake in western Arizona has produced many largemouths of modest size. Black River has fishing for small smallmouth bass.

The Verde River, which flows southward through central Arizona, connects two lakes: Horseshoe, to the north, and Bartlett. These two lakes furnish some fair to very good fishing. The Verde River, which joins the Salt below the dams, has smallmouth-bass fishing. The combined flow of the Verde and Salt rivers furnishes several more miles of fishing. North and west of Phoenix are Lake Carl Pleasant and Frog Tanks; the former produces some good largemouth fishing from time to time.

More information is available from the Arizona Game and Fish Department, 2222 West Greenway, Phoenix, AZ 85023.

Colorado

This is strictly a trout state, and a bass fisherman must look far to find sport of any quality. Virtually all the bass in the state are confined to farm and ranch ponds or irrigation ditches in the southeastern quarter of the state. Local inquiry is the only way to find these places.

Bobby Reservoir in Yuma County probably has the biggest bass. Horseshoe Reservoir, near Fort Collins; Lonetree Reservoir, at Loveland; and Two Buttes Reservoir have a few largemouths.

More information is available from the Colorado Division of Wildlife, 6060 Broadway, Denver, Co 80216.

New Mexico

Bass fishing for largemouth and smallmouth is possible in New Mexico year-round.

Conchas, one of the biggest lakes, is stocked with bass, as are Alamogordo Lake and Elephant Butte Lake. Bear Canyon Lake has trout as well as bass. There are bass in the small, deep lakes near Santa Rosa, and in Red Bluff Lake. Other lakes for fair to good bass fishing are Avalon, Bitter, Bottomless, Caballo, Jackson, Municipal, and Six-mile lakes. Cochita Lake, north of Albuquerque, and Navajo Lake often produce large bass.

The Pecos River contains bass from McMillan Dam south, the lower Pecos River being generally good. Berrendo and Hondo creeks and Felix River, all in the Pecos Valley, have or have had bass.

The lower Rio Grande and the drainage canals near Las Cruces and Socorro and south of Belen have limited fishing.

Boats are available at Elephant Butte, Caballo, and Conchas lakes and at several of the following bass waters: Alamogordo Lake, Anaconda Lake, Avalon Lake, Bass Lake, Bitter Lake, Bottomless Lake, Caballo Lake, Calley Lake, Chain Lakes, Conchas Lake, Dosher Lake, Elephant Butte Lake, El Paso lakes, Fin and Feather Lake, Harroun Dam, Harroun Lake, Hidden Lake, Mossman Reservoir, Municipal Lake, Ojo Caliente Lake, Pasamonte Lake, Power Dam Lake, Railroad reservoirs, Red Bluff Lake, Red Lake (Navajo Reservation), Riner Lake, Rio Grande Beach Lake, Zuni Reservoir, Belen-Riverside Drain (Los Lunas South), Belen-Riverside Drain (Los Lunas North), Berrendo Creek (tributary to Lower Pecos), Black River (tributary to Lower Pecos), Bosque del Apache Drains (tributary to Rio Grande), Conejo Creek (tributary to Pecos River), Del Rio Drain (tributary to Rio Grande), East Drain (tributary to Rio Grande), Felix River (tributary to Pecos River), Gila River (L) (tributary to Little Colorado), Isleta Drain (tributary to Rio Grande), La Mesa Drain (tributary to Pecos River), Mora River (tributary to Canadian River), Nemexas Drain (tributary to Rio Grande), Pecos River, and Penasco River (tributary to Pecos River).

More information is available from the New Mexico Department of Fish and Game, Villagra Building, Santa Fe, NM 87501.

Texas

Texans like to brag about their great bass fishing, but they rarely agree on which bass

Tournament angler Roland Martin with a good string of largemouths taken from a Texas reservoir.

waters are best. Although this also was a relatively waterless state originally, large reservoirs are fairly well scattered from border to border. More than likely there is more bass water here than anywhere else.

The biggest and probably the best bass lake is Toledo Bend, in the extreme east, with over 186,000 acres of flooded timber and other cover for largemouth bass. Quite possibly this is the best bass producer in the world. Vast, alligator-shaped Sam Rayburn Lake, not far away and similar, also offers splendid bass fishing in super-structure. Another of the giant reservoirs is Amistad, formed by Falcon Dam on the Rio Grande near Laredo. It is remotely located, but a red-hot bass lake year-round. A poll of Texas pro bass anglers reveals that in addition to the above three, the best bass lakes are Dow, near Freeport; Texoma, on the Oklahoma border; Lake of the Pines; Lake Belton; Mathis, near Corpus Christi; and Whitney, near Dallas.

There is some river bass fishing in Texas, the best of it centered in the eastern part of the state. Bass are available in oxbows of the Red River and in the Sulphur River, west of Texarkana. Add also Blue and Long lakes, northeast of Point Pleasant. Half of Caddo Lake is in Texas, northeast of Marshall. Fully as good is Black Cypress Bayou, which meanders into the lake from near Jefferson.

Much fishing is found in the waters of Davy Crockett, Angelina, and Sam Houston forests. The Big Thicket is a region of dense vegetation, lazy, interwoven bayous and sloughs. It is good sense to go in with somebody who knows the region well. Largemouth bass there run to fair size. Attoyac Bayou and Angelina and Neches rivers also furnish sport.

Lake Dallas, the Dallas water supply, is on Elm Creek. A series of dams has been built on Trinity River upstream from Fort Worth. Lake Worth is the older; others are Eagle Mountain Lake and Lake Bridgeport. Three reservoirs are near Wichita Falls: Lake Kemp, the largest; Diversion Lake, downstream; and Lake Wichita. All are good bass lakes.

Largemouths are numerous in picturesquely named Possum Kingdom Reservoir on the Brazos near Mineral Wells. Below there is fishing for bass in creeks and sloughs of the Brazos.

Cleburne fishermen visit Cleburne State Park, where there is a public lake. Bass can also be taken along Paluxy River southwest of Cleburne. Near Waco, fishermen have Lake Waco and the Leon River. Medina Lake, northwest of San Antonio, is a good possibility, as is the river above and below. The following lakes, widely scattered, also are excellent largemouth-bass prospects:

Lake Meredith, near Amarillo; Twin Butte Reservoir, near San Angelo; Belton Reservoir, near Belton; Benbrook Reservoir, near Fort Worth; Canyon Reservoir, near New Braunfeis; Dam "B" Reservoir, near Town Bluff; Garza-Little Elm Reservoir, near Denton; Grapevine Reservoir, near Roanoke; Lavon Reservoir, near Lavon; Navarre Mills Reservoir, near Silver City; Texarkana Reservoir, near Texarkana; Whitney Reservoir, near Whitney; Lake Livingston, near Trinity; Lake Conroe in Montgomery County; Houston County Reservoir, near Crockett; Lake Travis, near Austin; Lake Murval, near Carthage; Cedar Creek Reservoir, near Athens; Fairfield Lake, in Freestone County; Lake Casa Blanca, in Webb County; Lake Arrowhead, near Henrietta; Cypress Springs Lake, near Mount Vernon; Dunlap Lake, near Daingerfield; Alcoa Lake, in Williamson County.

More information is available from the Texas Parks and Wildlife Department, John H. Reagan Building, Austin, TX 78701.

Utah

Utah has one top-quality bass water, Lake Powell, formed by Glen Canyon Dam on the Colorado River in the southeastern part of the state. Largemouths strike especially well in spring, around Bullfrog Basin. Anglers at Powell often live and cruise on the lake in a rented houseboat; narrow canyons and coves can be fished from trailed skiffs.

Otherwise bass-fishing waters are scarce—extremely scarce, in fact. Some bass live in the Logan River north of Brigham in the northern part of the state. The Provo River and Deer Creek, both below Salt Lake City, furnish some bass fishing. But probably an angler's best bet is Utah Lake, just west of Provo.

More information is available from the Utah Division of Wildlife Resources, 1596 West North Temple, Salt Lake City, UT 84116.

Fishing in Lake Powell, Utah. Once a dry desert, this is now among the best bass-fishing impoundments in America.

A stringer of bass taken in Lake Powell, Utah.

Chapter 18

THE WEST

Except for the Sacramento perch (a close cousin of the black bass), which inhabited the Sacramento River drainage in moderate numbers, no members of the black bass family lived on the West Coast until seventy years ago. Today the largemouth bass, at least, is an important game fish in every Pacific Coast state because it has been introduced into nearly every new reservoir built in modern times. What is more, as new reservoirs continue to be built to serve an exploding human population, bass will be released in still other waters.

Largemouths have adapted especially well to their new West Coast homes; at times and in places, the fishing for them rivals that found anywhere. In addition, the bass are attaining a size similar to that of southeastern bass.

California

No species of black bass are native to California, but today the state is on the verge of producing a new world's record, if such is ever caught. Nevertheless, bass fishing today is confined, mostly, to the southern half of the state.

San Diego County is the current hot spot. Within that area, Otay, Miramar, Murray, San Vicente, El Capitan, Henshaw, Wolford, and Cuyamaca lakes all have produced bass beyond twelve pounds. Miramar produced the second largest bass known—twenty pounds, fifteen ounces, taken in 1973. In San Vicente, an eighteen-pound, nine-ounce largemouth was taken, and during one season (1978), anglers caught more than a hundred largemouths exceeding nine pounds apiece. That is astounding success, especially since the lake is relatively small, is

opened only four days a week (Thursdays through Sundays) and for only nine months (October through June) each year. More information can be obtained from the San Diego City Lakes Department, Balboa Park, San Diego, CA 92101.

Perhaps California's next best bet for bass, in the north, is Shasta Lake, formed by damming the Sacramento, McCloud, and Pit rivers north of Reading. Five- and six-pounders are not too rare here.

Clear Lake, north of San Francisco, the largest natural lake in the state, has good bass possibilities. So do Havasu Lake on the Colorado River; Isabella Lake, formed by a dam on the Kern River; and Santa Margarita Lake on the upper Salinas River. Although Sacramento Delta waters are best known for stripers, there's excellent largemouth fishing here too. Local inquiry is necessary to find out exactly when and where.

An example of how productive California waters can be is Irvin Lake, a few miles from Santa Ana. Although little more than a large pothole, it has produced many *Field and Stream* magazine contest winners. Other worthwhile waters are:

Cachuma Reservoir, East Park Reservoir, Folsom Reservoir, Millerton Reservoir, Berryessa Reservoir, Stony Gorge Reservoir, Burns Reservoir, Farmington Reservoir, Hansen Reservoir, Mariposa Reservoir, Pine Flat Reservoir, Salinas Reservoir, Pardee Reservoir, Hogan Reservoir, Melones Reservoir, Tullock Reservoir, Tinemaha Reservoir, Exchequer Reservoir, Railroad Canyon Reservoir, Vali Reservoir, Barrett Reservoir, Lower Otay Reservoir, Hodges Reservoir, Nacimiento Reservoir, Anderson Reservoir, Coyote Reservoir, Dallas-Warner Reservoir, Woodward

Reservoir, Turlock Reservoir, Don Pedro Reservoir, Piru Reservoir, Bullard's Bar Reservoir, Salt Springs Valley Reservoir.

More information is available from the California Department of Fish and Game, 1416 9th Street, Sacramento, CA 95814.

Hawaii

Though not native to any of the Hawaiian Islands, bass today are well established in a few waters. Fishing is possible at such public fishing areas as Wahiwa on Oahu Island, Kohala on Hawaii Island, and Wailua on Kauai Island.

Besides the public areas, there are a few streams and several reservoirs that contain fishable stocks of bass. Most are privately controlled, predominantly by sugar-cane companies, and permission must be obtained to fish on them. On the whole, permits are granted. The best and most plentiful bass fishing is on Kauai.

More information is available from the Hawaii Division of Fish and Game, 1179 Punchbowl Street, Honolulu, HI 96813.

Idaho

With a couple of notable exceptions, Idaho's bass fishing is very limited. Largemouths can be caught in a few small public lakes and reservoirs of state parks in the southern half of the state. But the best bass fishing—and it is excellent—is for smallmouth bass in the Snake River below Hells Canyon Dam. Most of this water is inaccessible, except by float-tripping in rubber rafts. The bass are not large, but they are plentiful.

More information is available from the Idaho Fish and Game Department, 600 South Walnut Street, Boise, ID 83707.

Montana

Especially in northwestern Montana, there is a moderate amount of bass fishing in small lakes, ponds, and potholes, a lot of these being on private land around Kalispell, Polson, and Bigfork. Lake Mary Ronan is public and has some good bass water. Pablo and Ninepipe Reservoirs also have bass. In eastern Montana, Fort Peck Reservoir contains some largemouths.

Lake Mary Ronan is one of the few bass lakes in western Montana.

More information is available from the Montana Fish and Game Department, Helena, MT 59601.

Nevada

All waters of the Colorado River reservoirs (see entry for neighboring Arizona) provide good largemouth-bass angling. The next best bet is Ruby Lake National Wildlife Refuge, near Ely. This is a 38,000-acre marsh where the largemouth fishing is often fast early in the season. Not all of the marsh is open during waterfowl nesting, though, and a small boat is necessary. Bass also are found in Lake Walker between Yerington and Hawthorne.

More information is available from the Nevada Department of Fish and Game, Box 10678, Reno, NV 89510.

Oregon

This is primarily a trout-fishing state, but a surprising number of first-rate bass waters do exist. Best by consensus is Owyhee Reservoir, Malheur County, in the southeastern corner of the state. It is not an easy lake to reach, and even launching a boat there can be a chore, but the bass fishing is worth any trouble, especially in spring. Klamath and Lake countries contain several lakes, including Lake of the Woods, with fair bass fishing.

Bass are found in many of the coastal lakes. On the north coast are Sunset and Cullaby lakes in Clatsop County and Devils Lake in Lincoln County. Farther south on the coast are Sutton, Mercer, Cleawox, Siltcoos, and Tahkenitch lakes. Still farther south are the Tenmile lakes in Coos County and Garrison Lake in Curry County. Fishing for bass goes on year-round, with the most productive period from May to October.

It is impossible to list the great number of very small bass ponds, including sloughs of the Columbia River, which contain good bass populations. But most of them are concentrated in the following counties: Multnomah (especially Sturgeon Lake), Columbia, and Clatsop. At times excellent bass fishing exists in the Willamette River above tidewater and within sight of downtown Portland.

Casting in the weedy fringes of a typical bass lake in western Oregon.

Smallmouth-bass fishing in the John Day River of central Oregon compares well with any river fishing for the species in America. The best areas are reached by float tripping, although at times (after early summer) the water level may be low enough to make this difficult.

More information is available from the Oregon Fish Commission, 307 State Office Building, Portland, OR 97201.

Washington

Washington has pretty good bass fishing in widely scattered waters, although the fish seldom ever approach trophy size. No doubt the best bet is Equalizing Reservoir below Grand Coulee; fishing is fast here. Another good bet is Moses Lake in central Washington.

The following counties each contain a number of public bass-fishing lakes. Many are not heavily fished, and fast action is certainly a possibility, especially when the water temperatures are ideal for the species. The counties are: Cowlitz, Grays Harbor, Island, Jefferson, King, Kitsap, Mason, Pacific, Pierce, San Juan, Skagit, Snohomish, Thurston, Wahkiakum, and Whatcom.

More information is available from the Washington Department of Fisheries, 115 General Administration Building, Olympia, WA 98504.

Wyoming

Except for Alaska, where no bass exist at all, this is the poorest bass state. Ocean Lake, near Riverton, is the only lake with fishing worth mentioning. Flaming George Reservoir, which is mostly in Utah, has largemouth and smallmouths, but virtually all are in the Utah end.

More information is available from the Wyoming Game and Fish Department, 5400 Bishop Boulevard, Cheyenne, WY 82001.

Chapter 19

BEYOND U.S. BORDERS

Canada

No other country contains such a high ratio of clear, cool, sweet waters to dry land. This is fine for the bass fisherman of North America because much of this water, in the southern parts of the eastern provinces, is good to excellent for bass. Many lakes contain either largemouths, smallmouths, or both.

Canada is not a promised land for an angler with a record bass on his mind because the shorter summer season in the North precludes their reaching great size. Still, bass fishing in Canada has an attraction all its own. Usually it means casting in an evergreen setting scented and air conditioned by nature. The smallmouths in particular are terrific performers in waters chilled year-round.

No fisherman will have any trouble finding accommodations or facilities to fit his budget, no

Fishermen trolling, during springtime, for smallmouth bass along a rocky shoreline in Ontario.

matter what it is, in any corner of Canada where bass fishing exists. He can enjoy his fishing from a plush American-plan resort or he can camp for a few dollars in a national or provincial park. There are cottages and cabins of every description. The more adventurous fishermen can plan a canoe trip deep into a wilderness area.

Ontario

Ontario has an honest claim to being a whole continent's favorite fishing ground, with a lake-and-river-surface area estimated at 80,000 square miles—one fifth the total extent of the province. In addition to the Great Lakes, all but one of which touch Ontario, there are numerous large bodies of water such as Lake of the Woods and Rainy Lake on the international border; and Nipissing, Nipigon, and Simcoe, completely contained within the province. Many other well-known waters average nearly one hundred square miles in area—for instance, the Rideaus, the Muskokas, and the Timagami chains of lakes. To these add countless smaller lakes that lie in an endless chain across the Precambrian Shield of northern Ontario—the count is well over 100,000. (According to expert geographers, only 40,000—less than half the total—are named.) And many of these waters are inhabited by bass. No Canadian province has more parks, camp grounds, or public facilities for visiting fishermen than Ontario.

There are five major fishing "regions" in Ontario where you can bass-fish from canoe, rowboat, motor launch, cruiser, or by wading. Usually the farther you go from the beaten track, the better are your chances of getting fish. However, some of the best bass fishing awaits you right off Long Point, on the north shore of Lake Erie—an hour's drive from Buffalo, two hours from Detroit.

Southeastern Ontario includes such famous waters as the St. Lawrence River, Lake St. Francis, the Rideau lakes, and Lake Ontario around the Isle of Quinte, plus hundreds of streams and pools lying north of the St. Lawrence, from Belleville to Pembroke.

Lake St. Francis and the St. Lawrence provide the best of trolling or casting for bass. Farther west, in Lake Ontario, around the Isle of Quinte, is smallmouth-bass territory. Less than fifty miles north of Belleville and Kingston begins the "Land O' Lakes" district, with many bass lakes

and streams. There are fishing camps and resorts around Napanee, Tweed, Madoc, Kaladar, Carleton Place, and Renfrew. Just east are the Rideau lakes, accessible from Kingston, with good fishing for largemouth and smallmouth bass early in the season.

Central Ontario covers the populated and industrial areas around Toronto and such vacation districts as Muskoka, Georgian Bay, and the Kawartha Lakes, with Bruce Peninsula on the west and the Haliburton Highlands on the east.

North and west of Lake Simcoe (fair bass) lies the Georgian Bay-Bruce Peninsula area with its good bass fishing. Simcoe is not an easy lake to fish, but with the right combination, it produces fine catches of largemouths and smallmouths. Midland, Penetanguishene, Honey Harbour, Go Home Bay, and the whole rocky shore of Georgian Bay to Parry Sound are good for smallmouths. This whole area, west of Orillia and covering the length of Georgian Bay, is good bass-fishing territory.

Huntsville marks the entrance to Algonquin Park, which contains numerous bass lakes. In this natural park the canoe is the ideal means of transportation. Any of the resorts or camps in the park, or around Dwight, will outfit you and provide bass guides.

East of Toronto are the seventy-five Kawartha lakes. At Rice Lake, Young's Point, Burleigh Falls, Fenelon Falls, and Bobcaygeon there's good fishing for bass. Lake Scugog is also good for largemouths.

In southwestern Ontario an angler will discover fine bass fishing along the reefs off Nanticoke, Port Dover, and Port Ryerse. At Rondeau Provincial Park, a forest area and game preserve, there are camping grounds as well as the usual good bass fishing associated with the Lake Erie region, as at Erieau Beach.

Northern Ontario begins at a line drawn from Mattawa to Georgian Bay. In Lake Nipissing there are plenty of bass, especially in the west arm, Trout Lake, and the French River. Eastward from North Bay, the waters connecting Lake Nipissing and the Ottawa River combine bass fishing with historic interest, for this is the time-honored route of Indians and *voyageurs*, the path Champlain took on his first trip into the Northland.

West of North Bay is Sudbury and Aiginawassi, Wanapitei, Ashigami, Kookagaming, Metagamasine, Oden, Thor, and Ivanhoe lakes, all containing bass. Farther north, in the Chapleau District, Onaping, Metagama, and Biscotasing lakes are good. On the road to Manitoulin Island, Lake Penage has good smallmouth bass.

Manitoulin Island is the largest freshwater island in the world. It is surrounded by Lake Huron, with its excellent summertime bass fishing. Also good are North Channel, Manitowaning Bay, South Bay, Honora Bay, Bayfield Sound, and Meldrum Bay.

Northwestern Ontario from east of Lake Nipigon to the Manitoba border includes Lake of the Woods, a vast lake with thousands of miles of irregular shoreline, making it ideal for fishing camps. South to Fort Frances and Rainy River, there is more good smallmouth water.

More information is available from the Ontario Ministry of Tourism, 900 Bay Street, Toronto, Ont. M7A 2E5 Canada.

Quebec

Because of widespread stocking during the past fifty years, smallmouth bass have been established in countless Quebec waters, a large percentage of which are closed to public fishing. Quebec has a policy of allowing "clubs" or companies to control vast areas of bush real estate, which means that only a few anglers are ever permitted to fish an entire chain of lakes in any season's time. Otherwise, as in Ontario, these same lakes might provide sport for thousands of bass anglers.

A few waters are worth mentioning. Lakes St. Louis (especially at the mouth of the Chateaugay River), St. Francis, St. Pierre, and Two Mountains on the St. Lawrence River have largemouths. Probably Quebec's biggest largemouths come from Missisquoi Bay of Lake Champlain. All the above also have smallmouths. Some good bets for smallmouths alone are Blue Sea and Bitobi lakes, near Gracefield; Wolf Lake, at Gatineau Provincial Park; Ottawa Lake, north of Quyon; Lac Mandeville, in Berthier County; Lac Clothier, in Joliette County; Nomininque, Durocher, and Ouimet lakes, in Labell County. More than half of the 50,000 lakes in the Outaouais region contain some smallmouth bass.

More information is available from the Quebec Department of Tourism, Fish, and Game, 150 St. Cyrille Boulevard, Que. G1R 4Y3 Canada.

Manitoba

Smallmouths have been stocked in a few Manitoba lakes, all in the Southeast, and the Whiteshell Forest Reserve. The best lakes are Crow Duck (very good), Caddy, Falcon, and the Winnipeg River, with spring and summer being by far the best periods.

New Brunswick

Smallmouth bass aren't widely spread through New Brunswick, but in those waters in which the fish have become established the fishing is excellent. These are confined to the southwestern part of the province, along or close to the Maine border. They include waters of the Chiputneticook Chain, the beautiful St. Croix River (float tripping is a good possibility here), Utopia, Palfrey, Magaguadavic, and Little Magaguadavic lakes.

The greatest fishing of all occurs in early June, when smallmouths are in very shallow water. At that time the bass bugging is unbelievably good. It is often good, but briefly, in September as well.

Saskatchewan

There is no important bass fishing in Saskatchewan, although smallmouths have been stocked in several places. Some are caught in Prince Albert National Park, principally in Lake Waskesiu, but that's just about the whole story.

Cuba

When Cuba reopened the country to sports fishermen in 1977, it suddenly made available an immense amount of bass fishing. Bass from the United States were stocked in Zapata Swamp in the 1920s and have thrived there as in few other places. Today the main fishing area, Treasure (or Tesoro) Lake, is almost as full of medium bass (if overfishing does not become a problem) as it is of vegetation. But world records have never materialized here, as some predicted. The heaviest largemouth to date has been a twelve-pounder.

During the 1960s and 1970s, when the country was closed to tourists, bass were transferred from Treasure Lake to many other new irrigation and water-supply reservoirs. The bass have prospered to such an extent that one (or more) of these is likely to become a superbass hole. In

Angler Dick Kotis grasps a good bass at Treasure Lake, Cuba.

1978 a fifteen-pounder was taken from 30,000-acre Lake Zaza. Other Cuban reservoirs (called *presas*) with great potential are La Guanabana and Viet Nam Heroico on the Isle of Pines; Ramirez and Juventuto, near Pinar del Rio; Malpoton, near Havana; Hanabanavilla, near Santa Clara; Caonao, near Camaguey; Alacranes, near Santo Domingo; and Cespedes, near Santiago de Cuba.

Mexico and Central America

There is much good bass fishing in Mexico, largely in the watersheds that drain into the Gulf of Mexico rather than to the Pacific. Some good waters are close to the United States border. One top example is Guerrero Lake; another is Obregon Lake, near Cuidad Obregon. Closer to the border is Angostura Reservoir, just south of Douglas, Arizona. It's possible to charter a small plane or go by group-package charter to

A fifteen-pound bass from Lake Zaza, Cuba, where even larger bass might soon be taken.

all of these from points in the southwestern United States.

A complete list of all Mexican bass-fishing waters has never been compiled, but the Mexican tourist director reports that the following waters have excellent bass fishing:

Don Martin Dam, Ojo Caliente, Yuriria Lagoon, Tuxpan Lagoon, Atezca Lagoon, El Estribon Dam, Valle de Bravo Dam, Patzcuaro Lake, Tacambaro Lagoon, Duero River, Tepuxtepec Dam, Zacapu Lagoon, Tequesquetengo Lake, Las Estacas, El Rodeo Lagoon, Cuatetelco Lagoon, Necaxa Dam, Valsequillo Dam, Vicencio Lagoon, El Centenario Dam, La Llave Dam, El Azucar Dam, and Mante River.

During the early 1970s, some very large (at least fourteen-pound) bass were taken in beautiful Lago Yojoa in Honduras, and the odds are fair that some just as large still exist. But the lake is difficult to reach and there is much subsistence fishing by locals. Lake Atitlan in the Guatemala highlands has largemouth bass, but very little sport fishing has been done for the species, often considered a nuisance.

APPENDIX

Manufacturers and Distributors of Bass-fishing Equipment

Tony Accetta & Son
932 Avenue E.
Riviera Beach, FL 33404
Telephone: (305) 844-3441

Acme Tackle Company
69 Bucklin Street
Providence, RI 02907
Telephone: (401) 331-6437

Action Lure Co., Inc.
4401 South Drive
P.O. Box 10529
Jackson, MS 39209
Telephone: (601) 969-5685

Al's Goldfish Lure Company
516 Main Street
Indian Orchard, MA 01051
Telephone: (413) 543-3324

American Luresmith Tackle Co.
P.O. Box 223
Tinley Park, IL 60477
Telephone: (312) 429-3388

Angler Products, Inc.
210 Spring Street
Butler, PA 16001
Telephone: (412) 285-4671

Angler Rod Co.
1426 Oakland Avenue
St. Clair, MI 48079
Telephone: (313) 329-2253

Aquasonic Lures, Inc.
101 South Main Street
Cibolo, TX 78108
Telephone: (512) 658-5363

Fred Arbogast Company, Inc.
313 West North Street
Akron, OH 44303
Telephone: (216) 253-2177

B & B Tackle Co.
P.O. Box 220
Lufkin, TX 75901
Telephone: (713) 632-2203

B & M Company
P.O. Box 231
West Point, MS 39773
Telephone: (601) 494-5092

Jim Bagley Bait Co., Inc.
Recker at Spirit Lake Road
Winter Haven, FL 33880
Telephone: (813) 294-4271

Bass Buster, Inc.
A Johnson Wax Associate
301 Main—Box 118
Amsterdam, MO 64723
Telephone: (816) 267-3217

Bay De Noc Lure Co.
800–810 Railway Avenue
P.O. Box 71
Gladstone, MI 49837
Telephone: (906) 425-0393

Bear Paw Tackle Co., Inc.
Route 2—Highway 620—Box 494
Bellaire, MI 49615
Telephone: (616) 533-8604

Berkley & Company, Inc.
Highways 9 and 71
Spirit Lake, IA 51360
Telephone: (712) 336-1520

Bingo Bait Co., Inc.
619 South Port Street
Corpus Christi, TX 78405
Telephone: (512) 882-5925

Blakemore Lure Company
North Highway 65, P.O. Box 505
Branson, MO 65616
Telephone: (417) 334-5340

Bomber Bait Company, Inc.
326 Lindsay—Box 1058
Gainesville, TX 76240
Telephone: (817) 665-5505

Boone Bait Company, Inc.
P.O. Box 571—Forsyth Road
Winter Park, FL 32789
Telephone: (305) 671-2930

Browning
Route No. 1
Morgan, UT 84050
Telephone: (801) 876-2711

Brule Corporation
P.O. Box 53
Iron River, WI 54847
Telephone: (715) 372-4215

Burke Fishing Lures
1969 South Airport Road
Traverse City, MI 49684
Telephone: (616) 947-5010

California Tackle Company, Inc.
430 West Redondo Beach Boulevard
Gardena, CA 90248
Telephone: (213) 323-5322

Charley's Wonderworm Company
917½ West Fourth Street
Mount Carmel, IL 62863
Telephone: (618) 263-3720

Lew Childre & Sons, Inc.
P.O. Box 535
Foley, AL 36535
Telephone: (205) 943-5041

Converse Rubber Company
Division of Eltra Corporation
55 Fordham Road
Wilmington, MA 01887
Telephone: (617) 657-5500

Cordell Tackle, Inc.
P.O. Box 2020
Hot Springs, AR 71901
Telephone: (501) 767-6766

Cortland Line Co.
67 East Court Street
Cortland, NY 13045
Telephone: (607) 756-2851

Covey Corporation
Division of Kelley Industries, Inc.
2727 Allen Parkway
P.O. Box 1317
Houston, TX 77001
Telephone: (713) 526-8461

Creek Chub Bait Company
113 East Keyser Street
Garrett, IN 46738
Telephone: (219) 357-3505

Creme Lure Co., Inc.
P.O. Box 87
Tyler, TX 75710
Telephone: (214) 593-7371

Cutter Laboratories, Inc.
Fourth and Parker Streets
Berkeley, CA 94710
Telephone: (415) 841-0123

Daiwa Corporation
Division of Daiwa Seiko, Inc.
14011 South Normandie
Gardena, CA 90249
Telephone: (213) 321-3211

Les Davis Fishing Tackle Co., Inc.
1565 Center Street
Tacoma, WA 98409
Telephone: (206) 272-0515

DeLong Lures, Inc.
85 Compark Road
Centerville, OH 45459
Telephone: (513) 885-7647

DeWitt Plastics
26 Aureliua Avenue, P.O. Box 400
Auburn, NY 13021
Telephone: (315) 253-6285

Dragon Fly Company
823 Broad Street—P.O. Drawer 1349
Sumter, SC 29150
Telephone: (803) 773-7815

E-Z Action Products Company
P.O. Box 403—113 South Union Street
Battle Creek, MI 49916
Telephone: (616) 968-8643

Emco Specialties, Inc.
2121 East Walnut
Des Moines, IA 50317
Telephone: (515) 265-6101

Lou J. Eppinger Mfg. Co.
6340 Schaefer Highway
Dearborn, MI 48126
Telephone: (313) 582-3205

Falls Bait Company
1440 Kennedy Road
Chippewa Falls, WI 54729
Telephone: (715) 723-3645

Fenwick
P.O. Box 729
Westminster, CA 92683
Telephone: (714) 897-1066

Fin & Feather Mfg. Co.
P.O. Box 179
Marshall, TX 75670
Telephone: (214) 938-5851

Fish Hawk Electronics Corporation
4220 Waller Drive (Ridgefield)
Crystal Lake, IL 60014
Telephone: (815) 459-6510

Fish It
Division of It, Inc.
P.O. Box 433
Canton, CT 06019
Telephone: (203) 482-3545

Flambeau Products Corporation
801 Lynn Avenue
Baraboo, WI 53913
Telephone: (608) 356-5551

Four Rivers Tackle Company
410 Eleventh Street
Greenwood, MS 38930
Telephone: (601) 453-4178

Gapen's World of Fishin', Inc.
Highway 10
Big Lake, MN 55309
Telephone: (612) 263-2655

The Garcia Corporation
329 Alfred Avenue
Teaneck, NJ 07666
Telephone: (201) 833-2000

Gladding Corporation (Executive Office)
Back Bay Annex—P.O. Box 586
Boston, MA 02117
Telephone: (617) 266-7570

Gladding-South Bend Tackle Co.
5985 Tarbell Road—P.O. Box 6249
Syracuse, NY 13217
Telephone: (315) 432-1921

Gott Mfg. Co., Inc.
P.O. Box 652
Winfield, KS 67156
Telephone: (316) 221-2230

Great Southern Tackle
Division of Great Southern Corporation
3607 Regal Boulevard
Memphis, TN 38118
Telephone: (901) 365-1611

Gudebrod Bros. Silk Co., Inc.
12 South 12th Street
Philadelphia, PA 19107
Telephone: (215) 922-1122

H & H Lure Co.
10874 North Dual Street
Baton Rouge, LA 70814
Telephone: (504) 275-1471

Harper-Willis Bait Co.
4835 Buffalo Gap Road
Abilene, TX 79605
Telephone: (915) 692-6021

Butch Harris Lures
421 Briarbend Drive
Charlotte, NC 28209
Telephone: (704) 527-0040

James Heddon's Sons
414 West Street
Dowagiac, MI 49047
Telephone: (616) 782-5123

Helin Tackle Company
4099 Beaufait
Detroit, MI 48207
Telephone: (313) 921-0888

John J. Hildebrandt Corp.
817 High Street—P.O. Box 50
Logansport, IN 46947
Telephone: (219) 753-2609

The Hobson Company
Outdoor Products Division
3283 Lakeshore Avenue
Oakland, CA 94610
Telephone: (415) 836-1669

The Hofschneider Corporation
848 Jay Street—P.O. Box 4166
Rochester, NY 14611
Telephone: (716) 235-1866

Hopkins Lures Company
1130 Boissevain Avenue
Norfolk, VA 23507
Telephone: (804) 622-0977

Igloo Corporation
P.O. Box 19322
Houston, TX 77024
Telephone: (713) 465-2571

Ray Jefferson
Main and Cotton Streets
Philadelphia, PA 19127
Telephone: (215) 487-2800

Luhr Jensen & Sons, Inc.
W. May Street Road
Hood River, OR 97031
Telephone: (503) 386-3811

Johnson Reels, Inc.
A Johnson Wax Associate
1531 Madison Avenue
Mankato, MN 56001
Telephone: (507) 345-4623

Keystone Fishing Corporation
1344 West 37th Street
Chicago, IL 60609
Telephone: (312) 927-4050

L & S Bait Company
1500 East Bay Drive
Largo, FL 33540
Telephone: (813) 584-7691

Lake King Rod Company
820 North Kansas
Topeka, KS 66608
Telephone: (913) 233-9541

Lazy Ike Corp.
P.O. Box 1177
Fort Dodge, IA 50501
Telephone: (515) 576-4118

Light Styx, Inc.
3303 Lee Parkway—Suite 404
Dallas, TX 75219
Telephone: (214) 528-0790

Lindly/Little Joe Famous
    Fishing Tackle
Ray-O-Vac Division, ESB, Inc.
Box 488
Brainerd, MN 56401
Telephone: (218) 829-1714

Lowrance Electronics, Inc.
12000 East Skelly Drive
Tulsa, OK 74128
Telephone: (918) 437-6881

Mann's Bait Company
State Docks Road—Box 604
Eufaula, AL 36027
Telephone: (205) 687-5716

Marathon Tackle, Inc.
Route 2, Highway XX
Mosinee, WI 54455
Telephone: (715) 359-6887

Martin Reel Company, Inc.
30 East Main Street—P.O. Drawer 8
Mohawk, NY 13407
Telephone: (315) 866-1690

Mercer Tackle Company, Inc.
6735 Atlanta—P.O. Box 5413
Lawton, OK 73504
Telephone: (405) 357-4811

Minn Kota, Inc.
A Johnson Wax Associate
201 North 17th Street—Box 759
Moorhead, MN 56560
Telephone: (218) 233-1316

O. Mustad & Son (U.S.A.), Inc.
185 Clark Street
Auburn, NY 13021
Telephone: (315) 253-2793

Nationwide Lure Mfg. Co., Inc.
P.O. Box 53
Beaver Dam, KY 42320
Telephone: (502) 274-7887

Ozark Lakes Tackle, Ltd.
West Highway 54
Camdenton, MO 65020
Telephone: (314) 346-2276

Paducah Tackle Co.
P.O. Box 23—701 Jefferson Street
Paducah, KY 42001
Telephone: (502) 442-7445

Penn Fishing Tackle Mfg. Company
3028 West Hunting Park Avenue
Philadelphia, PA 19132
Telephone: (215) 229-9415

Pfleuger Sporting Goods
Division of Shakespeare Company
1801 Main Street—P.O. Box 185
Columbia, SC 29202
Telephone: (803) 779-7331

Plano Molding Company
113 South Center Avenue
Plano, IL 60543
Telephone: (312) 552-3111

Plastics Research & Develop-
    ment Corp.
Rebel Lures
3601 Jenny Lind
Fort Smith, AR 72902
Telephone: (501) 782-8971

Rabble Rouser Lures
Factory Distributors
500 South 7th Street
Fort Smith, AR 72901
Telephone: (501) 783-5000

Ridge Runner Lures, Inc.
5025 Flournoy Lucas Road
Shreveport, LA 71109
Telephone: (318) 686-6309

Royal Red Ball
Division of Uniroyal, Inc.
1230 Avenue of the Americas
New York, NY 10020
Telephone: (212) 489-3123

St. Croix Corporation
Division of Kusan, Inc.
9909 South Shore Drive
Minneapolis, MN 55441
Telephone: (612) 540-0511

Scientific Anglers/3M
P.O. Box 2001
Midland, MI 48640
Telephone: (517) 832-8884

Shakespeare Company
1801 North Main Street
P.O. Box 246
Columbia, SC 29202
Telephone: (803) 779-5800

Sheldons', Inc.
West Center Street
Antigo, WI 54409
Telephone: (715) 623-2382

Smithwick Lures, Inc.
Box 1205
Shreveport, LA 71163
Telephone: (318) 929-2805

Speed Cast Lure Co.
Highway 75A North
P.O. Box 117
Denison, TX 75020
Telephone: (214) 465-6271

Stearns Manufacturing Company
P.O. Box 1498
St. Cloud, MN 56301
Telephone: (612) 252-1642

Stembridge Products, Inc.
2941 Central Avenue—P.O. Box 90756
East Point, GA 30344
Telephone: (404) 768-2330

Sunset Line & Twine Co.
Jefferson and Erwin Streets
Petaluma, CA 94952
Telephone: (707) 762-2704

Tack-L-Tyers
939 Chicago Avenue
Evanston, IL 60202
Telephone: (312) 328-2777

3M Company
Leisure Time Products Project
3M Center
St. Paul, MN 55101
Telephone: (612) 733-4751

U. S. Line Company
22 Main Street
Westfield, MA 01085
Telephone: (413) 562-3629

Umco Corporation
Highway 25—P.O. Box 608
Watertown, MN 55388
Telephone: (612) 472-4626

Uncle Josh Bait Company
524 Clarence Street
P.O. Box 130
Fort Atkinson, WI 53538
Telephone: (414) 563-2491

Weber Tackle Co.
1039 Ellis Street
Stevens Point, WI 54481
Telephone: (715) 344-9080

Weedless Bait Co.
Route 1, Box 2-B
Rogers, MN 55374
Telephone: (612) 428-4220

Whopper Stopper, Inc.
Highway 56 West—P.O. Box 1111
Sherman, TX 75090
Telephone: (214) 893-6557

Wright & McGill Company
4245 East 46th Avenue
Denver, CO 80216
Telephone: (303) 321-1481

Zebco
Division of Brunswick Corp.
6101 East Apache Street—Box 270
Tulsa, OK 74115
Telephone: (918) 836-5581

ELECTRONIC DEVICES

Allied Sports Company
One Hummingbird Lane
Eufaula, AL 36027

Fish Hawk Electronics Corp.
4229 Waller Drive
Crystal Lake, IL 60014

G & R Industries
Silvertrol Division
P.O. Box "H"
Pierce City, MO 65723

Garcia Corp.
329 Alfred Avenue
Teaneck, NJ 07666

Ray Jefferson
Division Jetronics Industries, Inc.
Main and Cotton Streets
Philadelphia, PA 19127

Jetco, Inc.
1133 Bararanca Drive
El Paso, TX 79935

Lowrance Electronics, Inc.
12000 East Skelly Drive
Tulsa, OK 74128

Stembridge Products, Inc.
East Point, GA 30344

Sure Power Products, Inc.
7415 S.E. Johnson Creek Boulevard
Portland, OR 97206

Telisons International Corp.
Marine Division
7075 Vineland Avenue North
Hollywood, CA 91605

Vexilar, Inc.
9345 Penn Avenue South
Minneapolis, MN 55431

Westmar Marine
905 Dexter Avenue North
Seattle, WA 98109

Johnson Outboards
Division of OMC
6715 Sea Horse Drive
Waukegan, IL 60085

Mercury Marine
Fond Du Lac, WI 54935

Minn Kota, Inc.
201 North 17th Street
Moorhead, MN 56560

Motor Guide
Box 825
Starkville, MS 39759

Pfleuger Sporting Goods
1801 Main Street
P.O. Box 185
Columbia, SC 29202

Ramglass Products, Inc.
618 East Markham
Little Rock, AR 72201

Shakespeare Co.
1801 North Main Street
P.O. Box 246
Columbia, SC 29202

TROLLING MOTORS

Byrd Industries, Inc.
Industrial Park
Ripley, TX 78063

The Eska Company
2400 Kerper Boulevard
Dubuque, IA 52001

Evinrude Motors
Division of OMC
4143 North 27th Street
P.O. Box 663
Milwaukee, WI 53201

G & R Industries
Silvertol Division
P.O. Box "H"
Pierce City, MO 65723

Jetco, Inc.
1133 Bararanca Drive
El Paso, TX 79935

OTHER ACCESSORIES

Fishmaster Manufacturing Co. (for fishing tubes and floats)
829 Portland
Oklahoma City, OK 73107

Moon-Glo (interior detachable lights)
Able 2 Products Co.
P.O. Box 543
Cassville, MO 65625

Q-Beam (spotlights)
The Brinkmann Corp.
4215 McEwen Road
Dallas, TX 75240

John Reb Anchors (electric anchors)
P.O. Box 46
Clinton, MS 39056

Weed Guard (for electric trolling motors)
Weed Master, Inc.
P.O. Box 5252
Fort Lauderdale, FL 33310

Offices of United States Corps of Engineers Throughout the United States

U. S. Army Engineer Division, Huntsville
Mail Address:
P.O. Box 1600 West Station
Huntsville, AL 35807
Office Location:
106 Wynn Drive
Huntsville, AL
Telephone: (205) 895-5460

U. S. Army Engineer Division, Lower Mississippi Valley
Mail Address:
P.O. Box 80
Vicksburg, MS 39180
Office Location:
Corner Crawford and Walnut Streets
Vicksburg, MS
Telephone: (601) 636-1311

U. S. Army Engineer District, Vicksburg
Mail Address:
P.O. Box 60
Vicksburg, MS 39180
Office Location:
USPO and Courthouse Building
Vicksburg, MS
Telephone: (601) 636-1311

U. S. Army Engineer Division, Missouri River
Mail Address:
P.O. Box 103, Downtown Station
Omaha, NE 68101
Office Location:
USPO and Courthouse
215 North 17th Street
Omaha, NE
Telephone: (402) 221-1221

U. S. Army Engineer District, Kansas City
700 Federal Office Building
601 E. 12th Street
Kansas City, MO 64106
Telephone: (816) 374-3201

U. S. Army Engineer District, Omaha
7410 USPO and Courthouse
215 North 17th Street
Omaha, NE 68102
Telephone: (402) 221-3900

U. S. Army Engineer District, Baltimore
Mail Address:
P.O. Box 1715
Baltimore, MD 21203
Office Location:
31 Hopkins Plaza
Baltimore, MD
Telephone: (301) 962-4545

Baltimore Harbor, Supervisor of
P.O. Box 1715
Baltimore, MD 21203
Telephone: (301) 962-4545

U. S. Army Engineer District, New York
26 Federal Plaza
New York, NY 10007
Telephone: (212) 264-0100

U. S. Army Engineer District, Norfolk
Fort Norfolk
803 Front Street
Norfolk, VA 23510
Telephone: (703) 625-8201

U. S. Army Engineer District, Philadelphia
U. S. Custom House
2nd and Chestnut Streets
Philadelphia, PA 19106
Telephone: (215) 597-4848

U. S. Army Engineer Division, North Central
536 South Clark Street
Chicago, IL 60605
Telephone: (312) 353-6310

U. S. Army Engineer District, Buffalo
1776 Niagara Street
Buffalo, NY 14207
Telephone: (716) 876-5454

U. S. Army Engineer District, Chicago
219 South Dearborn Street
Chicago, IL 60604
Telephone: (312) 353-6400

U. S. Army Engineer District, Detroit
Mail Address:
P.O. Box 1027
Detroit, MI 48231
Office Location:
150 Michigan Avenue
Detroit, MI
Telephone: (313) 963-1261

U. S. Army Engineer District, Rock Island
Clock Tower Building
Rock Island, IL 61201
Telephone: (309) 788-6361

U. S. Army Engineer District, St. Paul
1210 USPO and Customhouse
St. Paul, MN 55101
Telephone: (612) 725-7501

U. S. Army Engineer District, Lake Survey
630 Federal Building and U. S. Courthouse
Detroit, MI 48226
Telephone: (313) 226-6161

U. S. Army Engineer Division, North Pacific
Mail Address:
210 Custom House
Portland, OR 97209
Office Location:
220 Southwest 8th Street
Portland, OR
Telephone: (503) 226-3361

U. S. Army Engineer District, Alaska
P.O. Box 7002
Anchorage, AK 99501
Telephone: (907) 752-9114

U. S. Army Engineer District, Portland
Mail Address:
P.O. Box 2946
Portland, OR 97208
Office Location:
2850 Southeast 82nd Avenue
Portland, OR
Telephone: (503) 777-4441

U. S. Army Engineer District, Seattle
1519 Alaskan Way, South
Seattle, WA 98134
Telephone: (206) 682-2700

U. S. Army Engineer District, Walla Walla
Building 602, City-County Airport
Walla Walla, WA 99362
Telephone: (509) 525-5500

U. S. Army Engineer Division, Ohio River
Mail Address:
P.O. Box 1159
Cincinnati, OH 45201
Office Location:
550 Main Street
Cincinnati, OH
Telephone: (513) 684-3002

U. S. Army Engineer District, Huntington
Mail Address:
P.O. Box 2127
Huntington, WV 25721
Office Location:
502 8th Street
Huntington, WV
Telephone: (304) 529-2318

U. S. Army Engineer District, Louisville
Mail Address:
P.O. Box 59
Louisville, KY 40201
Office Location:
600 Federal Place
Louisville, KY
Telephone: (502) 582-5601

U. S. Army Engineer District, Nashville
Mail Address:
P.O. Box 1070
Nashville, TN 37202
Office Location:
306 Federal Office Building
Nashville, TN
Telephone: (615) 242-8321

U. S. Army Engineer District, Pittsburgh
Mail Address:
1828 Federal Building
1000 Liberty Avenue
Pittsburgh, PA 15222
Office Location:
Federal Building
1000 Liberty Avenue
Pittsburgh, PA
Telephone: (412) 644-6800

U. S. Army Engineer Division, South Atlantic
510 Title Building
30 Pryor Street SW
Atlanta, GA 30303
Telephone: (404) 526-6711

U. S. Army Engineer District, Canaveral
Mail Address:
P.O. Box 21065
Kennedy Space Center, FL 32815
Office Location:
Building K6-1146
Kennedy Space Center, FL
Telephone: (305) 856-2003

U. S. Army Engineer District, Charleston
Mail Address:
P.O. Box 919
Charleston, SC 29402
Office Location:
Federal Building
334 Meeting Street
Charleston, SC
Telephone: (803) 577-4171

U. S. Army Engineer District, Jacksonville
Mail Address:
P.O. Box 4970
Jacksonville, FL 32201

Office Location:
Federal Building
400 West Bay Street
Jacksonville, FL
Telephone: (904) 791-2241

U. S. Army Engineer District, Mobile
Mail Address:
P.O. Box 2288
Mobile, AL 36601
Office Location:
2301 Airport Boulevard
Mobile, AL
Telephone: (205) 473-0311

U. S. Army Engineer District, Savannah
Mail Address:
P.O. Box 889
Savannah, GA 31402
Office Location:
200 East Saint Julian Street
Savannah, GA
Telephone: (912) 233-8822

U. S. Army Engineer District, Wilmington
Mail Address:
P.O. Box 1890
Wilmington, NC 28401
Office Location:
308 Federal Building
U. S. Courthouse
Wilmington, NC
Telephone: (919) 763-9971

U. S. Army Engineer Division, South Pacific
Mail Address:
630 Sansome Street, Room 1216
San Francisco, CA 94111
Telephone: (415) 556-0914

U. S. Army Engineer District, Los Angeles
Mail Address:
P.O. Box 2711
Los Angeles, CA 90053
Office Location:
300 North Los Angeles Street
Los Angeles, CA
Telephone: (213) 688-5300

U. S. Army Engineer District, Sacramento
650 Capitol Mall
Sacramento, CA 95814
Telephone: (916) 449-2232

U. S. Army Engineer District, San Francisco
100 McAllister Street
San Francisco, CA 94102
Telephone: (415) 556-3660

U. S. Army Engineer Division, Southwestern
1114 Commerce Street
Dallas, TX 75202
Telephone: (214) 749-3336

U. S. Army Engineer District, Albuquerque
Mail Address:
P.O. Box 1580
Albuquerque, NM 87103
Office Location:
517 Gold Avenue SW
Albuquerque, NM
Telephone: (505) 843-2732

U. S. Army Engineer District, Fort Worth
Mail Address:
P.O. Box 17300
Fort Worth, TX 76102
Office Location:
819 Taylor Street
Fort Worth, TX
Telephone: (817) 334-2300

U. S. Army Engineer District, Galveston
Mail Address:
P.O. Box 1229
Galveston, TX 77550
Office Location:
Santa Fe Building
Galveston, TX
Telephone: (713) 763-1211

U. S. Army Engineer District, Little Rock
Mail Address:
P.O. Box 867
Little Rock, AR 72203
Office Location:
700 West Capitol
Little Rock, AR
Telephone: (501) 372-4361

U. S. Army Engineer District, Tulsa
Mail Address:
P.O. Box 61
Tulsa, OK 74102
Office Location:
224 South Boulder
Tulsa, OK
Telephone: (918) 584-7151

A Directory of Conservation Bureaus and Other Sources of Fishing Information in the United States and Canada*

Alabama Department of Conservation and Natural
   Resources
64 North Union Street
Montgomery, AL 36130

Alaska Department of Fish and Game
210 Ferry Way
Juneau, AK 99801

Arizona Game and Fish Commission
I and E Division
2222 West Greenway Road
Phoenix, AZ 85023

Arkansas Game and Fish Commission
No. 2 Natural Resources Drive
Little Rock, AR 77025

California Department of Fish and Game
1416 Ninth Street
Sacramento, CA 95814

Colorado Division of Wildlife
6060 Broadway
Denver, CO 80216

Connecticut Department of Environmental Protection
State Office Building
165 Capitol Avenue
Hartford, CT 06115

Delaware Division of Fish and Wildlife
P.O. Box 1401
Dover, DE 19901

District of Columbia Metropolitan Police
550 Water Street SW
Washington, DC 20024

Florida Game and Fresh Water Fish Commission
620 South Meridian Street
Tallahassee, FL 32304

Georgia Department of Natural Resources
270 Washington Street, SW
Atlanta, GA 30334

Hawaii Department of Land and Natural Resources
1151 Punchbowl Street
Honolulu, HI 96813

Idaho Fish and Game Department
P.O. Box 25
600 South Walnut Street
Boise, ID 83707

* Fishing seasons, license costs, and up-to-date information are available from state and provincial addresses
listed here.

Illinois Department of Conservation
34 West Broadway
Alton, IL 62002

Indiana Department of Natural Resources
607 State Office Building
Indianapolis, IN 46204

Iowa Conservation Commission
Wallace State Office Building
Des Moines, IA 50319

Kansas Fish and Game Commission
Box 54-A, RR No. 2
Pratt, KS 67124

Kentucky Department of Fish and Wildlife Resources
Capital Plaza Tower
Frankfort, KY 40601

Louisiana Wildlife and Fisheries Commission
400 Royal Street, Room 104
New Orleans, LA 70130

Maine Department of Inland Fisheries and Game
State Office Building
Augusta, ME 04330

Maryland Department of Natural Resources
Tawes State Office Building
Annapolis, MD 21401

Massachusetts Division of Fisheries and Wildlife
Westboro, MA 01581

Michigan Department of Natural Resources
P.O. Box 30028
Lansing, MI 48909

Minnesota Division of Game and Fish
390 Centennial Building
658 Cedar Street
St. Paul, MN 55155

Mississippi Division of Game and Fish Commission
Box 451
Jackson, MS 39205

Missouri Department of Conservation
2901 North Ten Mile Drive
Jefferson City, MO 65102

Montana Department of Fish and Game
Helena, MT 59601

Nebraska Game and Parks Commission
P.O. Box 30370
Lincoln, NE 68503

Nevada Department of Fish and Game
P.O. Box 10678
Reno, NV 89520

New Hampshire Fish and Game Department
34 Bridge Street
Concord, NH 03301

New Jersey Department of Environmental Protection
Division of Fish, Game, and Shell Fisheries
P.O. Box 1390
Trenton, NJ 08625

New Mexico Department of Game and Fish
State Capitol
Santa Fe, NM 87501

New York State Environmental Conservation Department
Division of Fish and Wildlife
50 Wolf Road
Albany, NY 12201

North Carolina Wildlife Resources Commission
Albermarle Building
325 North Salisbury Street
Raleigh, NC 27611

North Dakota State Game and Fish Department
2121 Lovett Avenue
Bismarck, ND 58505

Ohio Fish and Game Division
Department of Natural Resources
Fountain Square
Columbus, OH 43224

Oklahoma Department of Wildlife Conservation
Box 53465
Oklahoma City, OK 73105

Oregon Department of Fish and Wildlife
P.O. Box 3503
1634 SW Alder Street
Portland, OR 97208

Pennsylvania Fish Commission
P.O. Box 1673
Harrisburg, PA 17120

Rhode Island Division of Fish and Wildlife
Washington County Government Center
Wakefield, RI 02879

South Carolina Wildlife and Marine Resources
Department
P.O. Box 167
Dutch Plaza, Building D
Columbia, SC 29202

South Dakota Department of Wildlife, Parks, and
Forestry
Sigurd Anderson Building
Pierre, SD 57501

Tennessee Wildlife Resources Agency
P.O. Box 40747
Ellington Agricultural Center
Nashville, TN 37220

Texas Parks and Wildlife Commission
4200 Smith School Road
Austin, TX 78744

Utah Division of Wildlife Resources
1596 West North Temple
Salt Lake City, UT 84116

Vermont Department of Fish and Game
Agency of Environmental Conservation
Montpelier, VT 05602

Virginia Commission of Game and Inland Fisheries
P.O. Box 11104
Richmond, VA 23230

Washington Department of Game
600 North Capitol Way
Olympia, WA 98504

West Virginia Department of Natural Resources
1800 Washington Street
East Charleston, WV 25305

Wisconsin Department of Natural Resources
P.O. Box 7921
Madison, WI 53707

Wyoming Game and Fish Department
P.O. Box 1589
Cheyenne, WY 82002

CANADA

Manitoba Department of Renewable Resources and
Transportation Services
Fisheries and Wildlife Branch
1495 St. James Street
Winnipeg, Man. R3H OW9
Canada

Ontario Ministry of Natural Resources
Fisheries Branch
Queen's Park, Whitney Block
Toronto, Ont. M7A 1W3
Canada

Prince Edward Island Fish and Wildlife Division
P.O. Box 2000
Charlottetown, PEI C1A 7N8
Canada

Quebec Department of Tourism, Fish, and Game
Tourist Branch
Place de la Capitale
150 Boulevard St. Cyrille East
Quebec City, Que. G1R 4V1
Canada

Saskatchewan Department of Tourism and Renewable Resources
Extension Services
1825 Lorne Street
Regina, Sask. S4P 3V7
Canada